DRILLING

through the

CORE

Why Common Core is Bad
for American Education

DRILLING
through the
CORE

Edited with an introduction by Peter W. Wood

PIONEER INSTITUTE
PUBLIC POLICY RESEARCH

Mission

Pioneer Institute is an independent, non-partisan, privately funded research organization that seeks to improve the quality of life in Massachusetts through civic discourse and intellectually rigorous, data-driven public policy solutions.

Board of Directors

TABLE OF CONTENTS

Preface   7
Jim Stergios and Jamie Gass

Introduction: How the Common Core
State Standards Will Harm American Education   13
Peter W. Wood

1 How Common Core's ELA Standards   111
   Place College Readiness at Risk
   Mark Bauerlein and Sandra Stotsky

2 The Fate Of American History in a   143
   Common Core-Based Curriculum
   Ralph Ketcham, Anders Lewis, and Sandra Stotsky

3 The Fate of Poetry in a   179
   Curriculum for the Proletariat
   Anthony Esolen, Jamie Highfill, and Sandra Stotsky

4 Common Core's Mathematics Standards   225
   Still Don't Make the Grade
   Ze'ev Wurman

5 Lowering the Bar: How Common Core Math   247
   Fails to Prepare High School Students for STEM
   R. James Milgram and Sandra Stotsky

6 The Revenge of K–12: How Common Core and   267
   the New SAT Lower College Standards in the U.S.
   Richard P. Phelps and R. James Milgram

7 The Road to a National Curriculum: The Legal   303
   Aspects of the Common Core Standards, Race
   to the Top, and Conditional Waivers
   Robert S. Eitel and Kent D. Talbert, with Williamson S. Evers

8 National Cost of Aligning States and   341
   Localities to the Common Core Standards
   AccountabilityWorks

Preface

Jim Stergios and Jamie Gass

The debate over Common Core is a contest between two views:

- The Common Core standards are a state-driven effort to improve K-12 public education in America and help children in under-performing school districts.

- The Common Core standards are of dubious academic quality and constitute a federal intrusion into what is historically, legally, and financially, a state and local issue.

Drilling through the Core is a book that strives to treat the first view fairly while arguing that the second should prevail.

It is a much needed contribution given that the debate over Common Core has descended into a contentious political fight. The controversy was hardly unpredictable given that Common Core is:

- An issue that touches 50 million kids and tens of millions more parents, grandparents, and guardians.

- A wrestling match between the federal and state governments over who controls key domestic policy levers.

- The newest chapter in the long history of attempts to centralize standards and tests.

Then there is money. The effort to create and promote Common Core came with an influx of large amounts of new federal and philanthropic money into political, policy, and advocacy organizations. The effort also implies a significant shift in how public education funds flow to support new testing and textbooks, with benefits to some and not to other companies. So, of course, there is controversy.

Both sides in the debate make important points. The pro-Common Core troops argue that many states have not done the hard work to advance student achievement. This failure leaves the United States woefully behind other developed nations. The anti-Common Core groups argue the standards came about through anti-democratic and secretive steps, including an unprecedented alignment of federal overreach and philanthropic pressure on state governments.

Pioneer Institute is among the anti-Common Core groups. The Institute cut its teeth in Massachusetts on issues of K-12 education reform, where we helped the state make historic strides in improving its schools and establishing the highest performing charter public school sector in the nation. Massachusetts is now the nation's top performer on every measure of student achievement and ranks among the top six countries on international math and science tests. We are proud of our state and proud of our contribution to bringing about these results for our students. But with the arrival of the Common Core, Pioneer realized that we had to raise our sights beyond Massachusetts.

We have observed the corrosive effects of the hundreds of millions of philanthropic dollars spent on both developing and marketing Common Core. That spending has diverted state and local governments from wiser policies and also damaged the objectivity of the research community.

Drilling through the Core is the culmination of a multi-year research and evaluation initiative, examining the key elements of Common Core. This book synthesizes that body of work in order to provide facts that parents and others can use to draw their own conclusions about an education reform that emerged suddenly, and without public debate, across the country. For over six years,

Pioneer has been one of the few independent sources of factual information and peer-reviewed research about Common Core. We have focused our research on questions that matter to three important constituent groups:

- For **parents**, are the Common Core standards academically rigorous?
- For **states**, how much will it cost to implement?
- For **Congress**, are the Common Core standards and federally funded tests legal?

We have commissioned eminent education scholars, lawyers, and experts to research these issues without taking money from the large philanthropies that hold a predetermined view on Common Core—an approach that distinguishes us from other groups active in this debate.

Drilling through the Core reflects the emphasis of Pioneer's body of research on Common Core and the national tests. Peter Wood's introduction provides an overarching survey of the debate. The chapters that follow focus on the standards' academic quality and their probable effects on children's learning. Three chapters examine the English language arts standards and how they shape student learning generally in poetry and the associated area of American history. Three additional chapters focus on mathematics, comparing the Common Core math standards with those in several states; delving into the likely impact on high school graduates' readiness to undertake authentic college courses in science, technology, engineering, and math; and reviewing the overall impact of the Core and the new Core-aligned SAT on the quality of college course offerings. The final chapter probes the legal dimensions of Common Core and associated federal actions to persuade states to adopt and maintain adherence to it.

Some further words about our experience in Massachusetts. Massachusetts' reform efforts, initiated with our landmark 1993 Education Reform Act, have propelled the Bay State to the front of the line in American public education. In 2005 our students became the nation's first to post the best scores in every subject and at every grade level tested in the National Assessment of Educational Progress (NAEP). Since then we have repeated this feat on every subsequent administration of NAEP. In 2007, the state's eighth graders tied for first in the world in international science testing. Again, in 2013, our students were competitive with the highest-achieving countries and far outperformed the rest of the United States.

The state's 1993 reform built on the Bay State's educational heritage. The law was an explicit recommitment to Massachusetts' foundational purposes—purposes outlined in 1780 by John Adams in the Massachusetts Constitution. That constitution went on to serve as an important template for the subsequent United States Constitution, especially as regards organizing political principles like the separation and limitation of government powers.

What is less known about Adams' magisterial 1780 Constitution—the world's oldest continuously used written constitution—is its focus on education and character. In Article XVIII, Adams wrote that "A constant adherence to those [principles] of piety, justice, moderation, temperance, industry, and frugality, are absolutely necessary to preserve the advantages of liberty and to maintain a free government." He famously encapsulated that assertion in his dictum that a "free government could only exist among a virtuous citizenry"; the alternative being that any citizenry lacking in civic virtue "would only respond to force" and that "the government would have to be more intrusive."

If, for Adams, the viability of his commonwealth and the republic depended on the moral citizen's ability to fulfill his (or with Abigail's help, her) civic role, education was the means for ensuring and perpetuating the principles of a modern liberal democracy. Chapter V of the state's Constitution elevates the role of education in a manner unseen in the U.S. Constitution:

Wisdom, and knowledge, as well as virtue, diffused generally among the body of the people, being necessary for the preservation of their rights and liberties... it shall be the duty of legislatures and magistrates, in all future periods of this common-

wealth, to cherish the interests of literature and the sciences, and all seminaries of them.

Adams' Constitution and Massachusetts' 1993 Education Reform Act serve as an important backdrop for the contents of this book. Both documents start from the dual purposes Massachusetts sees for education: Developing informed citizens who can maintain America's great experiment in democracy, and ensuring their ability to pursue self-reliance and happiness. Those dual purposes are why Massachusetts' K-12 education reforms have prioritized an authentic liberal arts education, with particular emphasis on students' literary, historical, mathematical, and scientific development.

We have, in Massachusetts, chosen to provide various types of schools and choices for parents to meet the specific needs of each child, including traditional district schools, charter public schools, vocational-technical schools, and options to transfer among districts. Our view of strong state standards, modest standardized testing for teachers and students, adequate funding, and a broad array of choices for students and parents reflects an opposing view to a one-size-fits-all approach to education and to an anti-democratic, reductionist purpose for our public schools, whereby K-12 students are integrated into only a system of workforce development.

Drilling through the Core is meant to inform an important policy debate, but we hope it performs the additional role of serving as a reference point for how Americans think about public education. We will continue to work energetically to make sure the country gets both Common Core and larger public policy debates right. In doing so, we aim to serve the purposes not only of employers and the national economy, but, more importantly, those of our children in the schools, their parents, teachers, and this exceptional republic.

Introduction

How the Common Core State Standards Will Harm American Education

Peter W. Wood

The Common Core State Standards are a far-reaching effort to transform American K–12 schooling. They are not the first such effort and will not be the last, but for our time they are the most important. If they succeed in doing what proponents promise, they will create for the first time in American history a largely unified set of national educational standards for children from kindergarten through high school across the country. They will also transform higher education by ensuring that every college matriculant arrives with much the same kind of preparation.

But the Common Core State Standards have also attracted skeptics and, if the skeptics are right, the Common Core will damage the quality of K–12 education for many students; strip parents and local communities of meaningful influence over school curricula; centralize a great deal of power in the hands of federal bureaucrats and private interests; push for the aggregation and use of large amounts of personal data on students without the consent of parents; usher in an era of even more abundant and more intrusive standardized testing; and absorb enormous sums of public funding that could be spent to better effect on other aspects of education.

The Common Core is, in a word, controversial.

This book provides a tour of that controversy. It is written from the perspective of the skeptics and it aims, first, to persuade those who have not yet made up their minds that the Common Core State Standards are not a good way forward for the country. But this book also aims to engage the proponents of the Common Core and to improve the general debate. It does so by gathering in one place the full range of well-considered arguments against the Common Core; by examining the claims made on both sides of the debate; and by providing a historical account of how the Common Core came to be.

The Case in Favor

Those who favor the Common Core State Standards argue that the nation will be better served when students in every state are educated according to a single well-conceived and well-executed plan. They see that plan as sufficiently flexible to allow for regional and local variation but nonetheless powerful enough to bring students to the same high threshold of knowledge and skill. The threshold they have in mind is "college and career readiness," which combines college-readiness for most and workplace readiness for the rest.

The vision behind the Common Core emphasizes that students in rural Mississippi, coastal Oregon, the urban Midwest, and New England villages will all be taught to a shared standard. This consistency befits a country that in most respects is a unified nation. We have a common economy, a common airline industry, common telecommunications, and common entertainment. We should not tolerate a form of schooling that divides us into myriad communities that set different expectations for what children should learn. Algebra is the same whether one is in Key West or Point Barrow. Why should we expect that a child who goes to school in one should learn less algebra than a child who goes to school in the other?

This call for a nationally shared set of educational standards can be seen as an appeal to national pride. A common core is what a great nation should expect of itself. And other nations—great and even not so great—have long had one. Why not us?

The national standards set forth in the Common Core indeed are, for the most part, higher than the standards that have prevailed in recent years in many states. Proponents of the Common Core admit that there are exceptions. Massachusetts, for example, had to lower its standards to adjust to the Common Core. But the exceptions are excusable. To achieve the substantial advantages of having a genuinely national curriculum, some sacrifices were necessary.

I said "curriculum," but that's not quite right. The word "curriculum" refers to the exact content of what schools teach in their classrooms. The Common Core State Standards don't actually reach that far, at least not yet. They are "standards" that declare the goals that a curriculum ought to attain, but they aren't a detailed blueprint of a curriculum let alone a collection of actual classroom assignments.

For example, the Common Core State Standards for Grade 3 in the English Language (in Common Core notation "CCSS. ELA") includes "Literacy. RL 3.3" which prescribes that students at this level ought to be able to:

> *Describe characters in a story (e.g., their traits, motivations, or feelings) and explain how their actions contribute to the sequence of events.*

The Common Core, however, does not specify what story and, although the readings are picked for grade level, a lot is left open. Are students asked to discern motives that are clear-cut or are they to be challenged with characters who have conflicting motives? Will they face stories in which a character's actions contribute

15

plainly to the "sequence of events" or stories in which characters try but fail to influence events?

The Common Core points to a valid goal but leaves room for teachers and others to figure out the best way to achieve that goal. And this should be counted as one of its seeming strengths. It does not seem to overreach.

Those who favor the Common Core have other good arguments at their disposal. They point out—correctly I think—that American public schools on the whole do a mediocre job. For some segments of the population, our schools don't even achieve mediocrity. (One commentator recently noted that, "Out of 1.6 million high school graduates who took the ACT in 2011, only 25 percent met all four College Readiness Benchmarks" which are set by the ACT. "Even more disturbing is that 28 percent did not meet any of the benchmarks."[1]) The spirit of the Common Core, like that of previous attempts to overhaul K–12 schooling such as No Child Left Behind, Goals 2000, or America 2000, is to create the kind of high standards and tests that will help all students, not just a few.

This is commendable and I am ready to agree that in many school districts around the country a program that implemented the Common Core in good faith would probably represent a sizable improvement over the way things are now.

These arguments do not exhaust the reasons why the Common Core may be a good thing. Proponents also argue that the Common Core will do a better job than our current patchwork approach to K–12 education in preparing students to compete for positions in a global market. They note that Americans are frequently on the move, and, when they relocate across state lines, their children face educational disruptions that would vanish under the Common Core. And they argue that the Common Core would bring efficiencies in teacher education, textbook publishing, and the spread of best educational practices. I take it that these are add-on arguments and not among the primary reasons why the nation should embrace this far-reaching innovation.

The Case Against

Those who oppose the Common Core believe that the proposed reforms will backfire. Their most basic criticism is that the Common Core will result, ultimately, in lower standards.

But before I explain that criticism, I need to put up a fence between the critique I am going to develop and some criticisms I am not going to pursue. Because the debate over the Common Core is a very public matter in which feelings sometimes run high, some critics have at times suggested that the advocates of the Common Core are acting in bad faith: that the proponents of the Common Core know that it is bad and want to impose it on the nation anyway out of self-interest. Let's put that claim on the other side of the fence.

I will identify some of the major proponents of the Common Core, but there is no reason to think that they have bad motives. My criticisms of the Common Core focus on what it is and what its likely consequences will be and that's all.[2]

1 - Adoption

The critics of the Common Core have good reasons for their doubts. Chief among these reasons is that the Common Core was sped into place in most states without the benefit of careful review. The standards were developed by the National Governors Association (NGA) in collaboration with the Council of Chief State School Officers (CCSSO). These are private, non-governmental bodies—in effect, education trade organizations. The National Governors Association, despite its name, isn't just a group of sitting governors. It includes many ex-governors and current and former gubernatorial staff members. The deliberations of the NGA and the CCSSO are not open to the public, and the work that these bodies did to develop the Common Core State Standards remains for the most part unavailable to outsiders. Neither body, being private, is subject to Freedom of Information requests. The standards themselves are copyrighted by the NGA and the CCSSO.

So one important criticism is that a huge change in American public policy was designed behind closed doors. The reasoning, the evidence, and the arguments that contributed to the development of the Common Core remain beyond the reach of public scrutiny.

Moreover, the public had virtually no opportunity to look at the finished project before it was rushed through the approval of 46 states and the District of Columbia. (Texas, Alaska, Virginia, and Nebraska did not adopt the Common Core, and Minnesota adopted only part of it.) In many cases, the state education departments acted on their own initiative. In other cases, the state legislatures took up and passed hastily drafted bills based on the assurances of current or former governors that this pig-in-the-poke was worth buying. Few had the time to hold hearings, solicit public comment, or to look for themselves at the details.

Why the rush? It had something to do with the Great Recession that began in fall 2008. The states were in financial pain when all at once a potential new source of major federal funding appeared on the horizon—but a new source with a short shelf life.

When the Common Core was presented, the states found themselves confronted with a tight deadline. The U.S. Department of Education under Secretary Arne Duncan announced on July 24, 2009, a new program called "Race to the Top" (RttT). Race to the Top was funded from the federal "stimulus" that was part of the American Recovery and Reinvestment Act of 2009. RttT had several parts, but a key one was the prospect of significant new federal funding for some states that adopted new K–12 academic standards that matched certain specifications. Those specifications happened to be a perfect match for the Common Core State Standards—and for nothing else.

The new federal funding was not a firm promise. States that adopted the Common Core were awarded "points" on an application (40 out of 500) which might lead to the substantial new federal funding. But the state legislatures had to act quickly to adopt the Common Core in order to secure those points. The prospect of getting the RttT funding without the Common Core points looked negligible. Therefore, almost all of the states adopted the Common Core.

The $4.35 billion for RttT was a one-time, non-renewable source of funding distributed in three rounds to just 18 states and Washington, D.C.[3] The other states that adopted the Common Core in order to secure RttT points received no RttT funding but had acquired a new and expensive liability. Some have found that getting out of the commitment is a lot more difficult than getting in.

These circumstances do not, of course, mean that the Common Core standards are necessarily bad. Rather, they mean that the normal scrutiny that such proposed changes would have undergone was bypassed. That provides good grounds for wariness.

The critics of the Common Core, however, often go further than wariness. The role of the federal government in promoting the Common Core skirts the U.S. Constitution and three federal laws that prohibit the U.S. Department of Education from funding, directing, or validating national standards, tests, or curriculum. One of the studies included in this volume tackles this situation head-on with an analysis that aims to show that the Department of Education crossed the line. I don't need to settle these questions here, but I do need to flag them as a concern. Is the way the Common Core came about legal? Even if it was arguably legal, is the result—with its apparent evasion of the spirit of the law—legitimate?

Criticizing the process by which the Common Core came about is only one part of the case against the Common Core. We need also to look again at the purpose of the Common Core, its content, who controls it, the context in which it will operate, and the controversies that it has already set in motion. I will look at each of these carefully.

2 - Purpose

The Common Core State Standards embody a set of utilitarian goals that are too small for America. Our schools historically have been where children learn the meaning of freedom. The Common Core, by contrast, mainly teaches children the duty of being productive. The Common Core emphasizes "college- and career-readiness" as though the child's most important destination is his job. But we also need to be concerned with the child's development as someone who has a rich and rewarding inner life, who reads good books, understands important ideas, who can set worthy goals, and help to shape a well-ordered society. The Common Core claims to prepare children to be successful participants in the workforce. Indeed, most of the rationale for the Common Core focuses on national productivity and international competitiveness. These are not, of course, goals to brush aside. They are important but drastically incomplete.

3 - Content

The Common Core has two parts: English Language Arts (ELA) and Mathematics. But because of the way the Common Core pursues these two subjects, it spills over into other areas, including history/social studies and science. The English Language Arts, for example, are meant to include the study of historical documents. These ELA standards have been criticized for their emphasis on "informational texts" (70 percent of all reading by the senior year) at the expense of literature. To the extent that the ELA standards pay much attention to literature at all, they specify American literature. The only British literature included is a smattering of Shakespeare.

The Mathematics standards have been criticized for putting American students two years behind students in high-achieving countries. For example, under the Common Core, students will not learn long division until sixth grade instead of fifth grade where it was formerly taught, and completion of algebra is deferred until 9th grade, in contrast to the top-performing states that start and complete algebra earlier. That in turn means that calculus will no longer be available for most high school students. The Mathematics standards also put a great deal of emphasis on teaching students to explain mathematical ideas rather than on learning how to calculate. The Common Core also puts forward a new and unproven approach to teaching geometry in 7th and 8th grades. Two of the papers in this volume look with some depth at Common Core Mathematics.

While some critics say the Common Core is not rigorous enough and will leave students underprepared for college, other critics argue that the Common Core's approach to K–3 education is *too* rigorous and too focused on preparing children for the eventuality of college. Child psychologist Megan Koschnick says that the standards at this level are "developmentally inappropriate" and will put undue "stress" on young children.[4] Possibly both criticisms are valid: Common Core could be too demanding in primary grades but too lax in middle school and high school.[5]

Beyond these particulars, the "content" of Common Core is doubtful in another way. The standards are often vague and ambiguous and invite manipulation by those who are charged with filling in the details. Proponents of the Common Core say this is a strength: a great deal is left to the implementers of the Common Core. But skeptics tend to view the vagueness as making the standards prey for hijacking. They see three kinds of vulnerabilities.

First, the Common Core standards are meant to be realized through a system of standardized tests. The people who set the content of the tests will actually be generating most of the detail of the curricula that will be built to meet the standards.

Second, the Common Core emphasizes a collection of educational goals called "21st century skills." These include "media awareness," "systems thinking," and a number of other mischievously broad concepts that appear at odds with both traditional learning and the liberal arts.

Third, the Common Core's ambiguities mean that a great deal of the interpretation of the standards is left in the hands of those who were its primary architects, including David Coleman, who now is president of the College Board. Coleman is an advocate for a form of education that radically diminishes attention to historical context, especially in reading. His approach has already had an outsized influence on the way the Common Core standards have been translated in curricular choices and practical pedagogy. To many observers the Common Core has begun to be synonymous with purposely odd, out-of-context readings, such as reading Lincoln's *Gettysburg Address* without giving students the historical background that it was delivered on a battlefield while the Civil War was still underway.

That connection to the College Board raises other concerns that I will come back to later.

4 - Control

The Common Core takes control of our schools away from parents and communities. It vests that control of education in agencies and individuals remote from our lives and concerns. The Common Core is not, however, just another instance of the federal government assuming powers previously reserved for the states, local school boards, and the private sector. It is worse than that. The NGA and the CCSSO, as noted above, are private organizations. They own the copyright on the Common Core, and no one can change it without their permission.

There is an additional layer that pushes control out of the reach of parents. The two assessment consortia, Smarter Balanced Assessment Consortium (SBAC) and Partnership for Assessment of Readiness for College and Careers (PARCC), are also private organizations. In 2010 the Department of Education awarded $330 million for "assessments" needed to bring the Common core to life. SBAC and PARCC (the latter managed by another private group called Achieve) took on the task of developing tests to measure student achievement in making progress towards the Mathematics and ELA standards. SBAC has developed "computer-adaptive" tests. Both consortia have developed instructional and curriculum tools for teachers as well as the tests. If the Common Core pro-

ceeds as planned, most American school children within a few
years will be taught according to a curriculum that has been profoundly shaped around the tests and teaching materials of these
two consortia. Parents and communities have virtually no say and
no influence on what they do. Neither body has any discernible
avenue for receiving complaints from parents.

The federal government has a piece of this, too. The United
States Department of Education retains wide-ranging oversight
of the two testing consortia, conducting annual performance
reports, and maintaining regular communication with both the
SBAC and PARCC. In March 2013, a Department-sponsored
"technical-review panel" began monitoring the consortia's testing
item design and validation process, their assessment development,
planning and research, and the accessibility and accommodations
for non-native English speakers and students with disabilities. In
ensuring conformance to the Common Core, the Department of
Education is essentially hiring out the work it can't legally perform
itself.

For a time, PARCC seemed the dominant player. In 2011 it
had 24 member states and the District of Columbia and covered
over half of America's school children. But PARCC has lost favor.
In 2015, only seven states and the District of Columbia are sched-
uled to give the PARCC tests. One by one the other states have
pulled back. In 2015, Arkansas's board of education withdrew
from PARCC in favor of the ACT's Aspire tests.[6] And New York
went from keeping PARCC at "arm's length" to having "no current
plans to adopt the PARCC assessments."[7] A columnist writing in
the Boston Globe in summer 2015 declared PARCC had entered
"a death spiral."[8]

PARCC's catastrophe is symptomatic of the control problem.
Once the public began to see how much local power had been
stripped from the schools by this national consortium, it reacted
with fury.

Yet another aspect of the disappearance of local control over
schools is the outsized role played by the Bill & Melinda Gates

23

Foundation, which has financed most of the development of the Common Core and the public advocacy that has driven its rapid adoption by the states.

5 - Context

The Common Core arrives at a moment in U.S. history after several decades of large and growing public dissatisfaction with our schools. The Common Core is presented as a solution to long-standing problems. The critics of the Common Core doubt that the proposed solution will work. Moreover, they argue that the illusions the Common Core promotes will make some matters worse.

The Common Core follows a long line of reform efforts that dot the last century, culminating in the 2001 No Child Left Behind Act (NCLB). That legislation responded to Americans' recognition that academic achievement in our schools was on the whole lagging but that poor and minority students were especially ill-served. NCLB attempted to repair the situation with a regime of frequent "assessments"—standardized tests tied to accountability measures—which proved in time to be unpopular with teachers, expensive, and easily subverted. Many critics point out that tying instruction to assessments led to narrowed curricula because teachers began "teaching to the test." Among other things, the Common Core should be seen as an attempt to replace a failing reform with a different model that at least has the virtue of not having failed, yet. But Common Core only replaces one system of pervasive standardized testing with another system of pervasive standardized testing.

The United States is still left with a collection of educational problems for which we have no evident answer. High on this list is the "achievement gap" between black students (and, to a lesser extent, Hispanic students) and white and Asian students. Household income levels also broadly match student achievement, suggesting that our schools do not really provide equality of opportunity in that realm either. In the United States today more than a quarter of all children (and more than half of all African-American children) are raised in single-parent households—a situation that has strongly negative implications for children's academic achievement.[9]

In an increasingly desperate search for ways to overcome these problems, millions of parents have opted out of the old public school systems in favor of putting their children in charter schools or private academies, or even to homeschool them.

The Common Core is presented by its advocates as aiming to make American children "college- and career-ready," which seems to be an anemic answer to the profoundly difficult issues we face. The Common Core might, in this view, bring some marginal improvements, but it doesn't touch the deep discontents and abiding problems in our public K–12 system of education. By diverting time and energy from more important reforms Common Core may prove to be a squandered opportunity.

6 - Controversies

The Common Core, like the bad marriage described by Congreve, was adopted in haste and is being repented in leisure. Several of the states that rushed it through the legislative process or declared their adoptions of it without even legislative approval either now want out or have placed major restrictions on its implementation. Indiana, Oklahoma, and South Carolina officially reversed their adoptions of the Common Core. Michigan and Pennsylvania officially "paused" their adoption of the Common Core. Georgia, Utah, and Alabama have withdrawn from the Common Core testing consortia.[10] Kansas committed itself to a cost analysis before full adoption. According to a Kansas state audit, between 2012 and 2014, each district would have to spend between $16 million and $30 million to carry forward the Common Core.[11] South Dakota, having adopted the Common Core, after the fact decided to add four public hearings before its implementation. New Mexico, Iowa, California, North Carolina, and Maryland have added official reviews of standards or cost verification before moving forward. The Wisconsin state legislature, in its 2013 budget, called for a Joint Legislative Council to review the Common Core's rigor and costs and asked the state Department of Public Instruction to hold a series of public hearings. Legislation aimed at halting the Common Core was introduced but has so far failed to be enacted in several other states.[12]

This sounds complicated but it gets worse. Some of the states opting out of the Common Core or dropping out of PARCC are playing games. They officially leave Common Core but then officially adopt Common Core's identical twin. Apparently the goal is to placate popular opposition to the Common Core without going to the trouble to develop a real alternative. For example, the new South Carolina math standards are in "92 percent alignment" with the Common Core.[13] Critics of the Common Core are furious about this trickery.

Another line of controversy has erupted with the discovery by many parents that the implementation of the Common Core in some states involves detailed tracking of student performance in permanent national databases. The databases are being shared with private companies. Ironically, the companies have greater privacy rights to their databases than the students have to their own data. Additionally, even those states that choose not to provide data for the national databases are still required by RttT to enhance their own data systems. So all students, even those whose data will not be shared on a national level, will be far more closely tracked than ever before.

The Common Core also will cost an enormous amount of money. We are, in effect, redesigning the curriculum for—according to some estimates—42 million students.[14] Existing textbooks and teaching materials will be obsolete. This is a bonanza for the vendors who provide these materials; it is a huge burden on taxpayers. Most of the states that adopted the Common Core hoping to cash in on Race to the Top monies, of course, failed in that quest and face paying for the full cost of the Common Core implementation out of their own funds. But even the "winners" in RttT belatedly discovered that those funds cover only a small fraction of the new costs. For example, Massachusetts received $250 million in RttT funding, but the Common Core, it is now estimated, will cost the Bay State a lot more. *The Boston Globe* estimated the price tag to be $360 million.[15] RttT awarded $4.35 billion in total to states; according to a study included this book, it will cost states a total of $15.8 billion to implement. Teachers have to be retrained and districts need to buy computers to support the myriad digital tests that are part of the assessment structure. The computers, of course, are not a one-time cost, given the rapidly obsolescent nature of this technology.

And as the results of standardized tests based on a curriculum based on the Common Core standards have become available, the public along with teachers, teachers unions, and school officials has been dismayed to see a precipitous drop in scores. The school establishment fears the consequences, which might include penalization of schools for poor performance, while parents fear their children's future has been compromised by a heedless experiment with an unproved pedagogy.

In the last four years the controversy over the Common Core has become a many-sided affair, with liberals and conservatives on both sides of the battle lines. Some teachers unions support the Common Core; some oppose it. Some supporters have been begun to defect. The American Federation of Teachers, which publicly supports the Common Core standards, has thrown up its hands in disgust at the pell-mell rush to proctor and base administrative decisions on Common Core-aligned tests.

Timeline

Understanding the timeline of the adoption of Common Core is crucial to understanding the controversies and the opposition it has engendered.

The Common Core sped into existence on the wings of private philanthropies and federal incentives, rapidly flying from abstract idea to concrete standards to actual policy in a short period of time. Many states were left scrambling to decide whether they would

27

join or decline. In many cases, they agreed to adopt the Common Core before it was even finished.

During 2008, private organizations such as the Council of Chief State School Officers (CCSSO) and the National Governors Association (NGA) urged the development of national education standards. Achieve, a private education nonprofit, joined in the movement while the James B. Hunt Institute helped by sponsoring conferences and summits for state education leaders and officials. In 2008, CCSSO, NGA, and Achieve issued a formal call for the development of national K–12 standards, which set in motion the writing of the Common Core.

In July 2009, President Obama and U.S. Secretary of Education Arne Duncan announced Race to the Top, the federally-sponsored state education competition incentivizing the adoption of Common Core. This was four months before states had their first peek at the first draft of the standards, and eleven months before the standards were finished. Forty-one states applied for RttT money in Phase 1 of applications, due January 2010. At that time, an early draft of the standards had been released to the public just two months prior, and the validation committee had met only once. (They would meet again twice more to review new iterations of the standards.)

Phase 2 applications were due on June 1, 2010, the day that final Common Core State Standards were released to the states, and one day before the standards were released to the public. In November and December 2011, states had the opportunity to complete a two-part application for Phase 3 Race to the Top funding, just one year and five months after the final standards were made public. As mentioned above, now that states have had time to compare the new standards to their old state standards, calculate the costs of implementing the Common Core, and better examine what is being required of them, some states are seeking to back out of the Common Core.

Timeline

- **December 19, 2008** - NGA, CCSSO, and Achieve release a report *Benchmarking for Success* calling on states to create and adopt "a common core of internationally benchmarked standards in math and language arts for grades K through 12."[16] They begin working to launch the Common Core State Standards Initiative (CCSSI).

- **June 1, 2009** - NGA and CCSSO announce that 49 states and territories have joined the CCSSI to write new national K–12 education standards.[17]

- **July 24, 2009** - President Obama and U.S. Secretary of Education Arne Duncan announce the federally-backed Race to the Top grant application, which awards points for states who agree to adopt the Common Core.[18]

- **September 21, 2009** - An early, incomplete draft of the Common Core is released to the public for review and comment. Comment is closed on October 21, 2009.[19]

- **September 24, 2009** - The validation committee for the Common Core is announced. The members review drafts of the Common Core State Standards in December 2009, April 2010, and May 2010.[20]

- **January 19, 2010** - Phase 1 applications to Race to the Top are due. (40 states, plus the District of Columbia, apply for funding.)[21]

- **March 10, 2010** - The first public complete draft of the standards are released. Members of the public have 24 days to review and submit feedback before April 2, 2010.[22]

- **March 29, 2010** - Phase 1 winners of Race to the Top are announced. Two states, Delaware and Tennessee, are awarded grants.[22]

- **June 1, 2010** - Deadline for submitting Phase 2 applications.[24]

- **June 1, 2010** - The final Standards are released privately to the states, six months after the first round of Race to the Top applications were due, and the same day that Phase 2 applications are due.[25]

- **June 2, 2010** - The full Common Core State Standards are released to the public, one day after the states received them.[26]

- **August 24, 2010** - Phase 2 Race to the Top winners are announced. Ten states plus D.C. win grants: Florida, Georgia, Hawaii, Maryland, Massachusetts, New York, North Carolina, Ohio, Rhode Island, and Washington, D.C.[27]

- **February 23, 2011** - A bill, S 604, is introduced into the South Carolina General Assembly stating that the Common Core State Standards may not be imposed on the state. The bill elicited a statement from U.S. Education Secretary Arne Duncan scolding South Carolina for its low academic expectations. The bill floundered in committee but a reintroduced version passed and was signed by the governor in May 2014.[28]

- **November 22, 2011** - Part 1 of Phase 3 Race to the Top grant applications is due.[29]

- **December 16, 2011** - Part 2 of Phase 3 Race to the Top grant application is due.[30]

- **December 22, 2011** - Phase 3 winners are announced. Seven states, Arizona, Colorado, Illinois, Kentucky, Louisiana, New Jersey, and Pennsylvania receive federal money.[31]

- **August 2012** - A string of states begin revealing their doubts in the new standards as well as the associated standardized tests. Utah withdraws from the testing consortium SBAC.[32]

- **November 2012** - Kentucky, the first state to adopt the Common Core, released the first set of Common Core-aligned tests results (developed by Pearson), which showed proficiency ratings at about 30% lower than in 2011 when students were tested against Kentucky's state standards.[33]

- **January 24, 2013** - Missouri SB 210 is introduced, which states that "the state board of education and the department of elementary and secondary education shall not implement the Common Core State Standards developed by the Common Core Standards

Initiative." The bill passed both the Missouri Senate and House. A reconciled version was signed by the governor in July 2014.[34]

- **February 2013** - Alabama, which had joined each of the two testing consortia PARCC and SBAC, withdraws from both.[35]

- **April 2013** - Next Generation of Science Standards released. Not part of the Common Core but widely seen as a complement to the Common Core.

- **April 2013** - Indiana passes a bill halting the implementation of Common Core, which Indiana governor Mike Pence signs in May.[36]

- **April 12, 2013** - The Republican National Committee adopts a resolution condemning the Common Core as "one size fits all," "an inappropriate overreach to standardize and control," and a "nationwide straitjacket on academic freedom and achievement." The resolution also condemns the collection of student data without the students' or parents' knowledge and approval.[37]

- **April 25, 2013** - Eight U.S. Senators (Tom Coburn (R-Okla.), Ted Cruz (R-Texas), Deb Fischer (R-Neb.), James Inhofe (R-Okla.), Mike Lee (R-Utah), Rand Paul (R-Ky.), Pat Roberts (R-Kan.), and Jeff Sessions (R-Ala.)) sign onto a letter drafted by Iowa Senator Chuck Grassley asking the chair and ranking member of the Appropriations subcommittee overseeing the U.S. Department of Education's funding of the Common Core to require that no USDOE funds go towards any Common-Core related purpose.[38]

- **May 2013** - Pennsylvania governor Tom Corbett issues an order delaying the implementation of Common Core, after the Pennsylvania house and senate committees on education expressed division and uncertainty over adopting the new standards.[39]

- **June 2013** - Michigan governor Rick Snyder halts Michigan's implementation of Common Core by signing a budget that prohibits state funding for Common Core.[40]

- **July 19, 2013** - The U.S. House of Representatives passes H.R. 5, the Student Success Act of 2013, which includes provisions barring the Department of Education from any attempt to "influence, incentivize, or coerce" states to adopt the Common Core.[41]

31

- **July 2013** - Oklahoma and Georgia announce independently that they will pull out of the Common Core testing consortium PARCC.[42]

- **August 2013** - New York State Department of Education announces the first results of Common Core aligned tests in New York State, one of the first states to implement the new tests.[43] Only 31% of students in grades 3–8 met the proficiency standards in ELA and math, compared to 65% in ELA and 55% in math in 2012, under the old New York state standards and tests.

- **September 2013** - Twenty states begin full implementation of the Common Core. Officially 45 states have joined. Alaska, Nebraska, Texas, and Virginia have rejected the Common Core. Minnesota is half-in, half-out. Alabama, Indiana, Louisiana, Massachusetts, New York, Ohio, and Pennsylvania are weighing legislation to withdraw.

- **January 2014** - Pearson introduces Common Core app for iPad.[44]

- **March 2014** - College Board announces changes in SAT to align it with the Common Core.[45] Indiana becomes the first state to withdraw from the Common Core.

- **May 2014** - South Carolina governor signs a bill replacing the Common Core in time for the 2015-2016 school year.

- **June 2014** -
  - Rasmussen Poll shows plummeting support for Common Core among parents who have school-age children.[46]
  - Gates Foundation urges two-year moratorium on school decisions about Common Core tests.[47]
  - Oklahoma repeals the Common Core.
  - The National Education Association calls implementation of the Core "botched" and demands a "course correction."

- **July 2014** -
  - Controversy breaks out over College Board's revision of Advanced Placement U.S. History Standards, changed in part to align them with the Common Core.

- Ohio House Republicans introduce a bill to replace the Common Core.[48]

- Utah governor asks attorney general to review his state's adoption of Common Core to see if it was improperly influenced by the federal government.[49]

• **August 2014** - Republican National Committee commends anti-Common Core activists.[50]

• **October 2014** -

- 132 prominent Catholic professors release a letter to each Catholic bishop in the U.S. calling on them to rethink their support for the Common Core.[51]

- Obama administration punishes Oklahoma for dropping out of Common Core; rescinds its No Child Left Behind waiver.[52]

• **March 2015** -

- PARCC discovered monitoring social media accounts of students who took PARCC exams.[53]

- Two national studies released show minimal gains in student learning after five years of the Common Core.[54]

• **April 2015** -

- Public recognition that Common Core has eliminated handwriting instruction from the curriculum.[55]

- Public recognition that Common Core has replaced GED (General Educational Development test) as the high school equivalency measure.[56]

• **June 2015** - Oregon Governor Kate Brown signs a law easing the way for parents who want to opt their children out of Common Core testing.

• **July 2015** - New Jersey announces plan to replace the Common Core.[57]

• **September 2015** - Rhode Island and Nevada implement the Common Core.

The 2013–2014 school year was when many states began to implement the Common Core. That involved retraining teachers and preparing students for a slew of new tests developed by PARCC and SBAC. It should also have involved the adoption of new textbooks, and, although some publishers, notably Pearson, were ready with Common Core-aligned texts, this proved to be a bottleneck. The near future will determine the fate of the Common Core.

The Basics

The Common Core sounds more complicated than it is. Let's unpack it.

What the Common Core State Standards Are

Before it became the copyrighted name for a set of educational standards, "the common core" was the term we professors used to talk about the list of books and ideas that *all* the students in a particular school had to study. The common core contrasted with electives and majors and other forms of specialization. A college, for example may require every freshman to read Plato's *Republic*, take an English composition course, take a class on the American founding, and complete a multivariate calculus course. But beyond these "common core requirements," the student at that college would be free to take anything from interpretive dance to particle physics. This concept of the common core combines two things: the idea that students benefit from having a *shared* body of knowledge, and the idea that some *particular* knowledge is so fundamental that a student must master it before anything else. The former is the force behind the word "common"; the latter gives life to the word "core." Historically, America's primary schools were nothing but "common core." All the students in first, second, and third grade at any particular school studied the same things.

But that's not what the new "Common Core State Standards" are all about. What is "common" about them is not that they are the basic requirements in a particular school but that they are meant to be the same in every school in every state. And what is "core" about them is not that they identify the particular books and knowledge as fundamental but mostly that they organize the sequence and progression of what "skills" students learn from kindergarten through 12th grade.

That's a rough approximation. The Common Core does imply some judgments about what *kinds* of knowledge are most fundamental. For example, it puts a large emphasis on teaching students how to read "informational texts," in contrast to reading stories or literature. The Common Core emphasizes teaching students to think of what they learn as "evidence" that can be put to use in making "arguments," as opposed to "facts" that help the student to discern how things really are. For the most part, the Common steers away from giving students a concrete picture of the world. Instead it emphasizes abstract skills such as reasoning and evaluating competing interpretations of data and evidence.

A natural response to these contrasts is, "Why not do both?" Surely students need to learn to reason and to know some facts. And indeed, a good set of standards would strike the right balance and put the pieces in a sensible sequence. Some things are best learned by doing. Learning to tie shoelaces comes before studying the typology of knots. Some things require a little abstraction at the very beginning. Letters are symbols that represent sounds. Some things should be learned as facts before they are analyzed in depth. In 1492 Columbus discovered America.

Part of the argument against the Common Core is that it jumbles up these basic distinctions or throws the emphases in the wrong places.

Be that as it may, the Common Core State Standards amount to a set of specifications about what students across the country should be able to do at each grade level. As we have noted, at the moment the Common Core is limited to only two sets of standards: (1) English Language Arts (ELA) and (2) Mathematics.

The English Language Arts

The English Language Arts Standards are broader than teaching students how to read, write, speak, and listen. Its full name is "English Language Arts & Literacy in History/Social Studies, Science, and Technical Subjects," and its aim is to make sure that American students undergo a "progressive development" of skills that will make them "college and career ready in literacy no later than the end of high school."

In grades K–5, the English Language Arts Standards are broken into four sub-standards: reading, writing, speaking and listening, and language. History, social studies, science, and technical subjects are not explicitly broken out in these early grades, but the drafters of the standards make clear that these topics are supposed to be "integrated into the K–5 Writing standards." By grade 6, however, the standards become more specific about these components, which are treated in grades 6–12 as independent instructional strands with skill specifications of their own. Likewise in these higher grades, writing, once a general ELA sub-standard, becomes its own independent strand.

The divisions and separations of these subjects, however, may be more apparent than real. The Common Core envisions a great deal of team-teaching, and teachers of topics in History/Social Studies, Science, and Technical Subjects are expected to participate in teaching the core ELA subjects (reading, writing, speaking, and listening). The governing idea is that students are required to read, write, speak, etc. in every subject. This leads to some complications that we will get to later.

The Common Core sets up a fairly precise percentage of the balance of literary and "informational" texts that students should be reading in each grade. As students progress from K–12, they read more and more informational texts. By fifth grade, literature and informational texts are evenly balanced. By twelfth grade, student reading is apportioned as thirty percent literature and seventy percent informational texts.

The Common Core's authors specify which skills are developed by studying informational texts and which by literature. The rubric recognizes ten basic skills that derive from reading informational texts and nine that derive from reading literature and grow more complex as students advance.

By grade two, for example, the standards give as an informational text skill:

- *CCSS.ELA-Literacy.RI.2.5: Know and use various text features (e.g., captions, bold print, subheadings, glossaries, indexes, electronic menus, icons) to locate key facts or information in a text efficiently.*

The parallel skill that the standards specify for literature is:

- *CCSS.ELA-Literacy.RL.2.5: Describe the overall structure of a story, including describing how the beginning introduces the story and the ending concludes the action.*

By grade 12, the standards specify as an informational text skill:

- *CCSS.ELA-Literacy.RI.11–12.3: Analyze a complex set of ideas or sequence of events and explain how specific individuals, ideas, or events interact and develop over the course of the text.*

The parallel skill that the standards specify for literature is:

- *CCSS.ELA-Literacy.RL.11–12.3: Analyze the impact of the author's choices regarding how to develop and relate elements of a story or drama (e.g., where a story is set, how the action is ordered, how the characters are introduced and developed).*

The skills developed in History/Social Studies, Science, and Technical Subjects are likewise delineated by a "progressive" scheme.

The writing standards require that students master three types of writing: argumentation, informational/explanatory text, and narrative, each of which grows increasingly sophisticated with each grade. The emphasis on argumentation in first grade looks like a significant departure from traditional ideas about child development, but it is consistent with the Common Core's broad emphasis on practical reasoning. Under the Common Core students are required to write "opinion pieces" in grades 1–5 and "arguments" in 6–12.

Exceptions

The ELA standards are mainly a list of skills grade by grade. But there are two exceptions: some specific readings that are required and an additional standard that strongly influences the selection of other readings. The latter is a "range, quality, and complexity" standard. I'll describe that first and come back to the specific required readings.

"Range" refers to the variety of literature—story, drama, poem, etc.—or informational text—"literary nonfiction and historical, scientific, and technical texts"—students must read. "Quality" is undefined but presumably refers to a judgment as to whether something is worth reading. "Complexity" refers to the difficulty of a text, and the Common Core authors present a "three-part model for measuring text complexity." Teachers must take into account "qualitative dimensions," "quantitative dimensions," and "reader and task considerations."

This sounds to most of us laymen as bland and perhaps tedious. Of course teachers should think about range, quality, and complexity. Is the Common Core just reaffirming the obvious? Maybe, but its authors don't seem to think so, nor do many of the critics. What lies beneath these seemingly bland declarations is a determination to limit the discretion of actual teachers about what they should teach. The proponents of Common Core, however, are very wary of pushing this part of their agenda too hard or to be explicit about it. The Common Core is itself an "informational text" of unusual subtlety and complexity, if not necessarily of the highest quality. It disguises as much as it reveals.

The standards do provide a 183-page list of "text exemplars" (known as "Appendix B") which are deemed appropriate for each grade, genre, and task. This list provides one kind of hint as to what the Common Core is about. The novels, plays, poems, and "informational texts" on the list include the titles of numerous outstanding works. By grade 11, the exemplars include Chaucer's *Canterbury Tales*, Cervantes' *Don Quixote*, Austen's *Pride and Prejudice*, Shakespeare's *Hamlet*, Moliere's *Tartuffe*, Paine's *Common Sense*, Thoreau's *Walden*, and Mencken's *The American Language*. This suggests a very high standard indeed, and if the implication is that students would find the time and energy to read a significant number of the "exemplars" during a given academic year, we would end up with high school graduates with a far better liberal arts education than most Ivy League college graduates.

But hold on. The "exemplars" name many great books, but the Common Core doesn't actually recommend that teachers assign such books in their entirety or even in anything more than isolated fragments. Chaucer's *Canterbury Tales* is exemplified by the first 42 lines of the "General Prologue," rendered in modern English; *Don Quixote* rides forth in a series of paragraphs spliced together from parts of the opening chapter; *Pride and Prejudice* is truncated to "a truth universally acknowledged" and the opening dialogue; *Hamlet* is bound in the nutshell of King Claudius's soliloquy on his guilt; and so on.

My National Association of Scholars colleague, Carol Iannone, took on the task of reviewing the teacher's edition of a Pearson Education Group/Prentice Hall 11th grade reader created specifically for schools that had put the Common Core ELA Standards in place.[58] *The American Experience—Common Core Edition* weighs over ten pounds and includes over 500 readings, and the teacher's edition charts page-by-page how each reading connects to the Standards. Nothing is left to the teacher's discretion or the student's imagination. The meaning of every assigned text is pre-specified in detail. How exactly this paint-by-numbers instruction promotes "critical thinking" is a mystery. But one thing is clear: the students in 11th grade Common Core read very few works in their entirety except short poems. The only exception in *The American Experience* is Arthur Miller's allegory of the McCarthy era, *The Crucible*, which is presented in its entirety.

The Common Core "exemplars" are, to be sure, merely recommendations and the Common Core does not prohibit teachers from pursuing more ambitious reading assignments. But the "text exemplars" have the very large power of filling in the gap between "the standards" and the actual curricula that schools will have to pursue.

We should be careful—because the architects of the Common Core are careful—not to confuse the standards with the exemplars. In practice, schools that pursue the Common Core can ignore the exemplars altogether. A few appear to be doing just that. Yet even those that ignore the actual exemplars seem to be absorbing their spirit. That is, the "range, quality, and complexity" standard seems to lend itself to the practice of teaching bits and pieces of longer works and paying little attention to governing context.

Again, the emphasis in the Common Core of gradually mounting "complexity" in assigned readings is something that most of us would assent to without further thought. Start simple and add difficulty as the student acquires greater and greater ability. But the Common Core version of complexity displaces human judgment. Appendix A lists the "quantitative dimensions" of complexity as "word length or frequency, sentence length, and text cohesion," which, the writers admit, "are difficult if not impossible for a human reader to evaluate efficiently," so this will be "measured by computer software."

Required Readings

The Common Core emphasizes skills and trades mainly in recommendations and "exemplars," but in a few cases it specifies particular authors (e.g., Shakespeare) or texts (e.g., *The Declaration of Independence*) that students must read. They are not controversial choices. These specifications are for the most part left to the last two years of high school. In literature, students must:

*Analyze multiple interpretations of a story, drama, or poem...,
evaluating how each version interprets the source text. (Include
at least one play by Shakespeare and one play by an American
dramatist.)*

They are also required to:

*Demonstrate knowledge of eighteenth-, nineteenth-, and ear-
ly-twentieth-century foundational works of American literature.*

In "informational texts," in ninth and tenth grade, students must
"Analyze seminal U.S. documents of historical and literary significance." In eleventh and twelfth grade, they must, "Delineate and
evaluate the reasoning in seminal U.S. texts, including the application of constitutional principles and use of legal reasoning,"
which means they must read at least parts of the U.S. Constitution and some opinions in important Supreme Court cases. Most
specifically, students must "Analyze seventeenth-, eighteenth-, and
nineteenth-century foundational U.S. documents of historical and
literary significance (including the Declaration of Independence,
the Preamble to the Constitution, the Bill of Rights, and Lincoln's
Second Inaugural Address)."

So while it is true that the Common Core standards do not
amount to a curriculum, in a few cases they do specify which texts
students should read and when.

Politically Correct?

Several observers have also criticized the Common Core recommended texts as politically slanted to the left.[59] There are a substantial number of readings, perhaps an overrepresented subset,
that deal with racism and environmentalism. Some choices of
informational texts are distinctly odd, as in grades 9 and 10 a U.S.
Environmental Protection Agency/U.S. Department of Energy
document, Recommended Levels of Insulation; and U.S. General
Services Administration Executive Order 13423, Strengthening
Federal Environmental, Energy, and Transportation Management.
A reading for grades 11 and 12 is an essay from *The New Yorker* by

Atul Gawande, "The Cost Conundrum: What a Texas Town Can Teach Us about Health Care."[60] Perhaps all three of these are models of good English expository writing, but they also appear to be pushing a contemporary political agenda, and are not balanced by recommended readings on the other side of the relevant debates.

Mathematics

This volume includes three essays on Common Core Mathematics by individuals—Ze'ev Wurman, R. James Milgram, and Richard P. Phelps—who are experts in the field. I offer only a layman's summary. The Common Core Standards for Mathematics aim to simplify and regularize the teaching of math in the United States. Like the English Language Arts standards, the Mathematics Standards aim at preparing students for "college and career readiness." The rationale for the Mathematics Standards, however, includes some other distinctive claims.

The overarching theme is that they would give American math instruction "greater focus and coherence." The architects of the Mathematics Standards compare the math performance of American students to students in other nations to drive the idea that the United States needs standards that have greater "clarity and specificity." That corresponds to "greater focus." The pursuit of "coherence," however, draws a much more complicated explanation about the "sequence of topics and performances" that must be logical, hierarchical, discipline-related, "evolved from particulars," connected to "deeper structures," and respectful of "what is known about how students learn."

This is a lot of abstraction to take on board and few who have written either for or against the Mathematics Standards have attempted to unpack it. Instead, observers have focused on the standards themselves, which are bunched into two groups: "Standards for Mathematical Practice" and "Standards for Mathematical Content." Both are prefaced with one more declaration of epistemological purpose, titled "Understanding Mathematics." It seems to be a warning against teaching students to become mere calculators of correct answers. Learning "procedural skill" is important, but "equally important" is "mathematical understanding" in the form of "ability to justify, in a way appropriate to the student's mathematical maturity, why a particular mathematical statement is true or where a mathematical rule comes from."

The "Standards for Mathematical Practice" come first. There are eight of them:

1. Make sense of problems and persevere in solving them.

2. Reason abstractly and quantitatively.

3. Construct viable arguments and critique the reasoning of others.

4. Model with mathematics.

5. Use appropriate tools strategically.

6. Attend to precision.

7. Look for and make use of structure.

8. Look for and express regularity in repeated reasoning.

These broad and rather abstract standards are meant to apply to all grade levels and they are drawn variously from principles advocated by the National Council of Teachers of Mathematics and from the National Research Council's 2001 report, *Adding It Up*, which focused on teaching math "pre-k through eighth grade."[61]

The Standards for Mathematical Practice look wholesome. The Common Core's explanation is that they are meant to emphasize "standards of problem solving, reasoning and proof, communication, representation, connections…adaptive reasoning…strategic competence…conceptual understanding…procedural fluency… and productive disposition."

Subtractions

All this sounds good, and the student who achieved a high level of competency in all of them would surely be regarded as having achieved a robust foundation in mathematics. But it is important to pay some attention to what is missing from this list of goals. The Standards for Mathematical Practice are not much concerned, for example, with the old-fashioned ideas of getting the right answer, calculating efficiently, and performing mathematical functions in your head. "Understanding Mathematics" in the Common Core to some extent trumps actually doing math. That may be a worthy trade-off and it is certainly one over which the authors of the Mathematics Standards deliberated before committing themselves to the approach they published. But it is not clear that parents, teachers, school districts, and even the states that adopted the Core understood this trade-off in advance.

The other piece of the Mathematical Standards is the "Standards for Mathematical Content." These are organized, like the English Language Arts Standards, grade by grade. And there are a great many of them. Kindergarten alone has 22 standards, grouped into five subcategories and nine sub-sub categories. The five subcategories are: Counting and Cardinality; Operations and Algebraic Thinking; Number Operations in Base Ten; Measurement and Data; and Geometry. The sub-sub categories under "Counting and Cardinality," are "Know number names and count sequence," "Count to tell the number of objects," and "Compare numbers." An example of a standard under the first of these subcategories and sub-subcategories is:

- *CCSS.Math.Content.K.CC.A.3 - Write numbers from 0 to 20. Represent a number of objects with a written numeral 0-20 (with 0 representing a count of no objects).*

A related standard under the subheading "Number and Operations in Base Ten" is:

- *CCSS.Math.Content.K.NBT.A.1 - Compose and decompose numbers from 11 to 19 into ten ones and some further ones, e.g., by using objects or drawings, and record each composition or decomposition by a drawing or equation (such as 18 = 10 + 8); understand that these numbers are composed of ten ones and one, two, three, four, five, six, seven, eight, or nine ones.*

44

Number 20 is apparently left out of the K.NBT.A.1 as a tantalizing glimpse of things to come.

To most of us who give relatively little thought to how math is taught to kindergarteners, this emphasis on the numbers from 11 to 19 seems unremarkable, but again the thing to pay attention to is what goes missing. The Common Core Mathematics Standards, after all, announce their first purpose as "greater focus." In this case, the focus on numbers 11 to 19 comes at the price of dropping some topics. In New York State, as the *New York Times* put it, what was dropped was "rudimentary introductions to concepts in algebra and statistics."[62] Algebra and statistics in kindergarten? What that really meant was that children were taught to look for elementary patterns, but are now focusing on gaining a "deeper" understanding of how a number such as "14" can be said, written, and understood to represent "a group of 14 objects."

Division

All told, there are 382 Common Core Mathematics Standards. To those of us who are not math teachers, what does all this amount to? Critics have offered five related characterizations of the Mathematics Standards. (1) The Common Core rhetoric of "rigor" notwithstanding, the Mathematics Standards set a low bar. They pamper rather than challenge students and end up shortchanging Americans in this vital area of education. (2) The Mathematics Standards build on some novel and not well tested ideas about the proper content and the right sequence of mathematics instruction. (3) In their emphasis on "mathematical understanding," the Mathematics Standards scant basic number skills. (4) In their pursuit of a kind of theoretical purity, the authors of the Mathematics Standards have created unnecessary barriers both to students gaining practical math skills and to parents who seek to participate in their children's education. The Standards privilege the "experts" at the expense of the public. (5) The Mathematics Standards are highly susceptible to forms of implementation that magnify all these problems.

R. James Milgram, Stanford Professor of Mathematics, says of the Common Core Mathematics Standards that they are the result of "political" compromises among the members of the committee that drew them up, with the result that the Standards are "as non-challenging as possible." Milgram should know since he served on the Common Core Validation Committee and refused to sign off on the final product.[63]

There are so many standards involving so many aspects of math that it is difficult to get a sense of the overall tenor of the Common Core approach. To many of the critics, one component of the Mathematics Standards has come to represent this overall tenor: the elimination of Algebra I in the eighth grade. By pushing completion of algebra to the ninth grade, the Common Core compresses the possibilities for high school mathematics and pushes calculus out of the curriculum. The standards culminate with statistics and probability. What appears to be a problematic aspect of the Common Core to some, of course, is an opportunity for others. Private academies have begun to advertise that, in contrast to the Common Core Mathematics Standards which reach no further than "pre-calculus," they can offer high school students, as one academy puts it, "one year of calculus and therefore spend their last year(s) of Upper School covering concepts that exceed the Common Core State Standards."[64]

Milgram's critique is more detailed. He argues that the more advanced countries teach algebra in seventh grade and geometry in eighth, and enable "a huge percentage" of students to finish calculus by the end of high school.[65]

Milgram also draws attention to the Common Core's unusual and previously untried approach to teaching geometry. Beginning in grade 7, students are introduced to an approach that focuses on "rigid transformations." This is a mathematically rigorous version of Euclidian geometry that employs "rotations, translations, and reflections," in which the vector distances between pairs of points are preserved as an object is moved. A supposed advantage of this approach mathematically is that it also preserves the difference between right and left-handedness. Milgram concedes that the approach is mathematically sophisticated and rigorous but notes "it focuses on sophisticated structures teachers have not studied or even seen before," and may well result in teachers opting for a superficial treatment of geometry, "one where there are no proofs at all."[66]

Milgram's criticisms are paralleled by the analyses of Ze'ev Wurman, an electrical engineer who served on a California Commission which evaluated the Common Core. In a paper with Sandra Stotsky, Wurman argues that the Mathematics Standards are destined to leave students ill-prepared for college math and for basic courses in science and engineering. He has compared the Mathematics Standards to the old standards in California and Massachusetts, and to the recommendations of the National Mathematics Advisory Panel (NMAP).

In an effort to foster greater knowledge of math among American students, NMAP in 2008 set out a plan to help students to develop the skills to progress to algebra and beyond. It proposed three "clusters" of skills: fluency with whole numbers; fluency with fractions; and "particular aspects of geometry and measurement." In 2010, Wurman published an analysis of how the Common Core addresses some key topics in each of these clusters. His analysis is included in Common Core's Standards Still Don't Make the Grade, which is part of this volume.

Among his observations is that when it comes to fluency with whole numbers, the Common Core defers learning division until 6th grade. That's unlike what other high-performing nations do. It also crowds 6th grade instruction in ratios. "Students tackle this new and demanding concept without complete fluency with division, which may undermine their ability to learn the new concepts of ratio and proportional thinking."[67]

Wurman faults the Common Core in the second cluster for introducing decimal fractions "in grade 4, two years behind both California and Massachusetts." He notes that while the Common Core introduces the concept of negative numbers in grade 6, it has, contrary to NMAP's recommendations, no standards for developing fluency with multiplication and division by negative numbers. It likewise neglects teaching students about how to find least common denominators. Wurman argues that the Common Core overemphasizes visual models for teaching fractions.

Wurman's critique of the Common Core's handling of geometry, like Milgram's critique, focuses on "the Common Core's effort to replace the traditional foundations of geometry" with ideas about "rigid motions."

$3 \times 4 = 11$

Another line of criticism is that the Common Core Mathematics Standards embody an approach called "investigative math" or "investigations math." Glyn Wright, executive director of the Eagle Forum, has complained:

> The math standard focuses on investigative math, which has been shown to be a disaster…With the new math standard in the Common Core, there are no longer absolute truths. So 3 times 4 can now equal 11 so long as a student can effectively explain how they reached that answer.[68]

The Common Core Standards themselves make no reference to an approach called "investigative math," though the word "investigate" naturally occurs quite a few times in an appendix on designing high school mathematics courses. This plainly is not what Wright, who focused on elementary school math instruction, had in mind. Rather, she appears to be referring to *Investigations in Number, Data, and Space,* a K–5 mathematics curriculum developed by TERC, a nonprofit in Cambridge, Massachusetts that focuses on improving math, science, and technology instruction. *Investigations* was developed with National Science Foundation funding. TERC promotes *Investigations* as being in "full alignment" with the Common Core Mathematics Standards, and Pearson, the publishing house, sells the Investigations "companion materials" as an integrated part of Common Core.

Thus a distinction seems in order. Wright is correct that some (many?) school districts that implement the Common Core Mathematics Standards employ the TERC *Investigations* K–5 curriculum, but her indictment is really of the TERC curriculum, not the Common Core Standards. Presumably those standards could be implemented with a curriculum that differs a lot from *Investigations*. This is another instance of how the problematic aspects of the Common Core tend to become manifest in the implementation stages rather than the Standards themselves. But that doesn't let the Standards off the hook. After all, the Standards invite the kind of elaboration that TERC has provided, and no one at the Common Core appears to be concerned that *Investigations* has misinterpreted what the Common Core requires. The designers of *Investigations* and the publisher of the teaching materials see perfect alignment, and the alignment goes even deeper. The Gates Foundation, the single biggest non-governmental backer of the Common Core, has been a major contributor to the non-profit arm of Pearson, the Pearson Foundation, having provided, for example, a $3 million grant to Pearson in February 2011 to support the development of "open access courses for 6th and 7th grade mathematics," among other things.[69]

Wright is also correct that many parents find the *Investigations* curriculum to be odd, unnecessarily complicated, and an obstacle to learning basic math. For instance, one popular YouTube video shows a third grader demonstrating to her mom how she can solve a math problem that is "going to be very hard."[70] The problem:

Betty bought 1,568 stickers. For her birthday she got 1,423 more. On Monday she went back to Sticker Station and bought 680 more. How many stickers does Betty have now?

The child proceeds using the TERC – taught method to diagram the numbers into geometric cubes (for the number 1,000), squares (for 100), lines (for 10), and dots (for 1). She adds the squares, adds them to the cubes, and erases the drawings as she proceeds. It takes her about eight minutes. She gets the wrong answer (3,763 instead of 3,671). Afterwards she performs the addition by using a technique her mom has taught her at home, which she calls "stacking," i.e., putting the numbers in a column and adding them up. It takes her about a minute and she gets the right answer. The child tries to explain her error using the TERC method by saying the approach was "more confusing and things were all over the place." She called the traditional approach "more organized."

Many parents expressed outrage at the way the school had taught the third grader how to add. Some math teachers, however, defended the pedagogy. One wrote:

> I am a middle school math teacher with a Masters in Teaching. This girl is explaining and drawing pictures to represent place value. This is an important concept to understand which many students don't learn as thoroughly as she has. Once this conceptual understanding has been developed students can then add the standard way. Math is not just about finding the right answer, but understanding how you get there. From this video I see meaningful learning going on here.

"Math is not just about finding the right answer, but understanding how you get there." That is in a nutshell the Common Core philosophy for mathematics instruction. It clearly resonates with a substantial number of math teachers, but it is worrisome to parents.

The emphasis on "not just" finding the right answers seems a short step from treating the pursuit of right answers as a minor concern. And indeed, the tone of dismissal about "not just" finding the right answer in some cases skips directly to the idea that the right answer can be superfluous. What's crucial, in this view, is the evidence that the student swim in the right direction.

Another YouTube video that has attracted a lot of attention shows Amanda August, the curriculum coordinator for the school district in Grayslake, a Chicago suburb, addressing a group of parents at a townhall on the Common Core.[71] August explains that the Common Core is "based on very sound, solid research and practice." She says of the Math Standards, "There's fewer of them; they're much clearer; and they are much more rigorous." The part of her presentation that has garnered national attention, however, comes when she turns to the Common Core's emphasis on "understanding" math, rather than learning how to calculate:

Amanda August: "Even if they [the students] said '3 times 4 equals 11,' if they were able to explain their reasoning and explain how they came up with their answer, really in words and in oral explanations, and they showed it in the picture but just got the final number wrong— we're more focusing on the *how*.

Audience member: "You are going to be correcting them, right?"

Amanda August: Oh, absolutely, absolutely. We want our students to compute correctly but the emphasis is really moving more towards the explanation, and the how, and the why, and 'can I really talk through the procedures that I went through to get this answer,'"

R. James Milgram and Wilfried Schmid, professor of mathematics at Harvard, issued a joint statement some years ago in which they characterized TERC as "deficient."[72] They argued that good mathematics education must "strive for a proper balance between mathematical reasoning, problem solving, and computational facility." It seems a fair criticism of not just the *Investigations* curriculum but the Common Core Mathematics Standards themselves that they are disproportionately weighted toward mathematical reasoning at the expense of the other two. What Milgram and Schmid call "number skills" are eclipsed in the Common Core by an effort to achieve an abstract rigor that may please some theorists but leaves students with impoverished skills.

The essay in this volume by Phelps and Milgram rounds out the critique of Common Core Mathematics by comparing it to mathematics instruction in other countries. They argue, interestingly, that the Common Core approach lays a better foundation than most American schools used to provide, but they vigorously dispute the claims of Common Core proponents that the new standards bring American math education up to the level of mathematics instruction in other developed countries. Their essay also captures errors in the Common Core approach that most of us

51

would probably miss, but once pointed out seem like substantial faults.

Who's Behind the Common Core?

Those who like to say that "Personnel is policy" can find support for that idea in the gallery of people who originated and helped to shape the Common Core. The advocates of the Common Core prefer to present it as a great work of collaboration and consultation, as if it sprang directly from the collective minds of the state governments as filtered through the National Governors Association and the Council of Chief State School Officers. Nothing could be further from the truth. The insistence on the role of the states is part of the marketing of the Common Core. It serves the twin purposes of asserting that the Common Core is not a creation of the federal government and asserting that it has legitimacy as a bottom-up reform movement in American society.

The facts are more complicated. The Common Core did not originate in the offices of the federal government but it is now deeply entangled with the U.S. Department of Education and likely to become even more of a federal project in the years ahead. And there is virtually nothing in the Common Core that could accurately be described as either grass-roots or originating from the states. The Common Core was instead a project put together by a small number of educational entrepreneurs who "sold" their idea to some powerful financial and political backers.

David Coleman, now president of the College Board; Susan Pimentel, a second lead author of the Common Core ELA standards; and Jason Zimba, a physics and mathematics professor at Bennington College (where David Coleman's mother was president) were the inner core of the Common Core. Without them, there would be no Common Core. According to revised history, Coleman, Pimentel, and Zimba first developed the idea and persuaded the NGA and CCSSO to sponsor it.

Michael Cohen, president of Achieve, Inc.; Laura Slover, senior vice president at Achieve, overseeing the development and implementation of PARCC's tests; and Sandra Boyd, chief operating officer at Achieve take us into the second layer of the Common Core's origin. Achieve, Inc. was an organization that already existed. It was founded in 1996 as an outgrowth of the National Education Summit of governors and business leaders, and had done work to promote educational standards. Prior to its involvement in the Common Core, which started in 2009, Achieve, Inc. was best known for trying to set benchmarks for student achievement in English and math. Pimentel worked for Cohen and Slover on that benchmarking effort, the American Diploma Project. Achieve also connects the Common Core to several other nationally prominent organizations and to key politicians.

Marc Tucker, president and CEO of the National Center on Education and the Economy; Jim Hunt, former governor of North Carolina; and Chester Finn, president of the Thomas B. Fordham Institute have been the Common Core's evangelists, selling it to several distinct constituencies. Tucker is important as the voice of the utilitarian calculus of the Common Core: the idea that the fundamental purpose of education is not education itself but job readiness. The numerous organizations with which he has been involved are incubators of other Common Core supporters. Hunt is important as the primary gubernatorial face of the Common Core, though Jeb Bush, former governor of Florida, and Bob Wise, former governor of West Virginia, have also played conspicuous roles in giving the Common Core a semblance of coming from the states. Finn is the most prominent think-tank conservative to lend his support to the Common Core.

Arne Duncan, current United States Secretary of Education and former chief executive of the Chicago Public Schools; and Joel Klein, former chancellor of the New York City public schools, are known for their aggressive pursuit of centralization and top-down management in large urban school districts. Duncan worked his way up through the ranks in Chicago. Klein left a successful career as a lawyer and media executive to head the New York Public

Schools. As men who wrestled with the obdurate problem of the racial achievement gap and persistently underperforming schools, they were perhaps preconditioned to see the appeals of a reform proposal like the Common Core that appropriates the rhetoric of high standards for a program of fair-to-middling expectations. In any case, both have given the Common Core the sheen of credibility as an approach that might be made to work to advance the learning of inner-city students who have seemed immune to many other attempts to improve public education.

Our catalog of individual proponents of Common Core could, of course, be much longer, but the names we have given capture both the most important contributors and give a sense of the wider field. The list, however, is incomplete in another sense. Some of the key players in the debate are organizations rather than individuals. The Fordham Institute and the American Enterprise Institute are organizations generally considered conservative in outlook that favor the Common Core. The Pioneer Institute, which is publishing this book and has sponsored the essays that are collected here, is probably the most important opponent of the Common Core. The American Principles Project, The Heartland Institute, and the Pacific Research Institute have also played leading roles in organizing public opposition to the Common Core. Among the institutional contributors to the debate, however, by far the most important is the Common Core advocate, the Bill & Melinda Gates Foundation.

The Role of the Gates Foundation

The Bill & Melinda Gates Foundation funds research and work on 21 issues, 18 of them international, and most of them focused on matters of health. Its three U.S. programs, though, have a particular bent towards education. One of the three U.S. programs funds projects relevant to Washington State, home to the foundation's headquarters, but the other two focus on college completion rates and on K–12 education.

"College-Ready Education," the K–12 initiative, aims to "ensure that all students graduate from high school prepared to succeed in college." To that end, the Gates Foundation has taken on the Common Core issue as its own. It might not be overstating the case, though, to say that the Gates Foundation created the Common Core in the first place, or at least served as its midwife. As the "College-Ready" homepage says,

> More than 45 states have adopted the Common Core State Standards for student learning...We're working with our partners to help these standards become part of the fabric of schools around the country and will support ongoing efforts to ensure they are understood and implemented effectively.[73]

All told, the Gates Foundation has spent over $200 million dollars on the Common Core. The funds have covered large portions of the costs of writing the Common Core.[74] Those funds paid for companies to redesign textbooks and curriculum; hired teams of software developers to create digital education venues in line with the new standards; bought advocacy campaigns on the national and state levels; seeded grassroots initiatives; purchased teacher training material; and enabled cash-starved state school boards and county school districts to pay for implementation costs. An additional $16.7 million dollars helped build a database system, inBloom, meant to complement the Common Core by aggregating student data into a single, easily accessed resource. More speculatively, Gates funds went to some organizations that might otherwise have mounted opposition to the Common Core but which then fell silent or found surprising reasons to support it.

At each step of the Common Core's development, the Gates Foundation has played a major role. The Hunt Institute, buoyed by $8,308,244 in Gates grants from 2008–2013, worked with NGA and CCSSO to put into place a national institutional platform calling for national standards. NGA has itself received nearly $26 million from the Gates Foundation, $1.6 million of that amount specifically earmarked for Common Core purposes. CCSSO has also accepted Gates cash: $79 million since 2002, $6.6 million of which was used to strategize and develop the Common Core standards, implementation, and assessment.

Student Achievement Partners, the organization David Coleman and Jason Zimba founded to lead the writing of the standards, has received $6.5 million from Gates. And Achieve, which has led the way in helping states transition to the new standards and developing the assessment consortium PARCC, has gotten nearly $37 million.

Other recipients of Common Core-directed Gates grants include state departments of education (Georgia, Pennsylvania, Louisiana, Kentucky, and Delaware), local school districts (in Albuquerque, Cleveland, St. Paul, Puget Sound, and Boston), and research-eager colleges and universities (University of Missouri, MIT, Harvard, University of Florida, DePaul University, George Washington University, Michigan State, University of Arizona, University of Michigan, Regents University of California—Los Angeles, UNC-Chapel Hill, University of the State of New York, Purdue, and New York University). Gates has also funded Common Core advocacy within the United Federation of Teachers, National Congress of Parents and Teachers, the National Council of Teachers of English, and National Association of State Boards of Education.

Some recipients of Gates money have suddenly become Common Core supporters, such as the Thomas B. Fordham Institute, which benefited from over $4 million from Gates, including $1,961,116 specifically for Common Core-related work. The American Enterprise Institute, which has received over $4 million from the Gates Foundation, has come out in favor of the Common Core. (One of those grants, for $1,068,788, was directed to "support their education policy work in four distinct areas: Exploring the Challenges of Common Core, Future of American Education Working Groups, Innovations in Financial Aid, and Bridging K–12 and Higher Ed with Technology."[75])

The harshest critic of the Gates Foundation's expenditures on the Common Core is Diane Ravitch who has written extensively on "How the Gates Foundation Bought and Paid for Common Core." She says of the Standards:

Gates paid to develop them; to evaluate them; to promote them. There seems to be no part of the Common Core that was not bought and paid for by Gates.[76]

And she worries that Gates' effort to re-shape education will not stop with the schools:

> Just as it has done in K–12 education, the foundation has bought the research, bought the evaluations, bought the advocacy groups, and even bought the media that reports on what the foundation is doing.[77]

Ravitch links the Gates Foundation's support of the Common Core with an effort by corporate America to take over education to serve its own interests, and from time to time has engaged in spirited debate with Bill Gates himself or his apologists.[78]

The Gates Foundation's financial support for promotion of the Common Core is far out of scale with any other non-governmental source of financial support on either side of the debate. In a September 2013 article, "The Common Core Money War," published on the website *Politico*, however, Stephanie Simon and Nirvi Shah suggest that the opponents of the Common Core are also well financed:

> The think tanks and advocacy groups fighting the Common Core are supported by some of the wealthiest and most politically savvy conservative donors in the U.S., including the Pope, DeVos and Scaife families, according to tax records and annual reports.

Simon and Shah provide no dollar figures to back up this comparison, but they admit that the amounts provided by the Gates Foundation are far larger: "As for opponents, what they lack in Gates Foundation cash, they make up for in volume." To counter the cash-fed institutional force of the Gates Foundation, the opposition has mainly mounted a grassroots movement:

> Mobilizing on social media, activists pack school board meetings to protest the standards. They bombard state legislators with demands for public hearings. There have been Twitter

rallies and physical rallies, too, in cities as diverse as Augusta, Maine; Raleigh, N.C.; and Port Jefferson Station, N.Y., where more than 1,500 parents, teachers and students marched around the high school football field on a summer afternoon, brandishing signs proclaiming "Common Core Hurts Children."

Simon and Shah even credit the opposition with hiring "its own communications team, Shirley & Banister Public Affairs."[79]

Gates's work is part of an emerging trend known as "philanthrocapitalism." The term, invented by the *Economist's* U.S. business editor Matthew Bishop in a 2006 article, refers to the use of market tools and business practices to enhance the effect of charitable giving. These effects are most marked when used by very wealthy individuals who have the funds necessary to counteract and redirect regular market and government spending tendencies.

Bishop's book *Philanthrocapitalism: How Giving Can Change the World* (co-written with Michael Green) has sparked interest in coalescing massive philanthropic efforts, often by pooling donors to work in tandem. It's also helped create zeal to measure and catalogue outcomes. The idea is to capture the results of each project, analyze them according to some metric, identify promising endeavors, and scale those endeavors to their largest realistic size—sometimes nationwide. Many of those wealthy individuals, including Bill and Melinda Gates, who signed The Giving Pledge to give away half of their wealth before their deaths, have focused their giving in accordance with philanthrocapitalistic ideals.

Targeted giving can effect massive social changes. Sarah Reckhow, a political scientist at Michigan State University, has studied private philanthropy in education and in 2012 released a book with Oxford University Press, *Follow the Money: How Foundation Dollars Change Public School Politics*. Reckhow found that a handful of large foundations have dominated education's philanthropic sphere: the Walton Family Foundation, the Eli and Edythe Broad Foundation, and the Bill & Melinda Gates Foundation. Of the three, Gates is by far the largest. Where Walton has $1.7 billion in assets and Broad has $2.2 billion, the Gates Foundation boasts $37 billion, making it the largest private grant-making foundation in the world.

Reckhow found that private educational giving totaled about $1 billion each year, a hefty sum in itself, but relatively small compared to the $600 billion in annual governmental spending on U.S. K–12 education. Realizing that even their largest donations were dwarfed by governmental spending, foundations have begun ramping up their advocacy work instead. Rather than fund a particular charter school or after-school program, charities are increasingly trying to direct and influence the funding decisions of government agencies armed with bureaucratic power and cash. The Gates Foundation, according to Reckhow's research, has likewise turned towards national issues. Of the Gates Foundation's education-centered giving, the proportion slated for national-level policy research and advocacy has increased more than 7 times from 2000 to 2010.

Reckhow also found that charitable giving was most immediately effective when concentrated in areas with strong top-down control. New York City schools, for instance, with their heavily consolidated administration centered near City Hall, were ripe for philanthropic involvement. Donors focused in New York needed only to convince a few key personnel that their idea or experiment held merit. The danger, though, was that staff turnover would hinder any long-term benefits, since the philanthropist would need to work to convince each new administrator who stepped in later on.

Los Angeles, by contrast, with its more de-centralized school districts, required convincing greater numbers of administrators and government officials, as well as creating a grassroots network of local individuals who supported any reform initiatives. Potential donors would need to spend more time developing relationships with more people in such a district, meaning that the time from start to measurable successes would be longer, but presumably the successes would remain in effect longer, maintained by widespread support cultivated across the entire community.

Long-term reform, then, requires a grassroots campaign built and sustained over time—unless donors can instead go directly to the top of the educational bureaucracy, influencing the national education policy regardless of what local parents and school districts might object. Reckhow cautions that this strategy is risky. She criticized the Gates Foundation as reckless for staking its reputation on single national issues—though it does hold the most promise for immediate, short-term influence.[80] This strategy appears to be precisely what the Gates Foundation has adopted. The Foundation has created a network of well-funded, carefully placed institutional allies with the power to effect the changes the Gates Foundation could not have created or implemented on its own. Instead, it provided key seed money at the outset and at each step along the way located the tipping point, nudging institutional decisions towards adopting and implementing the Common Core.

Private manipulation of markets and policies yields troubling ethical questions about appropriate spheres and blurred boundaries. The Gates Foundation is a private entity, yet it appears to have played a significant role in shaping federal policy and driving significant changes down to the level of state and local jurisdictions across most of the country.

The Common Core does bear a certain resemblance to an operating system. The engineer develops a framework, works out the bugs, builds in enough flexibility to satisfy distinct subgroups of customers, but maintains sufficient consistency and uniformity to dominate the market, such that any later additions must align with it as well. The Gates Foundation has brought to the Common Core some of the business savvy that made Microsoft the dominant player in computer operating systems for the last 40 years.

If Not the Common Core, What?

A single set of academic school standards doesn't really fit the realities of American life or our national aspirations. The United States is not France. Our federal system has historically left education to the states and local communities. The fiction that the Common Core is a voluntary initiative that originated in the states and became a de facto national standard by acclamation is threadbare. A better approach would be one that respects our local and regional differences. That is the essence of the argument I made against the *Common Core in Common Core: Yea and Nay*. (Encounter Books, 2014). My co-author, Sol Stern, argued the "Yea" side.

The Common Core is not alone in violating this key principle of local control. No Child Left Behind in its promotion of universal testing devolved into unwelcome (and unforeseen) consequences; states adopted very low "cut scores" on tests to avoid penalties. We have experience stretching over several decades that federal efforts to bolster the nation's schools have produced little gain and may well have contributed to further erosion of student performance.

Federal involvement is not the sole source or even a primary source of what is hampering K–12 schools in the United States. Other factors loom much larger, including changes in family structure, changes in the labor market, poverty, immigration, and shifts in cultural expectations. The Common Core is a mistaken experiment in part because it attempts to put a curricular band-aide over much more grievous social wounds.

Some of the proponents of the Common Core acknowledge these larger problems by emphasizing that, for the Common Core to work its magic, it will have to be accompanied by shifts in school structure. They especially emphasize the need to "regionalize" school governance and in metropolitan areas combine urban and suburban districts into larger integrated units.

These ideas, even if they were to be implemented, do not come near to solving the root problems. Americans are an inventive and resourceful people, but those qualities work best in situations where they are free to discover for themselves what works best. In that light, a robust version of school choice is probably our best first step. Parents ought to have access to real options, including old-style public schools, charter schools, religious schools, private schools, and homeschooling. School choice is not a stand-alone answer to the larger problems either. The racial performance gap and the radically diminished interest in formal learning that have become endemic in the United States are problems that have to be addressed community by community, family by family. These are not problems that are not to be fixed by top-down policy prescriptions, though good public policy can help tilt communities and families towards fostering better conditions for children to thrive.

The Common Core State Standards, however, are not that policy. The rules they impose will only deepen the alienation from learning and the community disaffection with schools that afflict much of the country. The Common Core is a false promise, and false promises exhaust our good will, patience, and hope.

But if not the Common Core State Standards, what? School choice, as I said, is no cure-all, and it would be wise not to count too heavily on finding any single policy that will answer to and solve the myriad woes of American schools. We have a system of teacher preparation that leaves much to be desired. Teachers unions have proven over and over to be an obstacle to attempts to weed out poor teachers. But teachers do offer powerful critiques of their own. Faced with educating large numbers of children from single-parent families and from broken homes, they must deal with large numbers of pupils who are distressed or distracted, and who lack the disposition to learn. Poverty compromises their prospects still further. And even children from intact families are raised in a mass culture that does little to foster the habits of self-control and respect that form a basic pre-condition to effective instruction.

The litany of problems could be expanded, but this is surely enough to serve as a caution against thinking that there is some magic program of school reform that will make headway against all these problems at once. That said, some schools do seem to achieve remarkable results, even with students who fit the profile of unlikely-to-succeed. Maybe the most practical answer to "If not the Common Core State Standards, what?" is to pay closer attention to these schools.

But let's not necessarily abandon the idea of standards. Some curricula really are better than others. Some states have presented compelling evidence that their students at all levels of K–12 education outperform those in other states. Massachusetts, in the days before Common Core, established itself as a powerhouse of K–12 education largely on the basis of well-thought-out and well-implemented standards. What is true at the state level can also be true at the district level. Minneapolis and St. Paul have very similar levels of poverty and similar levels of minority enrollments. But St. Paul outperforms Minneapolis on every measure of academic success. These examples are not puzzles that have baffled fair-minded observers.

There are, in other words, reasonable standards that can contribute to broad-based improvements in student success, and there are known ways to manage schools so that students can, on the whole, thrive. But those are topics for another time. To round out this critique of the Common Core, we need to consider several of its other components, starting with the tests.

Testing, Testing, Testing

This is a book about an experiment that is still unfolding. The Common Core English Language Arts Standards and the Mathematics Standards have been decided on, written down, published, and endorsed by the controlling legal authorities in many states. But they have only recently reached the nation's classrooms and the crucial phase of testing the students who are the Common Core's guinea pigs has only run a few cycles. The two states that first reached that stage were Kentucky and New York. In both states the first standardized tests based on Common Core-aligned curricula showed dramatic drops in student performance. The immediate consequences were cries of alarm and defensive declarations on the part of the Common Core's proponents.[81] The longer-term consequences, after the tests were tried in some other states, was a rush to the exits. As I described previously, PARCC went from

24 members in 2011 to seven in 2015, and had begun what one observer called "a death spiral." How did that happen? It wasn't all PARCC's fault. The testing disaster began to unfold even before PARCC had produced its first test.

Kentucky

Kentucky was the first state to adopt the Common Core State Standards in 2010 and implement those standards in the 2011–2012 school year. Initial test results from that year, released in November 2012, showed disappointing results.

- The biggest drop came at the elementary level. On the previous Kentucky Core Content Tests, 76 percent of elementary students scored proficient or higher in reading in the 2010–11 school year. On the K-PREP tests, only 48 percent were proficient, a drop-off in proficiency of more than a third.

- In 2010–11, 73 percent of elementary students were proficient or better in math, but that fell to 40.4 percent. That drop represents a 45 percent decline in the share of proficient students.

- Middle schoolers: In reading, they dropped from a 70 percent proficiency level in 2010–11 to 46.8 percent in 2011–12, a decline of a third. In math, proficiency-or-better levels declined slightly more than that, from 65 percent in 2010–11 to 40.6 percent in 2011–12.

- The proficiency level in high school reading dropped from 65 percent to 52.2 percent (a figure 6 percentage points higher than the state's prediction), based on the end-of-course tests, while proficiency in math fell from 46 percent to 40 percent on the Algebra 2 test, beating the state's prediction by 4 percentage points.

New York

New York students in grades 3–8 began taking new Common Core-aligned tests in 2013, and saw similar drops in proficiency ratings. In 2012, under the old standards, 65 percent of New York students were proficient in math and 55 percent proficient in

English. In 2013, under Common Core, 31 percent were deemed proficient according to the new tests.

- 31.1 percent of grade 3–8 students across the state met or exceeded the ELA proficiency standard; 31 percent met or exceeded the math proficiency standard

- Only 16.1 percent of African-American students and 17.7 percent of Hispanic students met or exceeded the proficiency standard

- 3.2 percent of English Language Learners (ELLs) in grades 3–8 met or exceeded the ELA proficiency standard; 9.8 percent of ELLs met or exceeded the math proficiency standard

- 5 percent of students with disabilities met or exceeded the ELA proficiency standard; 7 percent of students with disabilities met or exceeded the math proficiency standard[82]

The sharp declines in test scores in Kentucky and New York were to some extent anticipated by school authorities who issued public warnings well before the test themselves were administered.[83] Kentucky outperformed the dismal projections it had initially made and New York City officials took solace that "the gap between scores in the city and statewide averages closed considerably."[84]

The reasons for these dramatic drops in test scores are many and, of course, disputed. Any major change in school curricula is typically accompanied by at least a temporary drop in test scores as teachers and students adjust to the disruption and adapt to new and unfamiliar teaching materials. Kentucky Commissioner of Education Terry Holliday explained:

It's going to take a little longer to see middle and high school growth on these tests. It'll take about five years to see an overall growth of significance at all levels.[85]

And New York Commission of Education John B. King, Jr. temporized:

These proficiency scores do not reflect a drop in performance, but rather a raising of standards to reflect college and career readiness in the 21st century. [...] The results we've announced today are not a critique of past efforts; they're a new starting point on a roadmap to future success.[86]

Gene Wilhoit, executive director of CCSSO at the time of Kentucky's tests, attempted to lower expectations for everyone. He foresaw that, "What you're seeing in Kentucky is a predictor of what you're going to see in the other states, as the assessments roll out next year and the year after."[87]

Why? The most benign explanation is that the Common Core is more "rigorous" than previous standards. For some schools this is clearly true. Thus the test scores could reflect the difficulty many students had in making up lost ground. But there are other possibilities. It may be that the Common Core-aligned curricula just are not that good, or that the pedagogy needed to teach a Common Core-aligned curriculum has yet to be developed despite the hasty roll-out of the Standards. Many parents have complained—with some justice—that their children are being used as guinea pigs.[88] And the lower test scores have reinforced the complaints of critics who have repeatedly pointed out that many of the Common Core Standards have never been adequately evaluated in small-scale trials (or in some cases subject to any trials at all) before being launched as a finished project.

Kentucky converted its curriculum to the Common Core so early that neither of the testing consortia, SBAC or PARCC, had yet written their tests. To proceed, Kentucky contracted with the testing division of the publisher Pearson to develop the state's own Common Core-aligned testing regimen for elementary and middle school students. Kentucky high school students took tests from the ACT QualityCore program, which was judged the best test option available at the time, but which was only about 80–85 percent aligned with the Common Core. Kentucky for a time belonged to the PARCC consortium, but in January 2014 it withdrew.[89]

SBAC and PARCC

As we noted much earlier, the testing consortia play a very large role in how the Common Core will actually unfold in the lives of students, teachers, school districts, and the nation as a whole.

The two assessment consortia, Smarter Balanced Assessment Consortium (SBAC) and Partnership for Assessment of Readiness for College and Careers (PARCC), are private organizations that are outside the reach of local and state authorities. They are answerable to no one, except that a state that is seriously dissatisfied with one can switch to the other or attempt to develop its own Common Core-calibrated instruments. The do-it-yourself option may prove unrealistic, as it could take many years to develop truly Common Core-calibrated tests and would end up being far more expensive than sticking with SBAC or PARCC. But faced with widespread public resistance to the tests, many states are attempting to build their own Common Core-aligned tests. If they succeed, of course, it will take much of what is "common" out of the Common Core.

Of all the doubtful aspects of the Common Core, the testing regime may be in the long run the most troublesome. In this arrangement, the consortia determine the questions that students will be asked, how those questions will be presented, and when they will be presented. The content of the tests will inevitably drive what teachers teach. In a practical sense, the testing regimen will outweigh the Standards themselves. The Standards, as their proponents point out, leave some room for interpretation. The tests don't. And the work of "interpreting" the Standards is, for the most part, delegated to the testing consortia. SBAC and PARCC get to decide what it is that students actually need to know.

Americans have some experience with this kind of testing. The SATs, SAT Subject Tests (formerly Achievement Tests), ACTs, and Advanced Placement Examinations are examples of national testing regimens that are to varying degrees keyed to high school curricula. The Common Core testing consortia will take this kind of testing all the way down to kindergarten. That is, the teachers will administer tests several times a year to their students in which student performance will be gauged on a uniform national scale. Again, the teachers themselves will have no say about this, nor will the schools, nor will the parents, and nor will the community.

Of course, some teachers, schools, parents, and communities will take comfort in this external locus of control. Standardization has real benefits. But the benefits of standardization have to be balanced against the indifference that sets in when some remote body assumes the authority to make key decisions. The testing consortia will displace local control far more thoroughly than any previous school reform movement in U.S. history. We are often told that parental involvement is key to the success of schools. An oft-cited figure is that 86 percent of the public believes that parental involvement is the most important way to improve schools.[90] The Common Core-aligned tests are a significant de-motivator for such involvement precisely because they vest nearly all the authority for what will be taught in the hands of a far-away and faceless bureaucracy.

This is not to say that SBAC and PARCC offer exactly the same thing, though the differences are fairly technical and not readily apparent to an outside observer. Analysts repeatedly focus on two differences:

> SBAC uses an "adaptive" technology, i.e., it employs a computer system that determines what the next question will be according to how the last one was answered. PARCC uses a "fixed-form" computer technology, i.e., all the students get the same questions.

> SBAC and PARCC have slightly different mixes of when students will take optional diagnostic and interim assessments throughout the school year.[91]

The similarities between SBAC and PARCC are more commanding. Both, as indicated, rely on computer-based assessment tools. Both use a variety of test techniques, including multiple choice, "constructed response," and what are called "complex performance tasks," such as reading several documents and drawing on them all to compose an answer.[92]

SBAC is also to be distinguished because of the involvement of its senior research advisor, Linda Darling-Hammond, a Stanford University professor of education, a key adviser to Obama in his 2008 campaign, and head of Obama's post-election transition team. Stanley Kurtz has characterized Darling-Hammond as "an influential proponent of a politicized curriculum" and an intellectual ally of Bill Ayers.[93] She was a candidate for Secretary of Education but was passed over in favor of Arne Duncan presumably because Obama judged her radical history too great a liability for confirmation. (Ayers said in an essay on the *Huffington Post* that Darling-Hammond would have been *his* choice for Secretary of Education.)[94]

Darling-Hammond is an advocate for using schools to promote "social justice" and unsettling the status quo by attacking the "unspoken privileges" of "white, middleclass, heterosexual" students and teachers.[95]

Whether these emphases will find their way into the SBAC standards is hard to say but one of the Common Core's leading apologists, Robert Rothman, credits her as having "heavily influenced" the SBAC "comprehensive assessment system."[96] Perhaps the safest thing to say is that regardless of whether her "social justice" commitments are reflected in the *content* of the tests, Darling-Hammond's conception of American education as a system of total social control coupled with her readiness to set aside long-established ways of teaching is manifest in SBAC's appropriation of the Common Core.

Darling-Hammond's influence should probably be understood as even a little more far-reaching. As an Obama adviser, she probably played a significant role in his decision to make the establishment of the Common Core a goal of his administration. And once SBAC had set out its approach, PARCC quickly emulated much of it. Moreover, SBAC and PARCC hold joint conference calls, coordinate their schedules, plan joint research, are working on a joint Web portal, and cooperate in numerous other ways.[97]

The number of states participating in SBAC and PARCC has shifted from time to time, most recently because a few states have resigned. In early 2011, SBAC had thirty states and PARCC had 25, with ten states participating in both. By July 2015, SBAC had shrunk to 15 states and PARCC seven. I've described the rush of states leaving PARCC, but something similar befell SBAC. Utah withdrew in 2012; Pennsylvania in 2013, then Alabama. (Alabama and Pennsylvania were among the ten states that initially signed up for both.) The Michigan legislature has defunded that state's involvement in SBAC. In June 2015, Maine also withdrew.

Tracking, Tracking, Tracking

One of the conditions of applying for Race to the Top grant money was the implementation of a State Longitudinal Data System that would track students throughout their academic careers. The tracking would permit "data-mining" of test scores and other performance markers; outcomes such as transferring, dropping out, graduating from high school, and enrolling in college; and demographic information. While the data was to be anonymous, and students were to be identified by markers rather than their names, each state was required to build a database system for schools that would communicate with databases for higher education as well. This meant that educational authorities (and others) could track each individual from kindergarten to adulthood.

Each state that applied for Race to the Top funding submitted a database plan to the Department of Education, which evaluated the plans on twelve criteria.[98] Race to the Top's 2009 guidelines for the data systems elaborate what the Department of Education had in mind. They specify that:

> the state's longitudinal data system are accessible to, and used to inform and engage, as appropriate key stakeholders (e.g. parents, students, teachers, principals, LEA leaders, community members, unions, researchers, and policymakers); [and] that the data support decision makers in the continuous improvement of instruction, operations, management, and resource allocation.[99]

By tracking each student, the Department of Education hoped states would be able to predict which students might be destined for difficulties in school. This would help the schools intervene early on. The Department also hoped to evaluate pedagogies, teachers, and curricula, and explore the effects of other social factors such as race, gender, and class. But parents, among others, might be alarmed to learn that the data on their children were destined for the use of such "stakeholders" as unions, community members, policymakers, and LEA ("local educational agencies") leaders. This level of screening doesn't seem to exclude anyone who might be interested and, in practice, will leave control over access to the discretion of those in charge of the systems.

RttT, Common Core, and Data-Mining

The State Longitudinal Data System (LDS) came about as an intervention of Department of Education. It is part of Race to the Top and another Obama administration initiative, the State Fiscal Stabilization Fund (aka the "Stimulus") and definitely not part of the original design of the Common Core. Common Core proponents have only been drawn into it because RttT became the instrument by which the Common Core was driven to adoption. That said, the Common Core, as we have seen, is inextricably tied to a testing regimen, and the testing regimen is being integrated with the State Longitudinal Data Systems.

The Stimulus (the 2009 State Fiscal Stabilization Fund) laid the initial groundwork for the educational data-mining. The administration offered $48.6 billion dollars to states "in exchange for a commitment to advance essential education reforms to benefit students from early learning through post-secondary education, including: college- and career-ready standards and high-quality, valid, and reliable assessments for all students; development and use of pre-K through post-secondary and career data systems; increasing teacher effectiveness and ensuring an equitable distribution of qualified teachers; and turning around the lowest-performing schools."[100] These were the same criteria used several month later when Race to the Top was announced.

True Grit

It was not immediately clear what data the Department of Education wanted to track, but in February 2013 the Department released a draft 106-page report, Promoting Grit, Tenacity, Perseverance: Critical Factors for Success in the 21st Century that laid out a detailed picture.[101] It is, however, a very odd picture. The authors, Nicole Shechtman, Angela H. DeBarger, Carolyn Dornsife, Soren Rosier, and Louise Yarnall, are enthusiasts for the idea that school should be about a lot more than a child's intellectual development and "content knowledge." They have in mind developing the "full potential" of students by focusing on "attributes, dispositions, social skills, attitudes, and intrapersonal resources, independent of intellectual ability." Among these factors, they are particularly interested in the three in their title: grit, tenacity, and perseverance, which concern how an individual deals with "challenges and obstacles encountered throughout schooling and life."

Shechtman, *et al.* pursue their interest in grit and the gritty virtues through a particular emphasis on "new and emerging" technologies that "can play in this paradigm shift." Thus they come to the need to measure "grit, tenacity, and perseverance" and are pleased to report on the advantages of "data mining techniques [that] can track students' trajectories of persistence and learning over time," but also "functional Magnetic Resonance Imaging and physiological indicators." They explore and find wanting various grit metrics including *self-reports*, which can be "lengthy and disruptive" and are prone to "failures of memory"; *informant reports*, which requires consistence among the judges, is "resource intensive" and may require "video recording," and presents "challenges in capturing information about an individual's mindset"; and *school records*, which are valuable but "are only broad indicators of perseverance."

They then turn to "new opportunities" for measuring "behavioral task performance." These are *educational data mining* (EDM), *learning analytics*, and *affective computing*. EDM is the most direct link to the Common Core. "Student data collected in online learning systems can be used to develop models about processes associated with grit." The new tests along with the new learning analytics can track "time on task, help-seeking, revisiting a problem, gaming the system, number of attempts to solve a problem, [and] use of hints."

The more arresting category is "affective computing" which deals with "systems and devices" that measure "discrete emotions particularly relevant to reactions to challenge" that "may be measured through analysis of facial expressions, EEG brain wave patterns, skin conductance, heart rate variability, posture, and eye-tracking." They describe appropriate "biofeedback devices" to study "student frustration," such as the Wayang Outpost which uses a "four sensor system," and the MIT Media Lab Mood Meter that provides a "smile intensity score." A helpful illustration, Exhibit 11, provides pictures of a facial expression camera, a posture analysis seat, a pressure mouse, and a wireless skin conductance sensor to be strapped to the student's wrist.

The Brave New World quality of these recommendations seems not to have struck the authors of "Promoting Grit, Tenacity, Perseverance," but it has registered with others such as Joy Pullmann of the Heartland Institute, who seems to have been the first to notice this visionary elaboration of the Common Core issued by the U.S. Department of Education Office of Educational Technology. As she observed:

> All of this looks like another step in the federal government's push to compile an intimate, cradle-to-grave dossier on every American. What they might intend to do with all that information remains a rather disturbing question.[102]

Achieve

The interconnections between the Common Core and the State Longitudinal Data Systems can be seen, too, in the involvement of Achieve, Inc. Achieve, which helped to develop the Common Core and which is the project manager for the testing consortium PARCC, has been an enthusiastic proponent of the Longitudinal Data Systems. Achieve in fact has an even more expansive vision of the data collecting. Instead of K–12 data collecting, Achieve favors "P-20," i.e., from preschool through graduate school.[103] This has exposed Achieve to the accusation that it wants to use PARCC to collect data, and to criticisms from those who wonder what it will do with the data and who will have access to it.[104] With PARCC's rapid decline, perhaps the Statewide Longitudinal Data Systems (SLDS) will stumble as well, but so far that hasn't happened. Federal backing for the big data initiative continues. As of July 2015, for example, the New Hampshire Department of Education posted a bid opportunity for a contractor to develop some additional part of that state's SLDS.[105] Programs like this take on a life of their own no matter the degree of public opposition.

Florescence

States can build their own data systems, or adopt an outside system, such as "inBloom," [*sic.* hereafter InBloom] a nonprofit data management system that aggregated student data. This is a story with a happy ending. InBloom, after facing ferocious public opposition in the nine states in which it contracted to snoop on students, closed down in April 2014. It wasn't a soft landing. Founded in 2011, InBloom had raised more than $100 million from charitable sources before six of its client states pulled out.[106]

InBloom tracked new data, set to be collected for the first time, with previously-collected data currently stored in dozens of school and district databases that didn't connect and "talk to" each other. The nine states that initially forged contracts with InBloom pledged to hand over student records. These states are Colorado, Delaware, Georgia, Illinois, Kentucky, Louisiana, Massachusetts, New York, and North Carolina.

Some states, however, opted out of sharing data (though they are still obligated to collect data on their own students). Oklahoma state representatives unanimously passed House Bill 1989 — the Student Data Accessibility, Transparency and Accountability Act — "to prohibit the release of confidential student data without the written consent of the student's parent or guardian."[107] In addition, on May 15, 2013, Georgia Governor Nathan Deal signed an executive order that "no personally identifiable data on students and/or their families' religion, political party affiliation, biometric information, psychometric data and/or voting history shall be collected, tracked, housed, reported or shared with the federal government."[108] In New York, however, when the question arose as to whether parents could opt out of the data collection, a state associate commissioner of education explained that the state's Race to the Top commitment prohibited anyone from opting out. The state has to provide "a statewide data set."[109]

InBloom was funded by the Gates Foundation and the Carnegie Corporation of New York, Marc Tucker's old organization that has long supported the ideological framework of the Common Core. InBloom collected information on over 400 data points, including students' addresses, economic status, race, immigration and disciplinary records, free lunch status, religious affiliation, parents' political affiliation, as well as test scores, special education status, and other academic data. This data-mining, however, outraged parents, because it meant information on their children was collected and shared by private firms. InBloom's privacy statement said, alarmingly, that it could not guarantee the security of the information stored in InBloom or that the information would not be intercepted when it was being transmitted.[110]

As Michelle Malkin has colorfully put it, the data collection is a "creepy Fed ed data-mining racket."[111] The InBloom version of that enterprise faded fast, but the bush on which it flowered still grows, rooted in the Common Core.

Big Data, Big Government

The Common Core arrogates to central government powers that constitutionally belong to states and localities. That power grab seems consistent with the creation of comprehensive and intrusive tracking of students in massive data bases. The Common Core's proponents insist that the Common Core was a spontaneous invention of the states while anyone who is paying attention knows that it was adopted due to the heavy-handed intervention of the Department of Education. That deception also seems consistent with the creation of tracking systems that were put forward as helping schools better manage their student records while it plainly serves the interests of remote officials pursuing their own policy goals. And the Common Core, backed by Gates Foundation philanthropy, puts computerized assessment at the center of students' educational experience. That circumstance chimes with the development across the country of Longitudinal Data Systems meant to record every step of every student's journey through school.

The appetite for Big Data has a totalitarian sensibility to it that the proponents of the Common Core have been unable to dispel. That has contributed forcefully to the backlash against the Common Core. The animus against the Longitudinal Data Systems is not based on any harm they have done. Indeed, the systems are not fully developed. But the prospect of such systems gives those who have apprehensions about the Common Core something specific on which to focus. Questions such as how much the English Language Arts should focus on "informational texts" and whether algebra should be taught in 8th grade or 9th grade rally a limited number of parents concerned about the quality of their children's instruction. Parents, however, do react strongly to the shadow of a Kafka-esque bureaucracy creating a secret, coded dossier on each of their children.

As the American Principles Project reported, Common Core's technological project is "merely one part of a much broader plan by the federal government to track individuals from birth through their participation in the workforce."[112] And because the Department of Education regards such activity as complying with federal privacy laws, states do not need to first get parents' approval. Parents cannot opt their children out of the data tracking. Like it or not, each child's performance will be measured, recorded, and stored indefinitely.

Waivers

Beginning in 2011, the U.S. Department of Education began selectively to grant "waivers" to states that appeared likely to fall short of a key legal requirement set under the 2001 No Child Left Behind law. The waivers have been issued largely as a way for the Obama administration to corral state support for the Common Core. The policy of issuing such waivers to garner support for another program may be illegal, but in any case is a dubious use of administration authority to circumvent the equal application of federal law. Moreover, the granting of waivers is a strong example of how much the Common Core State Standards have become a *de facto* federal policy. To understand this bit of bureaucratic skullduggery, however, we need to take several steps back.

The adoption of the Common Core is only possible because of prior federal involvement with K–12 education and because of the national standards movement which began in the 1980s. These two related but distinct histories eventually converged to produce the Common Core.

The federal government became directly involved in K–12 education with the passage of the Elementary and Secondary Education Act (ESEA) in 1965. ESEA was established to provide financial assistance to poorer schools and school districts and was initially authorized until 1970. ESEA has been reauthorized roughly every five years since. Its most important reiteration was the No Child Left Behind Act of 2001 (NCLB—commonly pronounced "nickel-bee").

The national standards movement, on the other hand, was touched off by the publication of *A Nation at Risk* in 1983, which warned against a "rising tide of mediocrity." The report's great concern was racial achievement gaps. Despite public alarm, however, until the adoption of the Common Core the national standards movement was a failure—most conspicuously so in 1994 when President Clinton's national history standards received only one vote in the U.S. Senate. The "national" standards movement seemed dead.

The federal government thus sought a new way to influence the states by requiring them to raise their own standards through "increased accountability." This influence came in the form of No Child Left Behind.

NCLB has widely been considered a disaster for American schooling, albeit one that began with good intent. And it paved the way for Common Core. Technically, the Common Core does not replace NCLB, which has not been repealed. But in practical terms, NCLB is becoming a dead letter while Common Core is becoming national policy.

NCLB has many important components. It requires (1) that all states participate in stringent annual testing and (2) that they demonstrate Adequate Yearly Progress. It also set a goal (3) that "all" students demonstrate "proficiency" in math and reading by 2014. That year is now past but it remains legally potent. The Department of Education is still extending "waivers" of law to favored states. In June 2015, for example, Secretary of Education Arne Duncan announced the renewal of waivers for Georgia, Hawaii, Kansas, Missouri, Nevada, New York, and West Virginia.[113]

The annual tests were developed and are administered by each individual state to measure the performance students in reading and math. The states were free to set their own standards and performance tests, which left room for wide discrepancies from one state to the next. Eliminating these discrepancies became one of the arguments in favor of the Common Core. Under NCLB students take these state exams annually in grades 3 through 8 and at least once in high school. These tests are designed to measure student "proficiency," an achievement line set by each individual state. In addition, a sample of students in each state take the National Assessment of Educational Progress exam, which has its own standard of proficiency, and which is truly national.

Adequate Yearly Progress (AYP), the second component, means that students have shown academic improvement every year. For example, this year's eighth graders from Michigan must outperform last year's eighth graders from Michigan. Schools that do not demonstrate AYP two years consecutively on the state administered tests are publicly labeled as "in need of improvement." Punishment becomes increasingly exacting each year, culminating in the fifth year of failure. If a school does not show AYP for five years straight, it will be closed.

The third component, that "all" students reach proficiency in math and reading by 2014, is often branded as utopian. While it very well may be utopian, "all" in this case actually means 95 percent of students. In addition, there are no penalties for failing to reach this goal, except for those already related to AYP.

NCLB's emphasis on testing and accountability has backfired. Under NLCB many teachers chose to "teach to the test," and many school districts, fearful of both the public reaction to low test scores and the possible consequences under AYP, adopted an encompassing "teach to the test" curriculum. The threat of school closure also led to a rash of major cheating scandals in cities that had histories of low student performance.[114] Furthermore, rather than raise standards, states set low "cut scores" to increase the number of "proficient" students. This became clear when state scores were compared to NAEP scores. For example, in 2004, according to Mississippi's standards, 87 percent of its fourth graders were considered proficient. But on the NAEP exam, only 18 percent of Mississippi's surveyed fourth graders were ranked proficient.[115]

If all of the states adopted Common Core, say proponents, we would have a single standard and the level of achievement in each state would be transparent. By convincing states to adopt the standards rather than making them federal law, it was hoped that the Common Core would avoid the legal obstacles that impeded the "national" standards movement. In this indirect way, the failings of NCLB paved the way for Common Core.

But because NCLB remains federal law, states that have adopted Common Core are still subject to its requirements. The United States Department of Education is a proponent of Common Core and is a critic of NCLB. The Department of Education knows that many states that adopted Common Core for Race to the Top funds have little incentive to implement fully the Common Core Standards. Only a few actually received RttT funds; implementation is incredibly costly; the Core is a political headache; and states that participate must cede educational authority to private organizations in Washington, D.C. The danger of states backing out is very real.

To head them off, the Department of Education took advantage of the failures of NCLB. As of 2011, states were allowed to apply to the Department for waivers that will release them from NCLB, provided they adopt "college- and career-ready standards" in English language arts and mathematics "that are common to a significant number of states."[116] As in the case of Race to the Top, it is fully clear which standards fill these criteria. The Department of Education calls this waiver program ESEA Flexibility or just Flexibility.

Many question the legality of such a move by the Department of Education.[117] It is true that the United States Secretary of Education has authority to grant waivers from NCLB.[118] But does he have the authority to grant waivers on the condition that states adopt the educational programs he prefers?

As of August 20, 2013, "45 states, the District of Columbia, Puerto Rico and the Bureau of Indian Education submitted requests for ESEA flexibility."[119] Of those, 41 states and the District of Columbia have been deemed eligible for Flexibility.

Teachers' Unions

Like many key issues related to the Common Core, the role of teachers' unions is unclear. A majority of teachers may support the standards themselves. According to a September 12, 2013 poll released by the National Education Association (NEA), America's largest teachers' union, more than three quarters of its members—which number 3.2 million—were pro-Core. Twenty-six percent endorse their adoption "wholeheartedly," and 50 percent endorse them with "some reservations."[120] In an official statement, NEA president Dennis Van Roekel said, "Our members support the Common Core Standards because they are the right thing to do for our children."[121]

But those "reservations" are important. What teachers disapprove of most with the Common Core is the high-stakes testing. On April 30, 2013, Randi Weingarten, President of the American Federation of Teachers (AFT), which has over a million members, gave a major speech before the Association for a Better New York, an AFT affiliate. New York was one of the first states to implement and test the Common Core. The test results had yet to be released, but early word was that they were disastrous. Weingarten was optimistic about the standards because "teachers want these standards to succeed," but, in the case of New York, she feared that the forthcoming accountability measures would "unfairly hurt students, schools and teachers." For that reason, she called for "a *moratorium* on the *stakes* associated with Common Core assessments."[122]

Similarly, on July 3, 2013, at the NEA's 2013 Representative Assembly, delegates approved New Business Item A, "which requires the NEA to support and guide affiliates, parent organizations, and community stakeholders in advocating, and transitioning to, the Common Core State Standards." But New Business Item 3 was also approved, which "requires the union to 'join with AFT' in calling for a moratorium on the 'outcomes' linked to testing associated with the common core."[123] Item 3 referred to Weingarten's speech. The role of the teachers' unions in the Common Core is only now unfolding, but if their resistance to the testing grows, the standards could be rendered ineffective.

Since then, the NEA and AFT have continued their internal disagreements. A recent movement to permit parents to opt out of Common Core standardized tests came up for discussion at the 2015 NEA convention. Members voted down a proposition to support the opt-out movement. Then days later, the membership voted again to endorse the opt-out movement.[124]

Common Core Goes to College

When I first heard of the Common Core in 2009, I wondered how it would affect higher education. It was pitched as promoting "college readiness" and, after all, if most students arrived at college with substantially the same preparation in their K–12 years, that would dramatically change the conditions in the college classroom. Professors like me would be able to draw on the students' fund of shared knowledge and face classes much more homogenous in skill sets. We would also know more decisively where to begin in light of where the Common Core ended. And, if the Common Core lived up to its billing, students generally would be better prepared for a rigorous college curriculum than the preceding generations.

Also, as a former college administrator, I could relish the prospect of no longer having to deal with cohorts of students who arrived on campus in need of remedial courses before they could begin the actual curriculum. Perhaps even the general standard would be set high enough that a new tool to combat grade inflation would be at hand. No longer would faculty members have to raise the bottom scores to carry the students who, post-remediation, were still struggling with the basics. Beyond this, the creation of a well-organized and coherent curriculum at the K–12 level might predispose students to treat college less as an exercise in wandering around among endless options and more as the purposeful pursuit of knowledge.

My initial enthusiasm, however, didn't last long. The Common Core's promise of "college readiness" turned out not to mean readiness for even a moderately demanding college. It means readiness for a community college.

The Common Core's published documents are evasive about this, but its architects have sometimes been more forthright when presenting the proposal in public. We owe to the alertness of R. James Milgram and Sandra Stotsky a transcript of a March 2010 meeting of the Massachusetts Board of Elementary and Secondary Education at which Bennington professor Jason Zimba, the architect of the Mathematic Standards, explained that the Common Core definition of "college readiness" is the "minimally college-ready student," and is not meant to prepare students for college study in science, technology, engineering, or math (the STEM fields.) Zimba expanded: "Not only not for STEM, it's also not for selective colleges."[125]

Zimba was, of course, speaking mainly about the Mathematics Standards and his motive appeared to be to assure the Massachusetts Board that the Common Core wouldn't set the bar unrealistically high. There was some irony to this, since to adopt the Common Core, Massachusetts had to lower its existing mathematics standards. But Zimba proceeded to explain that students who wanted to attend a selective university would have to take some courses outside the Common Core framework: "For example, for UC Berkeley, whether you are going to be an engineer or not, you'd better have precalculus to get into UC Berkeley." Precalculus, of course, is not part of the high school mathematics curriculum in the Common Core, and indeed the Common Core makes it difficult to teach even as a supplemental course since the sequence of prerequisites to it are deferred to later grade levels than the ones in which they have traditionally been taught.

Zimba subsequently changed his story and said:

> The definition of college readiness in the standards is readiness for entry-level, credit-bearing courses in mathematics at four-year colleges as well as courses at two-year colleges that transfer for credit at four-year colleges. It is incorrect to say, as critics sometimes claim, that the definition of college readiness in the Common Core is pegged to a community college level.[126]

Milgram and Stotsky teased out the rationale for Zimba's change of position, but he was more accurate in his March 2010 statement.[127]

Let's grant that the Common Core State Standards provide a floor for what students should learn in K–12 schools, not a ceiling. Some students will excel past what the Common Core requires regardless of whether their schools offer more challenging tracks, and some schools will indeed offer more advanced options, including pre calculus and calculus. But granting all that doesn't make the Common Core Standards any more attractive from the perspective of those of us concerned about the quality of preparation of students pursuing college careers. The Common Core has set the norm for "college readiness" quite low in math, and most students will settle for it. Milgram writing with Phelps makes the case (in this volume) that the Common Core Mathematics is so poor a foundation for further study that it actually impedes the more capable students from going further.

Such students will settle for the Common Core math standards because their high schools teach to that level, but also because the SATs and other exams are being re-jiggered by the College Board to match the Common Core Standards. David Coleman, the primary creator of the Common Core, and now head of the College Board, is delivering on his promise to "align" the SATs to the Common Core standards.

We should also consider the threat contained in the Common Core. For colleges and universities to align themselves with the Common Core, they will have to accept that students who graduate from high school are indeed "college ready," and, whatever the deficiencies in their math preparation, must be admitted to "credit-bearing courses." Remedial courses generally do not give students college credit. As Milgram and Stotsky point out, that means colleges and universities will have to offer lower-level math courses for college credit. In this way, the Common Core becomes a lever for lowering academic standards in higher education.

That lever will be especially powerful at state colleges and universities because Race to the Top gave state boards and departments of elementary and secondary education the authority to decide the content of all entry-level courses at colleges in their states. The reasoning is that the only way to ensure that Common Core-based high school courses truly make students "college ready" is to adjust the college curricula down to the level that Common Core-prepared students are ready for. There is a Tweedle-Dum, Tweedle-Dee logic to this. Words apparently mean whatever the

Common Core proponents want them to mean. In this instance, "college ready" appears to mean, "Colleges: you better get ready!"

And some colleges are indeed making the downward dive. In April 2015, four colleges in Delaware announced they would use the results of the SBAC tests to "measure college readiness," and would admit students on this Common Core basis in lieu of a separate entrance exam. According to Inside Higher Ed, "More than 100 colleges in California, 10 in Hawaii, 24 in Oregon, 49 in Washington, and 6 in South Dakota" have also agreed to use the SBAC test results to determine "college readiness." Other colleges and universities are using the PARCC exams in a similar way.[128]

This plainly realizes the goal of the Common Core advocates. Success in the Common Core, as measured by the SBAC and PARCC exams, is being accepted by colleges and universities as adequate proof that students are "college ready." That means those students will never be required to take a remedial course, no matter how little they know or how undeveloped their skills may be.

These are ill omens for the quality of undergraduate education in the United States. But not everyone thinks so. In June 2014, the chancellors of the University System of Maryland, the California State University System, and the State University of New York (SUNY) System jointly welcomed the Common Core as "a solution" to the problem of underprepared students enrolling in college. Along with "more than 200 other postsecondary leaders" they created a new college-based pro-Common Core collaboration, Higher Ed for Higher Standards.[129] It has since grown to over 300 members.[130] As one might guess, Higher Ed for Higher Standards has deep ties to the Common Core establishment. It explains itself as "a project of the Collaborative for Student Success." The Collaborative for Student Success in turn is "a grant-making initiative" created to channel foundation money to bolster support for the Common Core. It is backed by the Gates Foundation, the Broad Foundation, the Lumina Foundation and several other long-time, deep-pocketed backers of the Common Core.

Higher Ed for Higher Standards isn't the only organization aggressively promoting the idea that colleges need to get on board with the Common Core. The New America Foundation also joined the push in 2014 with a data-filled "policy brief," *Common Core Goes to College: Building Better Connections between High School and Higher Education*.[131] The author, Lindsey Tepe, tells a long story about why the Common Core came about, but eventually comes to the point, "A college-ready designation on the state-adopted Common Core standards-aligned PARCC assessment should be sufficient to meet minimum eligibility criteria for unconditional admission to the state's public universities."[132] Tepe was referring to Arkansas in particular, but she makes it clear she means every state.

The downward adjustment of college admission standards to meet the level of the Common Core is most conspicuous in math but is happening in English as well. The Common Core's diminished attention to literature makes that inevitable. Certainly students will arrive in college with thin preparation in literature, and little preparation in reading full-length books and sustaining attention to complex texts. The Common Core may succeed in preparing students to glean "information" and re-assemble it on demand. But the Common Core doesn't look like an especially good foundation for the sorts of analogical thinking and synthesis that college-level courses typically require.

Parochial Schools, Charter Schools, Home-Schooling

The Common Core's reach extends beyond public schools. Charter, private, and even home schools will also feel the weight of the Common Core's influence. Charter schools are required by law to abide by their state's chosen standards, though they enjoy more discretion in curricular choices and pedagogy. And with test scores serving as proxy for teacher evaluation and informing promotion and hiring decisions, the Common Core will likely play a rather prominent role in charter school administrative decisions.

Many private schools, though not required to adopt state standards, have begun to opt for the Common Core. In some cases, they've bought into the idea that the newly aligned curriculum will be stronger, and their own commitment to excellence drives them to conform. For other schools, adopting the Common Core is a pragmatic decision. Some states require private schools to use standardized tests in order to qualify for voucher funds, which means that private schools in those states face a hard choice between adopting Common Core or foregoing state vouchers. Loss of vouchers in turn would mean an exodus of students who depend on state aid. There is also fear that adopting the Common Core might become a condition of receiving state accreditation. Moreover, principals and administrators know that the SAT serves in many regards as a gatekeeper to the best colleges, and if they want their students to perform well on the SAT and get into those colleges, they will need to prepare for the new Common Core-aligned SAT.

Catholic schools, more readily than other private schools, have started to approve and implement the Common Core, according to Joe McTighe, executive director of the Council for American Private Education. The National Catholic Educational Association estimates that 100 dioceses have looked into implementing at least some parts of the Common Core. And to help schools approach the Standards with a distinctly Catholic perspective, the Center for Catholic School Effectiveness at Loyola University's School of Education in Chicago has started the Common Core Catholic Identity Initiative. But parents are less satisfied than Catholic school administrators seem to be. Many parents have petitioned their children's schools to turn away from the Standards. Some have even threatened to withdraw and home-school their students. One parent, Coleen Carignan, who co-founded Pittsburgh Catholics Against Common Core, worries that "institutionalized mediocrity" will replace Catholic schools' long "tradition of academic excellence and moral development."[133] Many worry about bureaucratic influence over private administrative matters.

But home-schooling isn't necessarily a safe option either. Home-schooling parents who want their children to perform well on the SAT, or to earn a GED (also slated for a Common Core redo), will likewise need to adjust if not re-think their curricular choices. A number of states also require home-schooled students periodically to take and pass the same standardized tests that publicly-school children take—tests that would be designed around the Common Core State Standards.

This Book

This book gathers several of the most significant research papers about the Common Core previously published by the Pioneer Institute. The eight papers are:

Chapter 1: Bauerlein and Stotsky, "How Common Core's ELA Standards Place College Readiness at Risk."

Chapter 2: Ketcham, Lewis, and Stotsky, "The Fate of American History in a Common Core-Based Curriculum."

Chapter 3: Esolen, Highfill, and Stotsky, "The Fate of Poetry in a Curriculum for the Proletariat."

Chapter 4: Wurman, "Common Core's Mathematics Standards Still Don't Make the Grade."

Chapter 5: Milgram and Stotsky, "Lowering the Bar: How Common Core Math Fails to Prepare High School Students for STEM."

Chapter 6: Phelps and Milgram, "The Revenge of K–12: How Common Core and the New SAT Lower College Standards in the U.S."

Chapter 7: Eitel, Talbert, with Evers, "The Road to a National Curriculum: the Legal Aspects of the Common Core Standards, Race to the Top, and Conditional Waivers."

Chapter 8: AccountabilityWorks, "National Cost of Aligning States and Localities to the Common Core Standards."

These chapters have been adapted from their first publication by the Pioneer Institute as individual white papers. I have shortened them, eliminated duplication, and condensed arguments with the aim of providing a reasonably full but readable critique of this important public policy issue. All of the papers in their original form are still available on the Pioneer Institute's website.

The United States is a wealthy nation and could afford the enormous expense of Common Core if it were purchasing something of real worth. But the Common Core is really just one experiment in a long line of experiments, and far less grounded in proven pedagogy than most such attempts to improve K–12 education. Even if we could get past the Constitutional objections; even if we could convince ourselves that "informational text"-based reading and writing is better than emphasizing literature; even if we decided as a nation that an easy-does-it approach to math suffices for students up to age 17; and even if we could relax about all that computerized testing and Brave New World database tracking of every wrong answer on every test; even if got past all these objections, the Common Core would still be a hugely expensive gamble on hugely uncertain results.

What Should Happen Next?

Many of the states that adopted the Common Core in 2009 and 2010 have had buyers' remorse and some have rescinded that commitment. In some cases legislative action has been proposed; in other states there has been so far only grassroots rebellion. The proponents of the Common Core, however, are not taking the rising opposition lightly. In February 2012, Secretary of Education Arne Duncan jibed that the critics of the Common Core had "a conspiracy theory in search of a conspiracy." He was referring to the idea that the Common Core Standards are "voluntary" in name only and are really a national program promoted by the Obama administration.[134]

Since then the backers of the Common Core have poured money and time into organizing armies of supporters. They have allied themselves to think tanks such as New America and, deeming that insufficient, gone out and created new organizations for the sole purpose of bolstering the appearance of broad support for the Common Core. That appearance is mostly an illusion. But a well-funded illusion repeated over and over has some effect. The portion of the public that has yet to pay much attention to the Common Core may be a little more inclined to believe some of the claims made on behalf of the standards.

But the main target of the public relations campaign for the Common Core is the education establishment itself. Many state education bureaucrats, legislators, and governors threw their support behind the Common Core early on. When it proved to be massively unpopular with parents and the general public, these early supporters were faced with hard choices.

Some of them publicly changed their minds and became opponents of the standards. Louisiana governor Bobby Jindal is perhaps the most famous example. He supported Louisiana's adoption of the standards in 2010, stood by the standards in 2013 when they had become controversial, but by April 2014, turned into an opponent.[135] Others stuck with their commitment to the Common Core even when it began to cost them politically. Former Florida governor Jeb Bush is the most famous loyalist. Bush has responded to his critics in a tone very similar to Duncan's. He has characterized the criticism of Common Core as "purely political" and the critics as people who are "comfortable with mediocrity."[136]

Public figures who chained themselves to the idea that the Common Core represents "state" standards are now in a complicated position. The Common Core did not originate with the Obama administration, nor did it grow out of a spontaneous effort among the states. It began and to a fair degree remains a *private* initiative started by an activist organization that adroitly sought and obtained the endorsement of the National Governors Association. The copyright to the Common Core remains in private hands; much of the funding to promote it came from the Gates

Foundation; and the testing consortia, SBAC and PARCC, that are essential to the Common Core's implementation, are non-governmental entities beyond the oversight of parents and the general public. While it is unfair to characterize the Common Core as an Obama initiative through-and-through—some have called it "ObamaCore"—it is entirely accurate to say that, without the Obama administration's intervention in 2009 through the financial incentives of Race to the Top, the Common Core would have had a very different career as a public policy proposal.

The endorsement, sponsorship, and advocacy of the Duncan-led Department of Education turned an idea that had the fervent support of some governors and ex-governors into a must-do agenda item. Why did the Obama administration adopt the Common Core as such a priority? It is hard to see that the program on its substantive merits was so compelling an idea as to warrant the heavy-handed political investment that the Obama administration gave it and the full-throated defense of those actions that followed. But the Common Core did have political appeal, even if its substance was sketchy. First, it represented an alternative to the Bush administration's No Child Left Behind Act. NCLB had largely worn out its welcome with teachers and parents and the time was ripe for the Obama administration to offer an alternative. Second, the Common Core looked like a relatively uncontroversial, centrist idea that had garnered endorsements from Republican as well as Democratic governors. It appeared safe. And third, it fit with the big government orientation of the Obama administration. Education, like health care and financial institutions, looked ripe for the sorts of administrative interventions that would lead to greater centralized control. It was a bonus that the veneer of voluntary state support for the Common Core would allow the centralization to proceed while maintaining the pretense that the federal government was playing a secondary role.

I've called this elsewhere "The Core Conundrum."[137] We are now faced with a situation in which centralized control at the national level of America's schools is proceeding but we have no clear way through the fog of obfuscation. Duncan's derision of "a conspiracy theory in search of a conspiracy" is part of the problem. The Common Core isn't and never was a conspiracy. It was a policy proposal that was brilliantly executed by its advocates to win political support while mostly avoiding the hazards of public review and debate. We are now at the stage where the by-passed public realizes what happened and is demanding accountability. Politicians—Republicans as well as Democrats—who had congratulated themselves on a successful maneuver are faced with a backlash.

My aim in this introduction and the aim of my fellow contributors is to give the critics a firm factual basis to carry forward their effort to set things right. It won't be easy. I've mentioned several times David Coleman's new role as head of the College Board. Coleman has adjusted the SATs and other College Board tests to align them with the Common Core. He has also implemented a controversial top-to-bottom revision of the Advanced Placement U.S. History standards, which brings the principles of the Common Core into yet another part of the high school curriculum. The efforts to institutionalize the Common Core apparatus, especially the new testing regime, are advancing quickly. Opponents have great cause for complaint but they seldom have any ready alternatives. The Common Core may be another of those massive changes in our society that few people like but no one seems able to reverse.

As a nation we arrived at the Common Core by a combination of blitzkrieg, circumvention of public oversight, closed meetings, confidentiality agreements, outsized foundation funding, skirting of Constitutional and statutory restrictions, and stealth maneuvers. Neither the general public nor the nation's legislators know much about the Common Core and teachers, despite their initial enthusiasm for the Common Core, are just beginning to awaken to the vast redefinition of their curricular responsibilities. Across the country school districts are discovering the extent of the changes they are charged with implementing and the costs they are expected to assume.

We need to step back from this brink. What should happen next is a pause in which Americans can assess for themselves whether we want national K–12 standards at all, and if we do, whether the Common Core State Standards are the best option.

I am on the side of those who think we can do a lot better. In fact, we have already done a lot better, if we take the pre-Common Core standards of Massachusetts and California as a benchmark. But doing better may well mean that we protect the right of the states to go their own ways in choosing the standards that suit their particular circumstances. The progressive ideal of one-size-fits-all when it comes to education seems to have a mesmeric appeal to a certain kind of would-be reformer, but that ideal is at odds with the restless, inventive, and independent genius of the American people.

Author Biography

Peter W. Wood is president of the National Association of Scholars and former provost of The King's College in New York City. Dr. Wood is the author of *A Bee in the Mouth: Anger in America Now* (Encounter Books, 2007) and of *Diversity: The Invention of a Concept* (Encounter Books, 2003) which won the Caldwell Award for Leadership in Higher Education from the John Locke Foundation. In addition to his scholarly work, Wood has published several hundred articles in print and online journals, such as *Partisan Review* and *National Review Online*, and the *Chronicle of Higher Education*. He received his Ph.D. in anthropology from the University of Rochester.

Endnotes

1. Gregory Linton, "Local Voices: Gregory Linton: Common Core Standards won't fix problems," *Knoxnews*, June 1, 2013, http://www.knoxnews.com/news/2013/jun/01/local-voices-gregory-linton-common-core-wont-fix/.

2. This book is only one of several that have been written on the Common Core. The principal pro-Common Core book is Robert Rothman's *Something in Common: The Common Core Standards and the Next Chapter in American Education* (Cambridge: Harvard Education Press, 2011 and 2012). Among the books written against the Common Core are Kirsten Lombard (ed.) *Common Ground on Common Core: Voices from across the Political Spectrum Expose the Realities of the Common Core State Standards* (Madison: Resounding Books, 2014); Donna H. Hearne's *The Long War & The Common Core* (St. Louis: Freedom Basics Press, 2014); and Orlean Koehle's *The Hidden C's of Common Core* (Santa Rosa: Turn the Helm Publishing, 2014). Lombard, Hearne, and Koehle assembled a wealth of relevant material and aimed their apparently self-published works mainly at activists organizing against the Common Core. Lombard's excellent collection of essays includes several authors who are represented in this volume as well.

3. Delaware ($119 million) and Tennessee ($500 million) on the first round; the District of Columbia ($75 million), Florida ($700 million), Georgia ($400 million), Hawaii ($75 million), Maryland ($250 million) , Massachusetts ($250 million), New York ($700 million), North Carolina ($400 million), Ohio ($400 million), Rhode Island ($75 million) on the second round; and Arizona ($25 million), Colorado ($18 million), Illinois ($43 million), Kentucky ($17 million), Louisiana ($17 million), New Jersey ($38 million), and Pennsylvania ($41 million). http://www2.ed.gov/programs/racetothetop/awards.html

4. "Early Childhood Standards of Common Core Are Developmentally Inappropriate." *American Principles Project.* September 18, 2013. http://americanprinciplesproject.org/preserve-innocence/2013/early-childhood-standards-of-common-core-are-developmentally-inappropriate/

5. https://www.bostonglobe.com/ideas/2015/06/13/common-core-killing-kindergarten/lydG3pnscVEnTEoELUZWdP/story.html?p1=Article_Related_Box_Article

6. http://arkansasnews.com/news/arkansas/state-board-education-oks-switch-act-tests

7. http://blogs.edweek.org/edweek/state_edwatch/2015/07/new_york_has_no_plans_to_give_parcc_arkansas_ditches_the_consortium_test.html

8. https://www.bostonglobe.com/opinion/2015/07/09/how-save-parcc-don-stupid/RBDpFdeCy5D8fVuxEUD2jK/story.html#

9. Kirsten Andersen, "The number of US children living in single-parent homes has nearly doubled in 50 years: Census data," *LifeSiteNews*, January 4, 2013, http://www.lifesitenews.com/news/the-number-of-children-living-in-single-parent-homes-has-nearly-doubled-in/.

10. Lindsey Burke, "Protecting Educational Freedom This Independence Day: Cracks in the Common Core," *The Foundry*, July 4, 2013, http://blog.heritage.org/2013/07/04/protecting-educational-freedom-this-independence-day-cracks-in-the-common-core/.

11. Andrew Ujifusa, "Common Core to Cost Kansas Districts up to $30M Annually," *Education Week*, December 14, 2012, http://blogs.edweek.org/edweek/state_edwatch/2012/12/common_core_to_cost_kansas_districts_up_to_12m_annually.html.

12. Karen Effrem, "States Starting to Rebel Against Common Core," *Education Liberty Watch*, September 29, 2012, http://edlibertywatch.org/2012/09/states-starting-to-rebel-against-common-core/.

13. http://www.nytimes.com/2015/06/16/opinion/meet-the-new-common-core.html?_r=0

14. "The Results Are In: Teachers Support Common Core," *The EdFly Blog*, Foundation for Excellence in Education, April 17, 2013, http://excelined.org/2013/04/the-results-are-in-teachers-support-common-core/.

15. Tom Birmingham. "Education Reform at 20." *The Boston Globe*. June 15, 2013. http://www.bostonglobe.com/opinion/2013/06/14/education-reform-act-reaches-mass-has-more/GMHHU8FdXLwR46qtAM7TgL/story.html?utm_source=MERA+Video+PR+-June+28+2013&utm_campaign=Jun+2013+MERA+vide&utm_

medium=email. The pro-Common Core Fordham Institute, however, has offered its own estimate, or actually three estimates, for every state. For Massachusetts, the Fordham Institute guesses that a bare bones implementation will save $22 million, a middle approach to implementation will cost $27 million, and a "business as usual" approach will cost $200 million. Patrick Murphy and Elliot Regenstein, with Keith McNamara. "Putting a Price Tag on the Common Core: How Much Will Smart Implementation Cost?" Thomas B. Fordham Institute. May 2012. http://edexcellencemedia.net/publications/2012/20120530-Putting-A-Price-Tag-on-the-Common-Core/20120530-Putting-a-Price-Tag-on-the-Common-Core-FINAL.pdf

16. "Benchmarking for Success: Ensuring U.S. Students Receive a World-Class Education." Achieve, Inc. December 19, 2008. http://www.achieve.org/BenchmarkingforSuccess

17. "Forty-Nine States and Territories Join Common Core Standards Initiative." National Governors Association. June 1, 2009. http://www.nga.org/cms/home/news-room/news-releases/page_2009/col2-content/main-content-list/title_forty-nine-states-and-territories-join-common-core-standards-initiative.html

18. "President Obama, U.S. Secretary of Education Arne Duncan Announce National Competition to Advance School Reform." U.S. Department of Education press release. July 24, 2009. http://www2.ed.gov/news/pressreleases/2009/07/07242009.html

19. "Process." Common Core State Standards Initiative. http://www.corestandards.org/resources/process

20. "Common Core State Standards Initiative Validation Committee Announced." National Governors Association. September 24, 2009. http://www.nga.org/cms/home/news-room/news-releases/page_2009/col2-content/main-content-list/title_common-core-state-standards-initiative-validation-committee-announced.html

21. "Phase 1 Resources." U.S. Department of Education. http://www2.ed.gov/programs/racetothetop/phase1-resources.html

22. "Reactions to the March 2010 Draft Common Core State Standards: Highlights and Themes from Public Feedback." Common Core State Standards Initiative. http://www.corestandards.org/assets/k-12-feedback-summary.pdf

23. "Race to the Top Awards." U.S. Department of Education. http://www2.ed.gov/programs/racetothetop/awards.html

24. "Race to the Top Guidance and Frequently Asked Questions." U.S. Department of Education. May 5, 2010. http://www2.ed.gov/programs/racetothetop/faq-addendum-7.pdf

25. "National Governors Association and State Education Chiefs Launch Common State Academic Standards." Common Core State Standards Initiative. http://www.corestandards.org/articles/8-national-governors-association-and-state-education-chiefs-launch-common-state-academic-standards

26. "Statement on National Governors Association and State Education Chiefs Common Core State Standards." U.S. Department of Education. June 2, 2010. http://www.ed.gov/news/press-releases/statement-national-governors-association-and-state-education-chiefs-common-core-

27. "Race to the Top Awards." U.S. Department of Education. http://www2.ed.gov/programs/racetothetop/awards.html

28. "Bills and Resolutions Against Common Core in: South Carolina, Indiana, Missouri, and Alabama." *What is Common Core?* http://whatiscommoncore.wordpress.com/2013/02/12/bills-and-resolutions-against-common-core-south-carolina-indiana-missouri-and-alabama/

29. "Phase 3 Resources." U.S. Department of Education. http://www2.ed.gov/programs/racetothetop/phase3-resources.html

30. "Phase 3 Resources." U.S. Department of Education. http://www2.ed.gov/programs/racetothetop/phase3-resources.html

31. "Race to the Top Awards." U.S. Department of Education. http://www2.ed.gov/programs/racetothetop/awards.html

32. "Utah Withdraws from Smarter Balanced Assessment Consortium Developing Common Core Tests." Huffington Post. August 7, 2012. http://www.huffingtonpost.com/2012/08/07/utah-withdraws-from-smart_n_1752261.html

33. Andrew Ujifusa. "Scores Drop on Ky.'s Common Core-Aligned Tests." *Education Week.* November 2, 2012. http://www.edweek.org/ew/articles/2012/11/02/11standards.h32.html?tkn=LTUFfO-pEpCAWut48lfLCsU4FHbuNRdCD%2F0qa&cmp=clp-edweek

34. "Bills and Resolutions Against Common Core in: South Carolina, Indiana, Missouri, and Alabama." *What is Common Core?* http://whatiscommoncore.wordpress.com/2013/02/12/bills-and-resolutions-against-common-core-south-carolina-indiana-missouri-and-alabama/

35. Evelyn B. Stacey, "Alabama Exits National Common Core Tests." Heartland Institute. February 13, 2013 http://news.heartland.org/newspaper-article/2013/02/13/alabama-exits-national-common-core-tests

36. "Indiana Legislature Latest to Halt Application of Common Core State Standards." *Washington Post.* April 29, 2013. http://www.washingtontimes.com/news/2013/apr/29/resistance-to-the-nationwide-k-12-school-standards/. Napp Nazworth, "Common Core Put on Hold in Indiana; Gov. Pence Agrees to More Review." *Christian Post.* May 13, 2013. http://www.christianpost.com/news/common-core-put-on-hold-in-indiana-gov-pence-agrees-to-more-review-95718/

37. "Resolution Concerning Common Core Education Standards." Republican National Committee. April 12, 2013. http://www.gop.com/wp-content/uploads/2013/04/2013_Spring-Meeting_Resolutions.pdf

38. Napp Nazworth, "Eight Senators Join Fight Against Common Core." *Christian Post.* April 29, 2013. http://www.christianpost.com/news/eight-senators-join-fight-against-common-core-94876/

39. Jan Murphy. "Corbett Orders Delay in Common Core Academic Standards' Implementation." *Penn Live.* May 20, 2013. http://www.pennlive.com/midstate/index.ssf/2013/05/corbett_orders_delay_in_common.html

40. Brian Smith. "Funding for Common Core Implementation Ends with Gov. Snyder's Signature on Budget." *Michigan Live.* June 14, 2013. http://www.mlive.com/education/index.ssf/2013/06/funding_for_common_core_implem.html

41. "H.R. 5 Student Success Act." Gov Track. http://www.govtrack.us/congress/votes/113-2013/h374

42. Andrea Eger, "State Pulling Out of Standardized Testing Through Consortium." *Tulsa World.* July 1, 2013. http://www.tulsaworld.com/article.aspx/State_pulling_out_of_consortium_to_develop_own_standardized/20130701_19_0_StateS605337?subj=298.

Susanna Capelouto, "Georgia the Latest State to Back out of K–12 PARCC Tests." *NPR*. July 25, 2013. http://www.npr.org/templates/story/story.php?storyId=205548324.

43. "State Education Department Releases Grades 3–8 Assessment Results." New York State Education Department. August 7, 2013. http://www.oms.nysed.gov/press/grades-3-8-assessment-results-2013.html

44. http://www.wsj.com/articles/SB10001424052702304558804579375583090338524

45. http://www.businessinsider.com/the-sat-is-getting-a-format-change-to-align-to-the-common-core-2015-6

46. http://www.rasmussenreports.com/public_content/business/general_business/june_2014/common_core_support_among_those_with_school_age_kids_plummets

47. http://www.nytimes.com/2014/06/11/education/gates-foundation-urges-moratorium-on-decisions-tied-to-common-core.html?_r=0

48. http://www.dispatch.com/content/stories/local/2014/07/28/common-core-elimination-bill.html

49. http://www.sltrib.com/sltrib/news/58191271-78/standards-utah-education-state.html.csp

50. http://watchdogwire.com/blog/2014/08/19/republican-national-committee-approves-two-anti-common-core-resolutions/

51. http://www.nas.org/articles/catholic_scholars_take_stand_opposing_the_common_core

52. http://www.breitbart.com/big-government/2014/08/28/obama-administration-punishes-oklahoma-for-repealing-common-core-standards/

53. http://newyork.cbslocal.com/2015/03/15/report-education-company-monitoring-social-media-accounts-of-common-core-test-takers/

54. http://www.usnews.com/news/articles/2015/03/25/five-years-in-its-unclear-if-common-core-is-helping-students

55. http://www.bostonglobe.com/ideas/2015/04/04/fighting-save-cursive-from-common-core/jM1p3rkH5dvlmc7jbbKnXM/story.html

56. http://www.breitbart.com/big-government/2015/04/04/new-common-core-aligned-ged-test-losing-edge-to-competition/

57. http://www.usatoday.com/story/news/nation/2015/07/06/new-jersey-to-discuss-common-core-pull-out-plan/29797119/

58. Carol Iannone. "Experiencing the Common Core." *Academic Questions*. Vol. 28. No. 2. Summer 2015. Pp. 182–194.

59. See, for example, Stanley Kurtz. "Obama and Your Child's Mind." *National Review Online*. December 5, 2012. http://www.nationalreview.com/corner/334878/obama-and-your-childs-mind-stanley-kurtz Or, "Common Core's Political Agenda." *Education Reformer*. April 2013. http://www.eagleforum.org/publications/educate/apr13/common-cores-political-agenda.html

60. Atul Gawande, "The Cost Conundrum: What A Texas Town Can Teach Us about Health Care." The New Yorker. June 1, 2009. http://www.newyorker.com/reporting/2009/06/01/090601fa_fact_gawande

61. Jeremy Kilpatrick, Jane Swafford, Bradford Findell, Editors. *Adding It Up: Helping Children Learn Mathematics*. The National Academies Press. 2001.

62. Kenneth Chang. "With Common Core, Fewer Topics but Covered More Rigorously." *The New York Times*. September 2, 2013.

63. Perry Chiaramonte. "Common Core Critics Warn of Fuzzy Math and Less Fiction." *Fox News*. September 4, 2013. http://www.foxnews.com/us/2013/08/30/new-age-education-fuzzy-math-and-less-fiction/

64. "Common Core State Standards in Math." Rutgers Preparatory School. http://www.rutgersprep.org/index.php/academics/upper-school/curriculum/43-us/uncategorized3/367-core-math

65. "James Milgram Testimony to the Indiana Senate Education Committee." Hoosiers Against Common Core. December 6, 2012. http://hoosiersagainstcommoncore.com/james-milgram-testimony-to-the-indiana-senate-committee/

66. Ibid.

67. Sandra Stotsky and Ze'ev Wurman, "Common Core Standards Still Don't Make the Grade," Pioneer Institute No. 65, July 2010.

68. Perry Chiaramonte. "Common Core Critics Warn of Fuzzy Math and Less Fiction." *Fox News*. September 4, 2013. http://www.foxnews.com/us/2013/08/30/new-age-education-fuzzy-math-and-less-fiction/

69. Gates Foundation Grants Database .http://www.gatesfoundation.org/How-We-Work/Quick-Links/Grants-Database/Grants/2011/02/OPP1031713

70. "The Unintended Consequence of TERC Investigations Math Curriculum." Youtube. February 20, 2011. http://www.youtube.com/watch?v=1YLlX61o8fg

71. "Common Core: 3*4=11 is Okay." Youtube. July 19, 2013. https://www.youtube.com/watch?v=DW0VxxoCrNo

72. "The Common Ground Report." *The Ridgewood Blog*. July 9, 2007. http://theridgewoodblog.wordpress.com/2007/07/09/the-common-ground-report/

73. "College-Ready Education: Strategy Overview." Bill & Melinda Gates Foundation. http://www.gatesfoundation.org/What-We-Do/US-Program/College-Ready-Education

74. Our own calculation based on a February 2013 calculation by Heartland Institute, which we have revised and updated with expenditures through September 2013. We have counted all reported expenditures by the Gates Foundation on the Common Core and in support of other organizations that promote the Common Core. Joy Pullmann. "Education Policies Led by Gates, not States?" *Heartland Institute*. February 11, 2013. http://news.heartland.org/newspaper-article/2013/02/11/education-policies-led-gates-not-states

75. Gates Foundation Grants Database http://www.gatesfoundation.org/How-We-Work/Quick-Links/Grants-Database/Grants/2012/06/OPP1062626

76. Diane Ravitch. "How the Gates Foundation Bought and Paid for the Common Core." *Diane Ravitch's Blog*. August 28, 2013. http://dianeravitch.net/2013/08/28/how-the-gates-foundation-bought-and-paid-for-common-core/

77. Diane Ravitch. "Now the Gates Foundation is Destroying Higher Education." *Diane Ravitch's blog*. July 17, 2013. http://dianeravitch.net/2013/07/17/now-the-gates-foundation-is-destroying-higher-education/

78. See Valerie Strauss. "Ravitch Answers Gates." *The Washington Post.* November 30, 2010. http://voices.washingtonpost.com/answer-sheet/diane-ravitch/ravitch-answers-gates.html?wprss=answer-sheet

79. Stephanie Simon and Nirvi Shah. "The Common Core Money War." *Politico.* September 18, 2013. http://www.politico.com/story/2013/09/education-common-core-standards-schools-96964.html

80. Reckhow, Sarah. "Reckhow: Savvy Walton Foundation," *This Week in Education.* January 11, 2013. http://scholasticadministrator.typepad.com/thisweekineducation/2013/01/are-philanthropists-good-at-picking-political-winners.html

81. Fawn Johnson. "Common Core's Testing Woes." *National Journal.* September 16, 2013. http://www.nationaljournal.com/insiders/education/common-core-s-testing-woes-20130916

82. "State Education Department Releases Grades 3–8 Assessment Results." New York State Education Department. August 7, 2013. http://www.oms.nysed.gov/press/grades-3-8-assessment-results-2013.html

83. Susan Edelman. "State Education Officials Brace for Test-Score Drop Due to Tougher Standards." *New York Post.* December 16, 2012. http://nypost.com/2012/12/16/state-education-officials-brace-for-test-score-drop-due-to-tougher-standards/

84. Dominick Rafter. "Common Core Test Scores Show Dramatic Drop." *Queens Chronicle.* August 8, 2013. http://www.qchron.com/editions/queenswide/common-core-test-scores-show-dramatic-drop/article_b6495a80-004f-11e3-89da-0019bb2963f4.html

85. Andrew Ujifusa. "Scores Drop on Ky.'s Common Core-Aligned Tests." *Education Week.* November 2, 2012. http://www.edweek.org/ew/articles/2012/11/02/11standards.h32.html?tkn=LTUFfOpEpCAWut48lfLCsU4FHbuNRdCD%2F0qa&cmp=clp-edweek

86. "State Education Department Releases Grades 3–8 Assessment Results." New York State Education Department. August 7, 2013. http://www.oms.nysed.gov/press/grades-3-8-assessment-results-2013.html

87. Andrew Ujifusa. "Scores Drop on Ky.'s Common Core-Aligned Tests." *Education Week.* November 2, 2012. http://www.edweek.

org/ew/articles/2012/11/02/11standards.h32.html?tkn=LTUFfO-pEpCAWut48lfLCsU4FHbuNRdCD%2F0qa&cmp=clp-edweek

88. "Classroom Chaos? Critics Blast New Common Core Education Standards." *FoxNews.com.* September 4, 2013, http://www.foxnews.com/us/2013/09/04/critics-claim-common-core-brings-chaos-not-accountability-to-classroom/

89. http://blogs.edweek.org/edweek/curriculum/2014/01/kentucky_withdraws_from_parcc_.html

90. L. Rose, A. Gallup, and S. Elam. "29ᵗʰ Annual Phi Delta Kappa/Gallup Poll of the Public's Attitudes Toward the Public Schools." *Phi Delta Kappan*, 79(1), 41–58. September 1997. See also "What Research Says about Parent Involvement in Relation to Academic Achievement." http://www.sheboygan.k12.wi.us/district/goals/documents/SASD%20Goal%204%20WHAT%20RESEARCH%20SAYS%20ABOUT%20PARENT%20INVOLVEMENT.pdf

91. Michael Keany. "Comparing the PARCC and Smarter Balanced Assessments." *School Leadership* 2.0. January 1, 2013. http://www.sheboygan.k12.wi.us/district/goals/documents/SASD%20Goal%204%20WHAT%20RESEARCH%20SAYS%20ABOUT%20PARENT%20INVOLVEMENT.pdf

92. Ibid. Robert Rothman. *Something in Common: The Common Core Standards and the Next Chapter in American Education.* Cambridge: Harvard Education Press. 2012. Pp. 148–161.

93. Stanley Kurtz. *Spreading the Wealth: How Obama Is Robbing the Suburbs to Pay for the Cities.* New York: Sentinel. 2012. P. 137.

94. Bill Ayers. "Obama and Education Reform." *The Huffington Post.* January 2, 2009. http://www.huffingtonpost.com/bill-ayers/obama-and-education-refor_b_154857.html

95. Kurtz. Op cit. p. 149.

96. Rothman. Op cit. p. 150.

97. Rothman. Op cit. p. 155.

98. "Key Requirements of Race to the Top Grants: Data Systems to Support Instruction." *Legislative Analyst's Office.* October 28, 2009. http://www.lao.ca.gov/handouts/education/2009/Key_Requirements_of_Race_to_the_Top_Grants_Data_Systems_to_Support_Instruction_102809.pdf. The criteria were:

1. Unique statewide student identifier that does not allow personal identification.

2. Student-level enrollment, demographic, and program participation information.

3. Student-level transcript information, including courses completed and grades earned.

4. Student-level exit, transfer, dropout, or continuation to postsecondary institution information.

5. Student-level college readiness scores.

6. Yearly test records for individual students.

7. Information on students not tested by grade and subject.

8. A capacity to communicate with higher education data systems.

9. Information regarding the extent to which students transition successfully from secondary to postsecondary education, including whether students enroll in remedial coursework at the postsecondary level.

10. Teacher identifier system with the ability to match teachers to students.

11. State data audit system assessing quality, validity, and reliability of data.

12. Other information determined necessary to address alignment and adequate preparation for success in postsecondary education.

99. "P-20 Longitudinal Data Systems." Achieve. http://www.achieve. org/files/RTTT-P20LongitudinalData.pdf

100. "State Fiscal Stabilization Fund." U.S. Department of Education. March 7, 2009. http://www2.ed.gov/policy/gen/leg/recovery/factsheet/stabilization-fund.html

101. "Promoting Grit, Tenacity, and Perseverance: Critical Factors for Success in the 21st Century." U.S. Department of Education Office of Educational Technology. February 2013. http://www. ed.gov/edblogs/technology/files/2013/02/OET-Draft-Grit-Report-2-17-13.pdf

102. Joy Pullmann. "Data Mining Kids Crosses Line." *Orange County Register*. March 11, 2013. http://www.ocregister.com/opinion/ data-499062-schools-information.html

103. "P-20 Data Systems." Achieve. http://achieve.org/P-20-data-systems

104. Susan Berry. "Parents Refused Right to Opt Out of Children's Private Data-Sharing." *Breitbart.* September 10, 2013. http://www.breitbart.com/Big-Government/2013/09/10/Parents-Refused-Right-To-Opt-Out-Of-Children-s-Private-Data-Sharing

105. http://www.newhampshirebids.com/bid-opportunities/2015/07/08/6430249-RFP--Statewide-Longitudinal-Data-System-Initiative-Opportunities.html

106. http://www.bloomberg.com/bw/articles/2014-05-01/inbloom-shuts-down-amid-privacy-fears-over-student-data-tracking

107. Michelle Malkin. "Time to Opt Out of Creepy Fed Ed Data-Mining Racket." *Real Clear Politics.* March 15, 2013. http://www.realclearpolitics.com/articles/2013/03/15/time_to_opt_out_of_creepy_fed_ed_data-mining_racket_117467.html

108. Nathan Deal. "State of Georgia Executive Order." May 15, 2013. http://gov.georgia.gov/sites/gov.georgia.gov/files/related_files/document/05.15.13.01.pdf

109. Susan Berry. "Parents Refused Right to Opt Out of Children's Private Data-Sharing." *Breitbart.* September 10, 2013. http://www.breitbart.com/Big-Government/2013/09/10/Parents-Refused-Right-To-Opt-Out-Of-Children-s-Private-Data-Sharing

110. "Breach Remediation." inBloom Privacy and Security Policy." *inBloom.* https://www.inbloom.org/privacy-security-policy

111. Michelle Malkin. "Time to Opt Out of Creepy Fed Ed Data-Mining Racket." *Real Clear Politics.* March 15, 2013. http://www.realclearpolitics.com/articles/2013/03/15/time_to_opt_out_of_creepy_fed_ed_data-mining_racket_117467.html

112. Michelle Malkin. "Rotten to the Core." National Review Online. March 8, 2013. http://www.nationalreview.com/articles/342483/rotten-core-michelle-malkin

113. http://www.usnews.com/news/politics/articles/2015/06/23/education-dept-extends-more-no-child-left-behind-waivers

114. The cities included Atlanta, Los Angeles, and Washington, D.C. See Motoko Rich. "Scandal in Atlanta Reignites Debates Over Tests' Role." *The New York Times.* April 2, 2013. http://www.

nytimes.com/2013/04/03/education/atlanta-cheating-scandal-re-ignites-testing-debate.html?_r=0

115. http://query.nytimes.com/gst/fullpage.html?res=9403E6DC 1338F93AA25752C0A9639C8B63

116. Eitel and Talbert, 16.

117. Martha Derthick and Andy Rotherham. "Obama's NCLB Waivers: Are They Necessary or Illegal?" *Education-Next*. Spring 2012. Vol. 12, No. 2. http://educationnext.org/obamas-nclb-waivers-are-they-necessary-or-illegal/

118. See, http://codes.lp.findlaw.com/uscode/20/70/IX/D/7861.

119. http://www2.ed.gov/policy/elsec/guid/esea-flexibility/index.html See also: Sarah Amandolare. "Flexibility, Accountability Key to Districts' NCLB Waiver." Ed Source. September 3, 2013. http://www.edsource.org/today/2013/qa-flexibility-accountability-key-to-districts-waiver-from-nclb/38112#.UkCHPNLktLc

120. Allie Bidwell. "Poll: Majority of Teachers Support Common Core." *U.S. News.* September 12, 2013. http://www.usnews.com/news/articles/2013/09/12/poll-majority-of-teachers-support-common-core

121. Ibid.

122. http://www.aft.org/newspubs/press/weingarten043013.cfm

123. http://blogs.edweek.org/edweek/teacherbeat/2013/07/nea_delegates_endorse_common-core-.html

124. http://blogs.edweek.org/edweek/teacherbeat/2015/07/nea_to_support_opt-out_oppose_.html

125. R. James Milgram and Sandra Stotsky. "Can This Country Survive Common Core's College Readiness Level?" Pioneer Institute White Paper No. 102, September 2013.

126. http://www.edexcellence.net/commentary/education-gadfly-daily/common-core-watch/2013/what-i-learned-about-the-common-core-state-standards-when-i-testified-in-indiana.html

127. Zimba defends his position against Stotsky, Milgram, and Wurman in a blog post at *Common Core Watch*, a site sponsored by the Thomas B. Fordham Institute, in "Critic's Math Doesn't Add Up." August 7, 2013. http://www.edexcellence.net/commentary/educa-

tion-gadfly-daily/common-core-watch/2013/critics-math-doesnt-add-up.html

128. https://www.insidehighered.com/news/2015/04/28/colleges-begin-take-notice-common-core

129. William E. (Brit) Kirwan, Timothy P. White, and Nancy Zimpher. "Use the Common Core. Use It Widely. Use It Well." *The Chronicle of Higher Education.* June 10, 2014. http://chronicle.com/article/Use-the-Common-Core-Use-It/147007/

130. 313 as of July 2015. http://higheredforhigherstandards.org/supporters/

131. http://www.edcentral.org/coretocollege/

132. Ibid. p. 10

133. Carol Zimmerman. "Common Core: Catholic School Community Gives Standards Mixed Grades." *National Catholic Reporter.* September 16, 2013. http://ncronline.org/news/faith-parish/common-core-catholic-school-community-gives-standards-mixed-grade

134. http://www.ed.gov/news/press-releases/statement-us-secretary-education-arne-duncan-1

135. http://www.usatoday.com/story/opinion/2014/04/23/common-core-louisiana-gov-bobby-jindal-editorials-debates/8071863/

136. http://miamiherald.typepad.com/nakedpolitics/2013/09/jeb-bush-pushes-back-against-common-core-critics-comfortable-with-mediocrity.html

137. http://chronicle.com/blogs/innovations/the-core-cunundrum/31719

1

How Common Core's ELA Standards Place College Readiness at Risk

Mark Bauerlein and Sandra Stotsky

Introduction

The English Language Arts Standards in the Common Core jeopardize students' ability to read and understand complex literary texts and to develop the higher order thinking skills associated with those texts. Students who read primarily information or literary nonfiction texts—as Common Core demands—will be less prepared for college.

Common Core's division of its reading standards into ten "for information" and nine "for literature" at all grade levels is unwarranted. Common Core itself provides no evidence to support its premise that more literary nonfiction or informational reading in English classes will make all students ready for college-level coursework. In addition, reading frameworks for the National Assessment of Educational Progress (NAEP), invoked by Common Core itself, provide no support for Common Core's division of its reading standards. Nor do they provide a research base for the percentages NAEP uses for its reading tests. Common Core's architects have inaccurately and without warrant applied NAEP percentages for passage types on its reading tests to the English and reading curriculum, misleading teachers, administrators, and test developers alike.

The deficiencies in Common Core's literature standards and its misplaced stress on informational reading in the English class[1] reflect the limited expertise of its architects and sponsoring organizations. Common Core's secondary English language arts standards were not developed or approved by English teachers and humanities scholars, nor were they research-based or internationally benchmarked.

Those states that have already *adopted* the Common Core should *adapt* the Standards to salvage their schools' curricula. State and local education policy makers should emphasize Common Core's existing literary-historical standards and add a new literary-historical standard of their own. This additional standard would require students to demonstrate knowledge of culturally important authors and/or texts in British literature from the Renaissance to Modernism.

Far from contradicting Common Core, these actions follow its injunction that, apart from "certain critical content for all students, including: classic myths and stories from around the world, America's Founding Documents, foundational American literature, and Shakespeare...the remaining crucial decisions about what content should be taught are left to state and local determination."[2] In other words, Common Core asks state and local officials to supplement its requirements with their own. It also expects them to help students "systematically acquire knowledge in literature." Common Core claims to make all students "college-ready." It fails to ensure that goal, and we urge state and local policy makers to bolster their literature standards and reading requirements before it becomes too costly to repair the damage.

Does College Readiness Depend on Informational Reading in the English Class?

No research we are aware of shows that college readiness depends on any percentage of informational reading in the English class—at the Common Core's 50 percent level or any other proportion. To the contrary, the relevant information prompts us to look elsewhere for reasons why large numbers of high school students fail to succeed in college. Consider the profile of the high school English curriculum since 1900, the increase in incoherent, less challenging secondary literature curricula from the 1960s onward, and the focus of the 1997 and 2001 Massachusetts English Language Arts Curriculum Framework and Bay State students' scores on state and national tests.

1 - Role of literary study in the high school English curriculum since 1900

Literary study assumed a central role in the high school English curriculum around 1900 due to the efforts of the Committee of Ten and a companion committee, both of which convened in the 1890s to work out uniform requirements for college entrance. Their work led to the development of syllabi in English and other subjects that came to be used in public as well as private schools. The English syllabi united literary study with composition and rhetoric, two subjects that had long been in the curriculum, although rhetoric was later removed from the English curriculum and often taught as part of a course in public speaking.

The syllabi developed for high school English classes hastened the evolution of literary content from classical works to chiefly British literature. By including some relatively contemporary British works, these syllabi helped to establish literary study as a significant part of a modern high school subject that could satisfy college entrance requirements (as Greek, Latin, and mathematics continued to do). These syllabi influenced the high school English curriculum for almost all students until well after World War II.[3] At no time was the focus on literary study in the English classroom considered an impediment to admission to a college; to the contrary, it was seen as an academic necessity. Or, to put it another way, no college recommended a reduction in the literature taught in the high school English class, or an increase in other types of readings, as a way to prepare students more effectively for college.

2 - An increasingly incoherent and less challenging high school literature curriculum from the 1960s onward

Despite the massive amount of money (public and private) poured into the K–12 educational system since 1965, when the Elementary and Secondary Education Act (ESEA) was first authorized, academic results have been consistently disappointing. In the area of English language arts, efforts to improve student performance have been undermined by a gradually weakening of the secondary English curriculum for the middle-third (by performance) of students. As a result, remedial coursework at post-secondary public institutions has exploded, abetted by low or open admissions requirements. Overall, the system has become dysfunctional, and the dropout rate for first-year students who need remediation is sky-high. As Michael Kirst has sagely observed, the placement tests given to incoming freshmen in reading, writing, and mathematics in post-secondary public institutions are the real high-stakes tests in this country.[4]

Structural changes from the 1950s on—including the break-up of the year-long high school English class, the proliferation of semester electives, and the conversion of junior high schools to middle schools—were accompanied by sweeping changes in what students read: more contemporary, shorter works as well as less difficult works.[5] The structural and content changes reduced the coherence and rigor of the literature/reading curriculum as well as the reading level of textbooks in other subjects. As Common Core's Appendix A acknowledges, "Despite steady or growing reading demands from various sources, K–12 reading texts have actually trended downward in difficulty in the last half-century" (p. 3). Given this background, it is not clear how assigning "informational" texts (sometimes in the form of literary nonfiction but often not) for more than 50 percent of reading instructional time in the secondary English class addresses the failure of "unready" students to acquire adequate reading and writing skills for college coursework.

3 - An emphasis on literary study correlates with high academic performance

The 50 percent division was clearly not needed in the one state where all groups of students regularly made gains in the English language arts: Massachusetts. Indeed, in Massachusetts, the English language arts curriculum was shaped by exactly the literary-historical richness that is threatened by Common Core's standards.

The Bay State's own English language arts curriculum framework, considered among the best in the country, was strongly oriented to literary study (and included literary nonfiction). Its major strand was titled Reading and Literature (the other three were Language, Composition, and Media), and it contained two appendices with recommended authors sorted by educational level (now accompanying Common Core's ELA standards, adopted by the state board in 2010, as part of the 15 percent extra allowable by Common Core). The K–8 lists have been vetted regularly by the editors of *The Horn Book* (the major children's literature quarterly in the United States) using only literary quality as the criterion. The Massachusetts high school lists have been vetted by numerous literary scholars.

The emphasis on literary study was the intent of those who developed the document, and their work met with the approval of the vast majority of Bay State English teachers, to judge from public comment on the document. Over the years (from 1997 to 2010), there was almost no criticism of the original document

115

(1997), the revised version (2001), or their literature standards by anyone including the assessment development committees, which met annually from 1997 onward to select passages and develop test items for the state's annual assessments (which were also considered the most rigorous in the country).

The results were impressive. Massachusetts students achieved the highest average scores on NAEP reading tests from 2005 onward in grade 4 and grade 8. The percentage of students enrolled in and passing Advanced Placement literature and language courses remains among the highest in the country.

When the Department of Elementary and Secondary Education surveyed the state's English and reading teachers in 2009 to find out if there were any changes they would recommend for another routine revision of the curriculum framework, fewer than 30 people in the state bothered to send in comments, only a few of whom were English teachers. At no point did the state's English teachers suggest that a reduction in literary study or an increase in informational reading would make Bay State students better prepared for post-secondary education.

4 - Why college readiness is increased by the study of complex literary texts

Massachusetts' performance casts doubts on Common Core's emphasis on informational texts. It makes sense that a state with literature-heavy standards and tests (about 60% literary/40% informational as recommended by the state's English teachers themselves) produced high rates of college-ready graduates. The reason lies in the very nature of college readiness as outlined in a document cited authoritatively by Common Core. Common Core's Appendix A, "Research Supporting Key Elements of the Standards," summarizes a 2006 ACT report titled "Reading Between the Lines," which reviewed ACT test scores and college readiness in reading:

> Surprisingly, what chiefly distinguished the performance of those students who had earned the benchmark score or better

from those who had not was not their relative ability in making inferences while reading or answering questions related to particular cognitive processes, such as determining main ideas or determining the meaning of words and phrases in context. Instead, the clearest differentiator was students' ability to answer questions associated with complex texts.

As ACT found, high school students who spend hours reading complex texts do better in post-secondary education than students who read chiefly simpler texts. Critical thinking applied to low-complexity texts, it concluded, is inferior to critical thinking applied to high-complexity texts. College readiness depends on skills developed through complex texts.

Unfortunately, Common Core draws the wrong conclusion from ACT's study. It claims that the importance of text complexity argues for fewer literary texts in the K–12 curriculum. The opposite conclusion is warranted. ACT's study shows that more complex literary texts in the English curriculum or a greater number of complex literary texts foster higher-level skills. ACT's delineation of the features of complex texts on page seven of the report demonstrates why.[6]

Complexity is laden with literary features. According to ACT, it involves "characters," "literary devices," "tone," "ambiguity," "elaborate" structure, "intricate language," and unclear intentions. Where is language more "intricate" than in Modernist poems? Where is structure more "elaborate" than in *The Divine Comedy* and *Ulysses*? Where are interactions "among ideas and characters" more "involved" than in a novel by George Eliot or Fyodor Dostoevsky? If complexity contains so much literariness, why reduce literary reading? The case of Massachusetts argues for elevating literary readings well above the 50 percent threshold—perhaps to 70 percent.

Common Core doesn't acknowledge the literariness of text complexity, though. Instead, it provides a spurious rationale for reducing the literary focus of the English classroom. In the section "Myths vs. Facts," Common Core tries to address a reasonable concern of many English teachers: that they will have to teach the content of other subjects.

Myth: English teachers will be asked to teach science and social studies reading materials.

Fact: With the Common Core ELA Standards, English teachers will still teach their students literature as well as literary non-fiction. However, because college and career readiness overwhelmingly focuses on complex texts outside of literature, these standards also ensure students are being prepared to read, write, and research across the curriculum, including in history and science. These goals can be achieved by ensuring that teachers in other disciplines are also focusing on reading and writing to build knowledge within their subject areas.

Note that the first sentence, while assuring English teachers that they will still teach what they've been trained to teach, doesn't imply that they will teach literature even 50 percent of the time, never mind most of the time. Then note the assumption in the next two sentences that not only does reading literature and literary nonfiction not develop college readiness (or much of it), but also that it is actually developed through complex texts "outside literature" and apparently in other subjects. That means, according to Common Core's architects, that all teachers, including English teachers, must teach reading and writing to "build knowledge" for college readiness. What that "knowledge" is in English classes we have yet to find out.

There are two problems with this reasoning, one practical and one theoretical. The practical problem lies in the error of making one discipline responsible for college readiness in several disciplines. Common Core may want the pressure to fall on teachers in other areas, too, but the common tests in reading and English will ensure that English teachers alone bear the accountability for readiness in reading. To tell English teachers that they "will still teach their students literature as well as literary nonfiction" is misleading. Once the results of reading-across-the-curriculum college readiness tests come in, reading assignments in the English class will become ever less literary. Moreover, English teachers are not secondary reading teachers; English teachers have been trained to teach literature, not reading across the curriculum.

The theoretical problem lies in assuming that studying literary texts will not help students in their comprehension of non-literary texts. In fact, given the high degree of "literariness" in complex texts (according to ACT) and the high college readiness of Massachusetts students, there are strong reasons to conclude the opposite. One likely reason that strong literary reading supports general college-readiness in reading is that classical literary texts pose strong challenges in vocabulary, structure, style, ambiguity, point of view, figurative language, and irony. In so doing, they build skills that can address a variety of non-literary complex texts. The only logical conclusion one can draw from ACT's report and its definition of complexity is that students need to read more complex literary works, not more informational ones, especially not popular and "relevant" ones.

How did the English class get its traditional content diminished and distorted in the name of making students more ready for college in general? A literature-heavy English curriculum, properly constructed, yields college-readiness in reading better than an information-heavy English curriculum. And we know of no research that shows otherwise.

Unwarranted Division of Reading Instructional Time

Common Core's emphasis on informational reading necessarily reduces the literary-historical content of English classes. The nine literature standards and ten informational standards in Common Core's grade-level standards for reading promote a 50/50 split between literature and informational reading. At the same time, Common Core indicates that the common tests in English language arts now being developed at the high school level must match the 30/70 percentages on the NAEP grade 12 reading test, and that English classes must teach more informational reading or literary nonfiction than ever before. In effect, Common Core yokes the English curriculum to a test of general reading ability.

NAEP never states that the percentages of types of reading in a curriculum should reflect the percentages designed for a test. There is good reason for NAEP's silence on the matter. NAEP percentages at all educational levels are merely "estimates" devised by advisory reading experts and teachers over the years, based on the unremarkable observation that most students do more informational than literary reading "in their school and out-of-school reading." NAEP's percentage-estimates have regularly been approved by its governing board and, for the 2009 reading framework for grade 12, were apparently also approved by "state reading or assessment directors."[7] Literary scholars, English department chairs, English teachers, and literature specialists were apparently never asked to examine and approve them, most likely because, since its inception, the grade 12 test had never been considered a test of the high school literature curriculum.

In 2004, NAEP's governing board asked Achieve to review the reading framework recommended by a committee authorized to revise the framework in place since 1992; it had recommended a 40/60 distribution of percentages. Achieve recommended an increase from 60 percent to 70 percent of the informational passages on the grade 12 NAEP reading test for 2009 onward and a decrease from 40 percent to 30 percent for the literary passages (20 percent fiction, five percent poetry, five percent literary nonfiction).[8]

Achieve's recommended percentages were not based on studies that had quantified the amount and kinds of reading students did inside and outside high school. No such studies exist. Nor were the percentages intended to reflect what students actually read just in the English class. They couldn't. There is no percentage for drama, for instance, because NAEP has never assessed drama (on the grounds that suitable portions of a play would be too long for a test item). NAEP has ignored the fact that Massachusetts has regularly assessed drama on its English language arts tests since 1998, and at all grade levels. Achieve, too, did not recommend assessment of drama.

Keeping in mind that nearly all high school literary reading takes place in English classes, we conclude that Common Core wants future high school English tests to assess informational reading more heavily than literary reading—and only some kinds of literary reading. Did Common Core's architects not know that NAEP's grade 12 literature tests do not assess what is typically taught in high school English classes?

Common Core pretends to soften the blow by maintaining that the 70 percent figure it took from the distribution of passages for the grade 12 NAEP reading test does not mean that grades 9–12 English classes should teach 70 percent informational texts. It goes on to say that this 70 percent must reflect informational reading across the entire high school curriculum. Nevertheless, this requirement inevitably affects the "distribution of texts" on the college readiness test for English language arts. As noted above, 70 percent of NAEP's high school reading test's weight rests on informational reading.

Two questions arise. How will teachers in other subjects be held accountable for some portion of this 70 percent? And how much of that 70 percent will English teachers be held accountable for? 10 percent? 50 percent? 60 percent? Common Core doesn't say, and in the absence of explicit percentages, we predict that it will fall entirely on the English class. It is hard to imagine that low reading scores in a school district will force grade 11 government/history and science teachers to devote more time to reading instruction. Instead, it is more likely that English teachers will be expected to diminish the number of their literary selections and align readings with test proportions. In any case, so far as we can tell at this point, English teachers are to be held accountable for an unknown percentage of the high school ELA test of college and career readiness.

1 - There is no justification for a 50/50 division in the classroom

NAEP doesn't outline instructional expectations for the English classroom or a school curriculum, only the distribution of types of passages for a test. In pushing an "instructional match" between passage types and readings assigned in English and other classes, Common Core misconstrues the purview of the test itself. It also misreports a key percentage.

NAEP specifications say that literary nonfiction should account for only 5 percent of the grade 12 test, not 50 percent or some portion thereof. Where did the architects of Common Core's ELA standards get the idea that literary nonfiction belonged in the informational category? Where did they get the 50 percent teaching division from? We don't know. Perhaps they thought that the 50/50 division between types of passages for the grade 4 tests was for the curriculum, and then extended NAEP's percentages for a grade 4 test to the entire public school curriculum. So far, the architects have provided no rationale for even organizing a 50/50 division of reading standards in grades 6–12 between informational text and literature, never mind a heavy emphasis on literary nonfiction.

2 - Misread source of the 30/70 mandate for the common test

The 30/70 mandate for the common test also reflects a misunderstanding of what NAEP reading tests purport to assess and whom NAEP considers accountable. The specifications for NAEP's current grade 12 reading test indicate that test items are to measure "students' comprehension of the different kinds of text they encounter in their in-school and out-of-school reading experiences." There is more: "Stimulus material must be of the highest quality, and it must come from authentic sources such as those students would encounter in their in-school and out-of school reading"; and "...the assessment as a whole reflects the full range of print and noncontinuous text that students encounter in their in-school and out-of-school reading."

In fact, both types of NAEP reading tests (the long-term trend tests beginning in 1971 and the main tests beginning in 1992) were designed to reflect the reading students do outside of school as well as across the curriculum. The distance of NAEP reading passages from a typical English class becomes obvious when we consider two examples. The first one, on the 2005 NAEP grade 12 reading test, is part of a pamphlet guide to the Washington, DC, Metro system; it generated such questions as, "According to the guide, how long are Metrobus transfers valid?" The second one, on the 2009 NAEP grade 12 reading test, is a copy of a housing rental agreement, followed by questions including "According to the rental agreement, what is the first action the landlord will take if the rent is not paid on time?" The reading tests include literary passages, too, but such flatly informational materials with no literary elements whatsoever (as opposed to literary nonfiction) mark a distance that the English curriculum cannot cross and remain an English curriculum. It is clear that the architects of Common Core's ELA standards improperly extended the purview of NAEP's assessment specifications.

The NAEP reading assessment frameworks also make it clear that student performance is the responsibility of more than teachers and schools.[9] On p. 6, we find:

NAEP assesses reading skills that students use in all subject areas and in their out-of-school and recreational reading. By design, many NAEP passages require interpretive and critical skills usually taught as part of the English curriculum. However, NAEP is an assessment of varied reading skills, not a comprehensive assessment of literary study. The development of the broad range of skills that the nation's students need to read successfully in both literary and informational texts is the responsibility of teachers across the curriculum, as well as of parents and the community.

123

That NAEP considers parents and the community also responsible for NAEP reading scores shows that NAEP percentages for reading passage types are inappropriate as a driver of the English curriculum. To use NAEP's percentages as a model for the English syllabus is, in effect, to convert the latter into a reading comprehension course and to make English teachers bear the full burden of reading skills, a burden properly shared by reading teachers, parents, and teachers across the curriculum.

Common Core's stipulations for the English class have no basis in research, in NAEP documents, or in informed consent, and NAEP's percentages for passage types have no basis in research at any educational level.

The Presence and Absence of Literary Study in Common Core

1 - What Common Core requires

Common Core's English Language Arts Standards could raise literary-historical study to rigorous levels. Much depends on how the states and local districts implement them. For Grades 9–10, the literature standards include:

> *RL.9-10.6. Analyze a particular point of view or cultural experience reflected in a work of literature from outside the United States, drawing on a wide reading of world literature.*

> *RL.9-10.9. Analyze how an author draws on and transforms source material in a specific work (e.g., how Shakespeare treats a theme or topic from Ovid or the Bible or how a later author draws on a play by Shakespeare).*

For Grades 11–12, the literature section goes further:

> *RL.11-12.4. Determine the meaning of words and phrases as they are used in the text, including figurative and connotative meanings; analyze the impact of specific word choices on meaning and tone, including words with multiple meanings or lan-*

guage that is particularly fresh, engaging, or beautiful. (Include Shakespeare as well as other authors.)

RL.11-12.7. Analyze multiple interpretations of a story, drama, or poem (e.g., recorded or live production of a play or recorded novel or poetry), evaluating how each version interprets the source text. (Include at least one play by Shakespeare and one play by an American dramatist.)

RL.11-12.9. Demonstrate knowledge of eighteenth-, nineteenth- and early-twentieth-century foundational works of American literature, including how two or more texts from the same period treat similar themes or topics.[10]

These requirements are supported by three standards for informational texts (note the presence of the term "literary significance" in two of them):

RI.9-10.9. Analyze seminal U.S. documents of historical and literary significance (e.g., Washington's Farewell Address, the Gettysburg Address, Roosevelt's Four Freedoms speech, King's 'Letter from Birmingham Jail'), including how they address related themes and concepts.

RI.11-12.8. Delineate and evaluate the reasoning in seminal U.S. texts, including the application of constitutional principles and use of legal reasoning (e.g., in U.S. Supreme Court majority opinions and dissents) and the premises, purposes, and arguments in works of public advocacy (e.g., The Federalist, presidential addresses).

RI.11-12.9. Analyze seventeenth-, eighteenth-, and nineteenth-century foundational U.S. documents of historical and literary significance (including the Declaration of Independence, the Preamble to the Constitution, the Bill of Rights, and Lincoln's Second Inaugural Address) for their themes, purposes, and rhetorical features.

Finally, the College and Career Readiness Anchor Standards for Reading terminate with this important pronouncement (or show it in a sidebar in some web-based versions):

Note on range and content of student reading

To become college and career ready, students must grapple with works of exceptional craft and thought whose range extends across genres, cultures, and centuries. Such works offer profound insights into the human condition and serve as models for students' own thinking and writing. Along with high-quality contemporary works, these texts should be chosen from among seminal U.S. documents, the classics of American literature, and the timeless dramas of Shakespeare. Through wide and deep reading of literature and literary nonfiction of steadily increasing sophistication, students gain a reservoir of literary and cultural knowledge, references, and images; the ability to evaluate intricate arguments; and the capacity to surmount the challenges posed by complex texts.[11]

The language is strong and clear: "wide reading of world literature," "foundational texts and documents," "historical and literary significance," materials from the 17th and 18th centuries, "classics." It articulates the premises of a vigorous literature curriculum, insisting on readings from long ago, prescribing certain texts and authors, and distinguishing the significant from the insignificant. These standards oblige high school English teachers to survey a wide range of great literature of historical consequence.

To acquire knowledge of "eighteenth-, nineteenth-, and early-twentieth-century foundational works of American literature," students must cover several thousand pages of complicated, profound, and influential literature, as well as 300+ years of social and historical context. The presence of "seminal U.S. documents, the classics of American literature, and the timeless dramas of Shakespeare" sets a high criterion for the reading assignments. The broad "range" and "exceptional" quality of selections decree that a few choices from the Bard and the American literary tradition won't suffice. Students must read a rich, cumulative corpus of great works.

These requirements presume breadth and excellence both in the readings and in the literary-historical knowledge of the teacher. The difficulty and remoteness of many of these works call for extensive scaffolding, for instance, historical information about the Puritans in order for students to understand the setting of Hawthorne's fiction. The "foundational" and "classic" nature of these required works adds another dimension as well, one that expands beyond the individual texts themselves. Students read "Bartleby," *The Red Badge of Courage*, "The Yellow Wallpaper," and other classics as distinct compositions, analyzing plot, character, theme, and style in each one. But they also contextualize them, fit them into relationships with elements outside them. These elements include other texts that came before and after them, aspects of American social and political life represented in the text, national ideals and character, and broader cultural movements and artistic schools.

We proceed past basic comprehension of the text and build up what the above Note terms "a reservoir of literary and cultural knowledge." The readings on the syllabus stand not merely as discrete samples of great literature. They accumulate into a tradition, a "story," so to speak, one that enriches each entry in it. If a teacher chooses *The Autobiography of Malcolm X* for a 10th-grade class, students comprehend it all the more if they explore the conditions of Jim Crow in the 1950s and read some of Frederick Douglass's *Narrative*, W.E.B. Du Bois's *Souls of Black Folk*, and Ralph Ellison's *Invisible Man*. Indeed, such contexts aren't external to basic comprehension, but essential to it. For instance, *Invisible Man* loses much of its meaning if students have no knowledge of Booker T. Washington.

In other words, knowledge of individual classic texts and awareness of American literary tradition are dictated by literary-historical statements in Common Core. There is no other way to interpret the blunt assertion "Demonstrate knowledge of eighteenth-, nineteenth-, and early-twentieth-century foundational works of American literature" or to narrow the range of readings to less than "across genres, cultures, and centuries." Common Core's high school English standards contain resolute literary-historical obligations, necessitating a syllabus filled with classics through the ages, instilling in students a broad, comprehensive awareness of tradition, not just familiarity with selected discrete texts.

127

2 - What the right hand giveth, the left hand taketh away

Unfortunately, these praiseworthy content requirements lack the accompanying machinery necessary to guarantee translation into curriculum and study in the classroom. They stand firm in the College and Career Readiness Anchor Standards for Reading and the grade-level reading standards for Literature. But Common Core fails to back them up by specifying the contents of literary-historical knowledge and the criteria by which a text would qualify for selection. Apart from Shakespeare and a few informational documents, authors and titles are missing. The terms "exceptional" and "foundational" are not defined, and the discussion of "text complexity" in Common Core's Appendix A does not emphasize texts whose difficulty derives from their literary-historical nature. The missing components of literary-historical machinery are easy to identify.

No list of recommended authors and titles

If the standards do not identify which works qualify as "foundational" and "classic," literary-historical knowledge remains vague. Teachers and schools must decide on their own what will fill the English curriculum, a system that promotes inconsistency and lower standards across districts. It suggests that the content of literary tradition is unsettled and arbitrary, a contention that may be true at the edges (for example, the discovery of a neglected author), but not at the center (Melville, Wharton, and Faulkner are fixtures now and in the future).

We recognize the discomfort many people feel with the reality that literature in English before 1830 is authored almost entirely by white males, but this is no reason to allow literary-historical knowledge of those areas to disappear from the classroom. We note, too, that under its grade-level standards for informational reading Common Core does single out specific texts for study, implicitly recognizing that those texts may drop off the syllabus if left unprotected. We see no reason for not doing the same for foundational literary texts.

No historical period coverage requirements

Literary history is arranged chronologically with subdivisions by cultural and social categories. Traditionally, dividing the history of literature written in English begins philologically with Old English (*Beowulf*), Middle English (Chaucer *et al.*), and Modern English (roughly, the Renaissance and after). The Modern Period has fallen into various sub-categories over the years: Elizabethan, Cavalier, Restoration, Augustan, 18th-century, Romantic, Victorian, and Modernist. American literature spans the Puritans, Colonial and Early Republic, American Renaissance, Realism and Naturalism, and Modernism. Some labels are no longer in use and we do not insist on maintaining them, but some chronological arrangement is necessary. Organizing assigned texts into meaningful groupings serves an educational purpose. Without them, the English curriculum is a random assembly of literary and non-literary texts. Common Core does order teachers to select works from different centuries, but imparts nothing about the connections between them. It solicits a mixture of older and newer, but doesn't ask students to interpret them together as pieces in one or more tradition.

No British literature aside from Shakespeare

On grounds of influence alone, the absence of British literature from Common Core is a serious deficiency. Schools may design a curriculum that fully aligns with Common Core yet produce students who never have to read anything produced in the British Isles save for two Shakespeare plays. Certainly the foundational authors in American literature avidly read the King James Version of the Bible, Milton, Swift, Pope, Wordsworth, Byron, and others, and their works become clearer in the light of British Romanticism, Restoration Satire, and later. British literature forms the literary heritage of our own language, too, and it offers models of prose style from Addison to Orwell that are still useful in composition classes. For much of the 20th century, British literature formed the center of high school English, and it still pops up in college courses in composition, English, history, linguistics, film, and cultural studies. We find no explanation in Common Core for dispensing with it.

No philology

One of the first principles of the language and literature fields is that language is a historical practice. It changes over time and from place to place. Words appear and disappear, styles rise and fall, verbal media are invented and abandoned. In Common Core's grade-level Language strand is a heading "Knowledge of Language," yet it completely overlooks the philological axiom, focusing instead on usage and comprehension (for example, "Use verbs in the active and passive voice and in the conditional and subjunctive mood to achieve particular effects"). In doing so, Common Core downplays the historical understanding of language, a capacity that advances students' ability to handle certain kinds of text complexity. Philology turns language into an explicit object of study, making students more conscious of the words they read and write. Philology also sets the history of the English (and American) language amidst a long foreground of world events and geography, including different regions and demographic groups. No literature curriculum is complete without a history of the language itself.

A 50 percent division

Common Core's reading standards for K–12 are divided into 10 for information and 9 for literature. Common Core's authors insist that at least half of English course readings be informational text (including literary nonfiction), leaving literary reading at one-half or less (although nothing in the standards themselves requires 50/50 teaching).[12] But the literary-historical knowledge demands of Common Core, if interpreted correctly, cannot be met on a half-time schedule. The amount of context and sheer number of pages exceed what even the most efficient teacher can assign and discuss, given the 50-percent informational text rule.

The only way to meet literary-historical standards and establish a 50 percent division of titles is for an English teacher to make all the informational assignments complementary to the literary assignments. Informational readings should either come directly from the foundational/classic corpus (we may treat Franklin's *Autobiography*, Emerson's essays, *Walden*, important speeches such as Lincoln's "Second Inaugural Address" and other non-fiction, non-poetic, non-dramatic classics as informational texts) or apply directly to them (for example, assigning essays about Huckleberry Finn as well as the novel itself). Informational texts should be part of the literary tradition or scaffolding for it. The 50/50 divide is a distraction. All the reading materials should reinforce one another and unite into a coherent literary curriculum. But Common Core makes no such recommendation for informational texts. A teacher may jump from William Dean Howell's *The Rise of Silas Lapham*, an 1885 novel about an awkward Yankee capitalist, to news stories about Occupy Wall Street without violating the standards, or skip from a poem by Phillis Wheatley to a commentary on the history of American racism by Henry Louis Gates (that says nothing specific about Wheatley's actual poems) and turn literary study into a social studies lesson, again without violating the standards.[13]

Restricted view of text complexity

Common Core rightly insists that students read progressively more challenging materials as they move from grade to grade. The elements of text complexity laid out in Common Core's Appendix A comprise obvious textual features such as "multiple levels of meaning," "unconventional structure," "sophisticated graphics," "ambiguous language," and "multiple perspectives."[14]

They also mention aspects of unfamiliarity that we might attribute to the historical distance of a text, citing "archaic language" and "cultural/literary knowledge." But neither one is expounded any further. Indeed, "knowledge" is related more to "readers' life experiences" than to readers' historical understanding. That is, knowledge deficits arise not because a text dates from 250 years earlier, but because the text broaches subject matter that the reader hasn't experienced first-hand. As a result, text complexity as defined by Common Core bypasses a common reason for complexity problems for high school students.

As NAEP U.S. history scores repeatedly demonstrate, the historical knowledge of 12th graders is meager. For most of them, the plot, setting, and society of, for instance, Kate Chopin's *The Awak-*

131

ening (1899) are completely alien. The difficulty students have in understanding the novel stems from the widespread problem that E. D. Hirsch addressed in the Core Knowledge curriculum: low background knowledge. In omitting historical remoteness from text complexity, then, Common Core not only lightens the literary-historical burden of the standards. It also overlooks a predominant reason why so many students falter when assigned complex texts.

These omissions and opposing pressures dilute and delimit the literary-historical standards in Common Core. Teachers dedicated to a strong literary-historical curriculum may cite Common Core in defense of a traditional syllabus of English literature from *The Canterbury Tales* to *1984*, but teachers uninterested in that tradition may satisfy Common Core standards with one Shakespeare play, The Declaration of Independence, some poems by Walt Whitman, and the rest contemporary literature. The intent of part of Common Core is to roster a rich literary-historical syllabus, but it won't be realized unless teachers share that intent. If teachers do not share it, Common Core poses little resistance.

How to Increase College Readiness and Analytical Thinking in the English Class

State law typically specifies only that state tests have to be based on state standards. Since most states have adopted Common Core's ELA standards as their state standards, and Common Core's College and Career Readiness Anchor Standards for Reading are mainly generic reading skills, states can generate state-specific guidelines for a secondary literature curriculum addressing what we recommend above without conflicting with Common Core's grade-level literature standards. They can ask English teachers to teach literature for 70 percent of the time, and literary nonfiction (or other informational texts) for no more than 30 percent of the time.

In essence, they can create an additional set of state standards focused only on literature. The literature standards will have subsets to them: (1) standards that clarify and build upon the existing literary-historical standards in Common Core (some world literature, classic myths and stories, Shakespeare, foundational American literature); and (2) standards that extend literary-historical study in the directions outlined above that are not in Common Core (British literature from Chaucer to Joyce and some history of the English language). The first general set will be assessed by the common tests. The second set, including all subsets, can be assessed by a state-level assessment similar to the old New York Regents exam (essay-type). No law or regulation says that states cannot have an additional set of literary standards or that they must be similar across states. A legislature or state board of education can make the additional assessment mandatory for schools and require a passing score for a high school diploma or college admission.

Because Common Core's standards require neither the systematic, copious study of literary traditions nor sufficient acquisition of literary-historical knowledge, it is up to state and local education policy makers and legislators to develop curricular materials that do. To ensure an intellectually and civically sound literature curriculum in our public schools, state and local education leaders need to set forth guidelines they want local curriculum developers to follow in constructing a secondary literature curriculum. These guidelines could encompass an extra 15 percent allowed by Common Core itself or state-specific literature standards if their state does withdraw from Common Core.

Conclusions

Common Core's standards for English language arts, their organization, and their division, in effect, make it unlikely that American students will study a meaningful range of culturally and historically significant literary works in high school and learn something about their own literary tradition before graduation. A diminished emphasis on literary study will also prevent students from acquiring a rich understanding and use of the English language, a development that requires exposure to the language and thinking of the most talented writers of English through the centuries. But Common Core's requirements will do more damage. The emphasis on more informational reading in the English class will likely lead to a decreased capacity for analytical thinking in all students. Why?

Informational texts (whether or not literary nonfiction) are often assigned today not for their complexity and promotion of college readiness in reading but for their topical and/or political nature. Clear examples can be found in a volume published in 2011 by the National Council of Teachers of English (NCTE) to show teachers how to implement Common Core's standards. It bears the title *English Language Arts, Grades 9-12.* The main author is Sarah Brown Wessling, a high school English teacher in Iowa who was named 2010 Teacher of the Year, a prize given by the Chief Council of State School Officers, sponsor of Common Core. Where better to find an authoritative derivation of the English curriculum from Common Core standards in order to judge both the fate of literary study and the kinds of reading an informational emphasis will evoke?

Wessling's informational preferences were revealed in a March 14, 2012 article in *Education Week.*

> [Wessling's] students are analyzing the rhetoric in books about computer geeks, fast food, teenage marketing, the working poor, chocolate-making, and diamond-mining. They were allowed to choose books about those real-world topics as part of a unit on truth. Students are also dissecting the sources, statistics, and anecdotes the authors use to make their arguments in books like *Branded* by Alissa Quart and *Nickel and Dimed* by Barbara Ehrenreich.

134

Branded: The Buying and Selling of Teenagers is a 2003 trade book about marketing to teens, and *Nickel and Dimed* is an anti-capitalist tract presented as a diary about the author's three-month experiences as a low-wage worker.

The NCTE volume follows the same track, showing how even works with literary-historical importance are subordinated to contemporary informational texts. To contextualize and "scaffold" *The Odyssey*, for example, Wessling doesn't add readings in ancient Greek history and social life or assign other ancient poems. Instead, she chooses "*Star Wars* and some excerpts from Joseph Campbell... juxtaposing *The Odyssey* with an NPR piece on veterans and violence along with excerpts from the *Frontline* episode 'A Soldier's Heart'" (p. 26).

Clearly, an understanding of *The Odyssey* on its own terms and literary-historical knowledge in general isn't the aim. Rather, certain ideas about heroism, war, and society are, and the presentation ends up focusing on "context texts" that "create a reservoir of prior knowledge that gives context to the complexities of further reading." These context texts comprise a mode of "pre-reading" that purports to disclose the main text and expand its significance to broader cultural and social realities. But will students pay closer attention to *The Odyssey* after they watch *Star Wars*? Or will they, instead, "modernize" *The Odyssey* to the point that it loses its literary-historical character and no longer stands as the main text?

Wessling and her co-authors turn this contemporary contextualization into a set practice. Their list of context "text genres" includes film excerpts, blogs, radio shows, podcasts, and graphic novels—materials that often work against the purpose of unveiling the main text. The authors of the NCTE volume do not try to justify these kinds of "context" texts as superior to contextual materials that emerge out of the same historical situation as the main text. We have no rationale for why, for instance, a blog about Charles Dickens' *A Tale of Two Cities* is preferable to 18th- and 19th-century accounts of the French Revolution. Indeed, the whole question of which texts and contexts are the best ones disappears. The selection of contextual materials is given not a content-based rationale, but a methodological one, namely, pedagogy: "How the texts are used to scaffold the reading experience takes precedence over which texts are chosen" (p. 25). In other words, the mandated literary-historical content of Common Core is gone.

Indeed, its literary-historical standards and the "Note on range and content" exercise no influence. For the authors of this NCTE volume, Common Core lays out only what students should be able to do, not what they should know. Even at the high school level, when college readiness increases in importance, they write: "the CCSS focus is on skills, strategies, and habits that will enable students to adapt to the rhetorical demands of their future learning and contributions" (p. 16). Nowhere do the authors distinguish between popular and contemporary works and the "seminal" and "classic" works required by Common Core.

More informational texts in the English class will produce less rigorous English classes than we already have if teachers assign more topical, present-oriented, and "relevant" readings that lack the literary craft and historical remoteness demanded by Common Core's literary-historical standards and text complexity requirements. Common Core builds in no constraints to their use as invitations to address adolescent "relevance" or to turning the analysis of a literary text into a social studies lesson.

Because Common Core's 50/50 division for the English class cannot help but reduce the presence of literary fiction, poetry, and drama in the curriculum, the responsibility for restoring British, American, and World literary traditions to the curriculum falls upon K–12 curriculum directors, English departments, and publishers of literature anthologies. Syllabi (and anthologies) for each course or grade need to include readings of high literary quality that contribute to a coherent understanding of specific literary and cultural histories—for instance, a 10th-grade syllabus made up of some of the recognized works of Russian literature from the early 19th to the late 20th century, or a 12th-grade syllabus made up of recognized works of British literature from the Renaissance to the Victorian period. Syllabi and anthologies also need to incorporate nonfiction texts written by important authors that complement the imaginative literary content in some way, for instance, Aleksandr Solzhenitsyn's lecture for the 1970 Nobel Prize in Literature, Samuel Johnson's preface on Shakespeare, and John Keats's letters on poetry.

We can't help but wonder if the case for more informational texts and increasing complexity (but not necessarily text difficulty) is a camouflage for lowering academic challenge so that more high school students will appear college-ready upon (or perhaps before) graduation. The next battle, we predict, will determine how many of these weak students can graduate from college and be considered eligible for graduate-level work or employment.

Author Biographies

Mark Bauerlein, professor of English at Emory University since 1989 and former director of the office of research and analysis at the National Endowment for the Arts, sat on a feedback committee for the ELA portion of the Common Core. He offered suggestions for the improvement of the Common Core standards. While some of those suggestions were adopted, Bauerlein has expressed disappointment with the Standards and frustration with the secretive nature of the Common Core's development. Bauerlein, who has a Ph.D. in English from UCLA, is the author of numerous books, including *The Digital Divide* and *The Dumbest Generation.*

Sandra Stotsky is professor emerita of the University of Arkansas Department of Education Reform. Unlike many of the testing experts who drafted the Common Core, she had significant experience, prior to being on Common Core's validation committee, writing content standards, having helped to develop Massachusetts' highly regarded English content standards during her time as Senior Associate Commissioner at the Massachusetts Department of Education from 1999 to 2003. Stotsky has taught elementary school, French and German at the high school level, and undergraduate and graduate courses in reading, children's literature, and writing pedagogy. She has written numerous books, including *The Death and Resurrection of a Coherent Literature Curriculum* and *Losing our Language.* She earned an Ed.D from Harvard Graduate School of Education.

Endnotes

1. From Common Core: "Fulfilling the Standards for 6–12 ELA requires much greater attention to a specific category of informational text—literary nonfiction—than has been traditional. Because the ELA classroom must focus on literature (stories, drama, and poetry) as well as literary nonfiction, a great deal of informational reading in grades 6–12 must take place in other classes if the NAEP assessment framework is to be matched instructionally. To measure students' growth toward college and career readiness, assessments aligned with the Standards should adhere to the distribution of texts across grades cited in the NAEP framework."

2. http://www.corestandards.org/assests/CoreFacts.pdf. As we note elsewhere, we do not know how these "other classes" will be assessed on informational reading instruction. Nor is it clear how much informational reading must take place in the English class to achieve the "instructional match" desired by Common Core.

3. See John Valentine, *The College Board and the School Curriculum: A History of the College Board's Influence on the Substance and Standards of American Education*, 1900–1980 (New York: College Entrance Examination Board, 1987); see also George Tanner, Report of the Committee Appointed by the English Conference to Inquire into the Teaching of English in the High Schools of the Middle West, *School Review*, 1907, 15: 37–45.

4. http://www.highereducation.org/crosstalk/ct0107/voices0107-kirst.shtml

5. Sandra Stotsky, *The Death and Resurrection of a Coherent Literature Curriculum*, Rowman & Littlefield, 2012.

6. According to ACT, a complex text can be described with respect to the following six aspects:

   Relationships: Interactions among ideas or characters in the text are subtle, involved, or deeply embedded.

   Richness: The text possesses a sizable amount of highly sophisticated information conveyed through data or literary devices.

   Structure: The text is organized in ways that are elaborate and sometimes unconventional.

   Style: The author's tone and use of language are often intricate.

139

Vocabulary: The author's choice of words is demanding and highly context dependent.

Purpose: The author's intent in writing the text is implicit and sometimes ambiguous.

7. Terry Salinger, Michael Kamil, Barbara Kapinus, and Peter Afflerbach. (2005). *Development of a New Framework for the NAEP Reading Assessment.* National Reading Conference Yearbook. 54, pp. 334–348.

8. Achieve. (2005). Analysis of the 2009 Reading Framework in the context of the college and workplace preparedness benchmarks of the American Diploma Project: Report of the major recommendations of the Achieve panel.

9. http://www.nagb.org/publications/frameworks/reading-2011-framework.pdf

10. During the early spring of 2010, Sandra Stotsky was asked by Michael Cohen, president of Achieve, Inc., and by Sandy Kress, with the James B. Hunt Institute at the time of his call, for suggested standards to add to Common Core's English language arts standards. To address the lack of cultural/historical markers in the "Anchor" reading standards, she recommended adding the first two literature standards in Achieve's 2004 end-of-high school benchmarks in English language arts: "H1. Demonstrate knowledge of 18th and 19th century foundational works of American literature" and "H2. Analyze foundational U.S. documents for their historical and literary significance (for example, The Declaration of Independence, the Preamble to the U.S. Constitution, Abraham Lincoln's 'Gettysburg Address,' Martin Luther King's 'Letter from Birmingham Jail')." Both standards were reworded and added to Common Core's grade-level standards for grades 9/10. Just before release of the final draft of Common Core's ELA standards on June 2, 2010, these two standards were moved to grades 11/12.

11. Mark Bauerlein, at the request of Common Core's staff, helped to draft this statement in the early stages of the project. He was approached specifically to strengthen the literary-historical aspect of the standards, and the staff welcomed the language of "foundational" and "classic" literature. Their request demonstrated Common Core's interest in mandating certain materials, even against

the wishes of educators and administrators who object to any required authors, texts, or traditions at all.

12. S6ee, for example, David Coleman's remarks in "Bringing the Common Core to Life," April 28, 2011. http://usny.nysed.gov/rttt/docs/bringingthecommoncoretolife/part4transcript.pdf. That's the first shift—50/50—informational text and literary text in K–5 required by the standards and required in both the standards and assessments that measure them. We were explicit about this...[the document] extends that same interest in the broad base of literacy... to 6th to 12th grade." Here, as in other remarks Coleman's has made on the matter, it is hard to interpret his comments to mean anything other than a requirement for at least 50 percent informational reading in grades 6–12 in the English class, given ten standards for informational reading and nine standards for literary reading from K–12. Coleman never says that the vast bulk of the readings in the secondary English class should be literary, only that teachers of other subjects are also responsible for ensuring that 70 percent of the reading students do in high school is informational. He has been consistently coy about stating what percentage of that reading should take place in the English class.

13. See Chapter 5 in Sandra Stotsky *The Death and Resurrection of a Coherent Literature Curriculum*, Rowman & Littlefield, 2012, for examples of how the English class has been turned into an ersatz social studies class.

14. Common Core. (2009). *Why We're Behind: What Top Nations Teach Their Students But We Don't. A report by Common Core*. Washington, DC. Pp. 25–33.

2

The Fate Of American History in a Common Core-Based Curriculum

Ralph Ketcham, Anders Lewis, and Sandra Stotsky

Introduction

This essay puts the Common Core's treatment of U.S. history into the context of the broader decline in history instruction in K–12. The Common Core is focused on English Language Arts and Mathematics. It does not include standards for instruction in history. Thus the relation between the Common Core and history instruction is indirect. The authors of this essay show how Common Core displaces traditional history instruction while emphasizing a particular approach to history as part of the English Language Arts standards.

The Crisis in K–12 American History

U.S. history is in trouble. Though many Americans take their children to the battlefield of Gettysburg, read the latest book by historian David McCullough, or watch the latest video on the History Channel, the teaching and learning of history in our nation's schools is in disrepair. James Madison would wonder if we have reached the point of farce or tragedy that he worried about—a nation with a democratic political system but one with a populace lacking in historical and civic knowledge.

The signs of trouble are widespread. At the elementary level, the National Council for the Social Studies (NCSS) warns the growing focus on mathematics and reading in the 2001 No Child Left Behind Act and in the Common Core State Standards adopted by over 45 states have cut into the time previously devoted to instruction in history. The NCSS has also noted that "abundant research bears out the sad reality that fewer and fewer young people, particularly students of color and students in poverty, are receiving a high quality social studies education, despite the central role of social studies in preparing students for the responsibilities of citizenship." According to one recent (and massive) study, elementary students spend less than 3.5 hours a week on "social studies." "We do not have time," one elementary social studies teacher noted, "and no one in the district cares about social studies."[1]

The teaching and learning of civics and history (let alone the amorphous subject of "social studies") is no longer a priority in our elementary schools, nor a priority among most of our nation's leaders. A bipartisan group of scholars known as the Commission on Youth Voting and Civic Knowledge recently issued a report in which they noted that "Civic education for most policy makers" is a "low priority." The overwhelming majority of states, the writers of the report stated, do not assess school and student performance in the field of social studies or history. Further, the overwhelming majority of states do not require certification in U.S. government for government teachers.[2] Another recent study conducted by the Center for Information and Research on Civic Learning and

Engagement found similar results. Education in social studies, the report concluded, is not a priority at the state or national level. In 2001, the report noted, only 34 states administered social studies assessments. By 2012–2013 that number had dropped to 21.[3]

Absent a focus on social studies, history, or civics at all levels of our K–12 public school system, it is not surprising that student knowledge of our own nation's history is minimal. For 25 years, in fact, student scores on the National Assessment of Educational Progress (NAEP) tests have been dismal. In 1986, for example, 60 percent of seniors failed to understand that the goal of the *Federalist Papers* was to support ratification of the Constitution. In 1995 more than 80 percent of students in all tested grades failed. In 2006, only 13 percent of seniors scores proficient and in 2010, only 12 percent of seniors were proficient. The 2010 NAEP test demonstrated that almost 100 percent of graduating seniors could not explain the importance of *Brown v. Board of Education*.[4]

Some prominent public figures have voiced concerns over these trends. In 2008, former Supreme Court Justice Sandra Day O'Connor and Congressman Lee Hamilton of Indiana wrote that a healthy democracy requires informed, knowledgeable citizens but "too many people today do not understand how our political system works."[5] In a 2011 article, O'Connor and U.S. Secretary of Education Arne Duncan wrote that "Civic knowledge is not inherited through the gene pool. It is learned – at school and at the dinner table. And, too often, our schools are doing a poor job of transmitting civic knowledge."[6] O'Connor and Duncan also pointed out that the crisis of historical and civics-based learning is most acute among African Americans and Hispanics. NAEP statistics confirm this. On the 2010 NAEP tests over 50 percent of Hispanic 12th graders and over 60 percent of African Americans failed to achieve a basic understanding of civics.[7] Results for African Americans and Hispanics were similar on the 2010 NAEP U.S. history test. To earn a score that demonstrates a "basic" understanding of U.S. history content required a cut score of 294. The average score for African Americans was 268. For Hispanic Americans it was 275. For white Americans it was 296.[8]

145

Such gaps in educational achievement on issues that are fundamental to the life of our democracy warrant state and national attention. Instead, most state and national leaders seem to be looking the other way. NAEP administrators, for example, have decided to eliminate two of their U.S. history and civics assessments (for grade 4 and grade 12). Massachusetts, which has one of the highest-ranked set of history standards for K–12, has suspended its history assessments.[9] The crisis of history extends all the way to the College Board and a course taken by almost half a million high school students. In the fall of 2014, the College Board implemented a re-designed Advanced Placement U.S. History curriculum in which U.S. history has been depersonalized and reconceived largely as the story of identity groups struggling under the oppression of the privileged and the powerful.

History teachers see that their subject now plays second fiddle to mathematics and English. They also see that a core part of American history (the philosophical and historical antecedents to the Constitutional period, as well as the contentious issues with which the Framers grappled) has been minimized or distorted by the College Board in its redesigned A.P.U.S. history curriculum. How did a nation that once believed the learning of history was fundamental to the success of a democracy become a nation in which the evolution of democracy and of a republican form of government is minimized, ignored, left to chance, or politicized?

The Founders' Views on the Study of History

The current decline in K–12 history instruction stands in contrast to the views of the men most responsible for launching the American experiment in democracy. These were practical men who were primarily concerned with launching a revolution and building a new Constitutional republic, but they regarded the study of history as indispensable.

When asked to comment on and support a plan for public education in the new western state of Kentucky in 1822, Madison responded with a theory of good republican self-government. It required, Madison insisted, intelligent, responsible, public-spirited citizens, who would have knowledge of "the globe we inhabit, the nations among which it is divided, and the characters and customs which divide them."[10]

Education, Madison insisted, "cannot be too much applauded." A government deriving its power from the people, and a people without "popular information, or the means of acquiring it, [was] but a Prologue to a Farce or a Tragedy, or perhaps both," he asserted. "A people who mean to be their own Governors, must arm themselves with the power which knowledge gives." His pleasure at Kentucky's plan was "not a little enhanced," he said, "by the enlightened patriotism which is now providing for the State; a plan embracing every class of Citizens." He explained: "Cheaper and nearer seats of Learning [would allow] parents with slender incomes...to place their sons in a course of education putting them on a level with the sons of the Richest." This would provide "Learned Institutions...diffused throughout the entire Society, the education needed for the common purposes of life." He confimed: "wherever a youth was ascertained to possess talents meriting an education which his parents could not afford, he would be carried forward at the public expence,...to the completion of his studies at the highest [seminaries]."

Madison thus promoted education for all citizens regardless of wealth, a plan which was later formalized in systems of universal public education. It addressed the needs of citizens and political leaders, and the development of the talents needed for the professions and occupations that he hoped would flourish in a free and self-governing society. A plan of education encompassing these broad, history-focused, objectives, Madison believed, was the only way to avoid the Farce or Tragedy of an uneducated self-governing electorate.

In turning to the content of the proper education for free and self-governing citizens, Madison, John Adams, and Thomas Jefferson, began with their collegiate studies at Princeton, Harvard, and William and Mary, where they learned the ancient languages of the Greek historians Herodotus, Thucydides, Polybius, and Plutarch, and of the Romans Livy, Sallust, Caesar, and Tacitus. When Madison and Jefferson drew up a list of 307 works they proposed for a Library of the Continental Congress in 1783 (blocked by the anti-government-spending delegates), they included books by the latest, often radical European historians such as Pierre Bayle, Voltaire, Montesquieu, and Barbeyrac, as well as contemporary English and Scottish historians such as Gibbon, Hutcheson, Robertson, Priestley, Hume, and Adam Smith. The list also included the four "books of elementary right" that Jefferson would declare were at the root of American thinking about government at the time of the Declaration of Independence: "Aristotle, Cicero, Sydney, and Locke."

The two Virginians recommended long lists of histories, exploration accounts, tracts, laws, and treaties about the Americas since the Columbian discovery. Then lawmakers might work with knowledge of the needs, dangers, and accomplishments of the people from whom they derived their "just powers" of government. The study and understanding of history, that is, was deemed essential to those taking part in the public life of the self-governing republic formed under the Constitution.

It was crucial to these founders that history be studied; that citizens have an awareness of its importance in understanding the United States of America, the nation which in 1776 was "conceived in liberty and dedicated to the proposition that all... are created equal" in 1776; and knowledge of the Constitution, the nation's operating framework. Benjamin Franklin, for example, as a nine-year-old growing up in Boston in 1715, heard Increase Mather preach about the rumored death of "that wicked old Persecutor of God's People, Lewis XIV." When sixty and moving toward the Declaration of Independence, Franklin remembered this sermon as his first recollection of commentary on public affairs. It placed not only historical knowledge at the center of his world view but also a view that saw the world as dominated by a struggle between "persecutors" of the people and a community seeking to live in political freedom. Thus Franklin's vastly important and useful public career arose in part from both his study of history and a moral perspective on it. Three years after his recollection of Mather's sermon he signed the Declaration of Independence, and 11 years after that the Constitution.

Franklin noted in his autobiography that though he had had only two months of formal schooling, "from a child I was fond of Reading and all the little money that came into my Hands was ever laid out in Books." Apprenticed to his brother's printing shop, he had access to a bounty of books and pamphlets which he read voraciously through the night. From an English translation of *Plutarch's Lives* he learned not only the facts of the history of the ancient world, but also its concern for the commonweal and for the public character of its leaders. Plutarch admired leaders who were not only great but also good. Thus he extolled Cicero's career in the Roman Senate, especially for showing "how invincible right and justice are [when] eloquently set forth," but condemned him for acquiescing in Caesar's dictatorship, "a more grievous and greater tyranny" than that of the Roman Senator Catiline, which Cicero had led in suppressing.[11]

From his study of virtue in history Franklin learned important lessons in how to fulfill diligently his dual citizenship roles, to rule and be ruled, with honor, responsibility, and public spirit. This was a message he conveyed to the members of the Constitutional Convention of 1787 when, in considering suffrage requirements, he asked that they do nothing to "depress the virtue and public spirit of our common people; of which they had displayed a great deal during the war."

Franklin elaborated the effects of his early reading of history in his 1749 *Proposals Relating to the Education of the Youth in Pensilvania.* He explained that "the Causes of the Rise or Fall of any Man's Character, Fortune, Power, &c., ... indeed the general natural Tendency of Reading good History, must be, to fix in the Minds of Youth deep Impressions of the Beauty and Usefulness of Virtue of all Kinds, Publick Spirit, Fortitude, &c....History," he added, "will also give Occasion to expatiate on the Advantage of Civil Orders and Constitutions, how Men and their Properties are protected by joining in Societies and establishing Government; their Industry encouraged and rewarded, Arts invented, and Life made more comfortable: The Advantages of Liberty, Mischiefs of Licentiousness, Benefits arising from good Laws and a due Execution of Justice, &c. Thus may the first Principles of sound Politicks be fix'd in the Minds of Youth."

The study of history for its own sake, then, was the indispensable path to the upright character of the public-spirited citizen and to the establishment of a good government of just and socially useful laws.

Madison, the future "father of the Constitution," acquired a strong general knowledge of history in preparatory school and college, but he read works of history more vigorously as the colonies moved toward the *Declaration of Independence* to deepen his understanding of public affairs. He studied Adam Ferguson's *An Essay on the History of Civil Society* and Joseph Priestley's *An Essay on the First Principles of Government*, which prepared him to take learned part in the Virginia conventions and legislatures which arose after the American victory in the war for independence. In his most momentous use of history for public purposes, in the months before the Constitutional Convention of 1787, he gathered around him his own growing library and the "literary cargo" of books that Jefferson had carefully selected for him from the book stalls of Paris, London, and Amsterdam.

Madison had at his disposal the latest Enlightenment, multi-volume works of French scholarship such as Diderot's *Encylopedie Methodique* and de Thou's *Historie Universalle,* and other histories reflecting the critical spirit of Voltaire and the French philosophes. Madison also had available to him classical works such as *Plutarch's Lives* and the histories of Polybius, the historical orations of Demosthenes and Cicero, and modern "Whiggish" (Jefferson's term) histories such as Sir William Temple's *United Provinces of the*

Netherlands and Abbe Raynal's *History of England*. From this study he compiled a booklet of forty-one pocket-sized pages "Of Ancient and Modern Confederacies" that he used in 1787–1788 at the Federal Convention and at the Virginia Ratification Convention.

He publicized his study of history and its linkage to the common good of the nation by using what he learned to build his arguments in Federalist 18, 19, and 20. He explained that a sovereign confederation of sovereign states (as the Articles of Confederation was) was a "solecism in theory," and in practice was "subversive of the order and ends of civil society." Such a political form substituted "the destructive coercion of the sword...[for] the mild and salutary coercion of the magistracy."

The result was that, he concluded, the United States had lost sight of its general welfare and of the need for a disciplined respect for law. The need was clear. He wrote to Washington a month before they took their seats in the Constitutional Convention of 1787, saying, "an individual independence of the States is utterly irreconcilable with their aggregate sovereignty," it was necessary at once "to support a due supremacy of the national authority, and not exclude the local authorities whenever they can be subordinately useful."[12] The lessons of history confirmed that "a more perfect Union" was necessary.

The founders insisted and assumed, then, that understanding human, especially American history, was essential to a union "conceived in liberty and dedicated to the proposition that all... are created equal." To proceed without the knowledge of history that undergirded essential public-spirited citizenship and good laws was a sure path to "a tragedy or a farce." All would have agreed on the shared obligation of all social agencies, government and non-government, public and private, to foster these qualities. And, thus, Franklin's aspiration might be achieved that "the first Principles of a sound Politicks might be fixed in the Minds of Youth."

The History of History Education

Prior to the American Revolution, schools focused on religious instruction. Throughout the 1600s and 1700s, most colonists received little to no history education. The American Revolution began to change this. Although the founders insisted that political success depended upon a citizenry educated in history, the reforms were slow to be realized.

In Massachusetts, Horace Mann led efforts to create the first common school system—schools that would be supported by taxpayers and teach a common curriculum. In the 1830s and 1840s, Mann (who became the state's first secretary of education) was concerned that the ideas of Jefferson were not being implemented. Many children, he argued, received no schooling at all and the schools that existed were often in poor shape. Students, in turn, sat for long hours on benches and did little more than practice writing, learn the alphabet, and memorize texts. The learning of history was at best an afterthought. Deep historical content was not in the curriculum. To change this, Mann urged the creation of common schools that would provide all children an opportunity to acquire the knowledge that would help them advance in society. "Education," Mann argued, "is the equalizer of the conditions of men, the great balance wheel of the social machinery."[13]

In 1852, Massachusetts became the first state in the nation to require all children to attend school (they could be private or public). Along with reformers like Mann in Massachusetts, reformers in New York, including Governor Silas Wright, called for the creation of common schools for the purpose of imparting knowledge to all students. "On the careful cultivation in our schools, of the minds of the young," Wright declared, "the entire success or absolute failure of the great experiment of self-government is wholly dependent." [14]

In response to the efforts of reformers and in response to the concerns many Americans had with the rising numbers of immigrants who, many felt, did not have the habits and values needed for self-government, common schools grew in number across the states. More and more children began to receive at least some education. Still, the history that students learned was limited. Many students read from popular books such as *McGuffey's Eclectic Readers* that were light on history but emphasized moral tales focused on admirable personality traits.

Nineteenth-century educators who supported the teaching of history did so in an effort to instill a common knowledge that all citizens would need to fulfill their democratic responsibilities. Charles Goodrich, a writer of popular 19th-century textbooks, declared that his goal was to make students "so familiar with the lives and sayings of famous Americans that they will have no difficulty in understanding" any modern reference to them.[15] One popular history textbook that teachers used for many years was Salma Hale's *History of the United States.* Hale made his goals clear. The preservation of American freedom, he wrote, depended on "the universal diffusion of knowledge" and "this truth should sink deep into the hearts of the old and the young." American citizens, he continued, "should never forget the awful responsibilities resting upon them."[16]

Regardless of the quality of instruction, history had become a recognized part of the school curriculum. Americans had been writing and publishing histories of the colonies from early on (e.g. Colonial Massachusetts' governor Thomas Hutchinson's 1764 *History of the Colony of Massachusetts Bay, The History of the Colony of Massachusett's Bay)* and new historians began to emerge such as Francis Parkman. Moreover, popular writers mined the young nation's past for stories and poems. The interest of American's in American history was strong and deep, but history instruction in public schools did not keep pace.

By 1900 common schools existed across the nation. Spending on schools increased as did student enrollment, spurred on by increasing immigration. Though history education was limited, there was widespread acknowledgment among educators that the teaching and learning of history merited a growing place in the school curriculum. In 1899, for example, the American Historical Association created the "Committee of Seven" to examine high school history curricula and make proposals for reform. The committee's report recommended four years of history at the high school level: ancient history in grade 9, medieval and modern Europe in grade 10, English history in grade 11, and American history and civics in grade 12.[17]

The committee's report was a moment of promise for history educators. It did not last long. At the turn of the century a new group of "progressive" educators began an attack upon the teaching of rigorous academic history that continues to this day and, in many respects, has now triumphed. In 1913 a committee led by Thomas Jesse Jones, a Welsh immigrant deeply interested in the education of African Americans, created a report titled "Cardinal Principles of Secondary Education." Jones and other members of the committee believed that education had to be made "relevant" to students. And history, according to Jones, was not relevant to the vast majority of students who would, after a few years of schooling, go off into factories and never have to bother themselves with the boring, arcane facts of the past. In place of history, schools should offer "social studies" classes that would help children accept their lot in life by teaching them skills they would need in the factories of the modern world.[18]

Jones' belief that history was superfluous to some students eventually became part of a report created by the National Education Association's (NEA) Commission on the Reorganization of Secondary Education issued in 1918 and reflective of the larger progressive trend in the field of education. The authors of the NEA report argued that the purpose of schools was to promote "social efficiency." Schools had to help each student "find his place and use that place to shape both himself and society toward ever nobler ends." One way to do this was to do replace history with social studies which the report defined as "subject matter related directly to the organization and development of human society, and to man as a member of social groups." History was too far removed from the immediate needs and wants of children. It was too arcane, too academic, and too likely to involve abstract thoughts. The fragile minds of so many American youngsters simply could not handle history. A separate Committee on Social Studies argued that "Facts, conditions, theories, and activities that do not contribute rather directly to the appreciation of methods of human betterment have no claim." Social studies, the NEA insisted, had to trump history.[19]

Progressive reformers latched onto newly created Intelligence Quotient (I.Q.) tests to argue that most students were not suited to serious academic subjects such as history. It was far better, they insisted, to train people for "real-world" work. The head of the Stanford University Department of Education argued that "We should give up the exceedingly democratic idea that all are equal and that our society is devoid of classes. The employee tends to remain an employee; the wage earner tends to remain a wage earner..."[20]

The progressives gained momentum. In response to their theories, state after state and district after district began to dramatically revise their curricula, eliminating history and other core academic subjects, replacing them—as Virginia did—with activities focused on the "major functions of social life," or the "Production of Goods and Services and Distribution of the Returns of Production." At the elementary level, schools ditched content in favor of fun-filled activities like block building.[21] Schools also began to track students. Only those deemed worthy would receive rigorous academic training in all subjects, including history. Some critics of progressivism sought to challenge these changes.

Changes after World War II

After World War II—and with more and more students attending school (80 percent of teenagers were enrolled in high school in 1950)—a few academics wondered if we were on the verge of producing a large class of citizens without the necessary knowledge to be self-governing citizens in a democratic society.[22] A leading critic of the progressive trend was University of Illinois historian Arthur Bestor. Bestor sought to rally opposition to progressivism by calling for a greater emphasis on academic subjects for all students. "One can search history and biography in vain," Bestor argued, "for evidence that men or women ever accomplished anything original, creative, or significant by virtue of narrowly conceived vocational training or of educational programs that aimed merely at 'life adjustment.'"[23] The Soviet launch of *Sputnik* in 1957 also convinced many Americans that we were falling behind our rivals in core academic subjects.

Change, however, came slowly in the field of history. Many educators continued to dismiss the importance of history as irrelevant to the lives of students. In 1951, A.H. Lauchner, speaking before a convention of high school principals, declared that "We shall some day accept the thought that it is just as illogical to assume every boy must be able to read as it is that each one must be able to perform on a violin..."[24] Learning how to read, let alone learning history, Lauchner insisted, is simply unnecessary for many children. In 1967 one social studies educator, Edgar Wesley, wrote an article titled "Let's Abolish History." In it, he emphatically declared that "no teacher at any grade level... should teach a course in history as content. To do so is confusing, unnecessary, frustrating, futile, and as illogical as to teach a course in the World Almanac, the dictionary, or the Encyclopedia."[25] After World War II, day in and day out, most students did not take much history and certainly did not benefit from a clearly defined, grade-by-grade history curriculum; instead, they took social studies classes that focused on current events, "social living" classes, or classes on problems such as drug use. History, when taught, was based on student interest and "hands-on" activities.

The Sixties and Seventies

By the 1960s and 1970s, proponents of history education could rightly feel dispirited. Two main forces were aligned against any substantive change. First, most schools of education had become centers of progressivism. Year after year, education schools graduated teachers who possessed little content knowledge but plenty of "child centered" teaching methods. In tandem with state and local governments, as well as school administrators, there emerged what Bestor referred to as "an interlocking directorate of professional educationists."[26] Second, alongside the continued anti-academic focus of progressives, there emerged new political and educational movements (characterized by terms such as "New Left," "radical," and "multicultural") that spawned out of the heated politics of the 1960s and in most cases melded with the ideas of progressive education.

New Left, radical, or multicultural historians, commentators, and educators urged a dramatic revision in the way that history was taught at all educational levels. It was time, they said, to move beyond Western triumphalism and American exceptionalism and focus on people and movements that have often been ignored. At its best, this new movement called for more attention to the history of American Indians, African Americans, Hispanics, and women, topics that had previously received little attention in history classes. On the other hand, the ideas of this new movement tended to verge into simplistic and polemical views of the past. So too did it promote the idea of the teacher as an activist—a person who should seek to change the views of students through historical study. Thus, Howard Zinn, author of the popular *A People's History of the United States,* declared that it was his goal to "awaken a great consciousness of class conflict, racial injustice, sexual inequality, and national arrogance."[27] Students, for Zinn and his followers, were not autonomous—they could not make up their own minds but, instead, had to be led along the path of proper historical thinking.

Progressive educators believed that their ideas were in the best interests of students. But facts began to tell a different story. All the changes progressive educators had made did not lead to better results, either on history tests or on SAT verbal and math tests. From 1963 to the late 1970s, SAT verbal scores dropped from an average of 478 to the 420s. Math scores dropped from an average of 502 in 1963 to 466 in 1980. Student knowledge of history and civics, as NAEP tests would soon demonstrate, was also minimal. Most damaging, the theories of progressive and multicultural educators were clearly not working for low-income students who face an enormous education gap in all major subjects, including history.[28]

At Risk

By the early 1980s, when a commission appointed by President Reagan issued a stinging indictment of American education titled *A Nation at Risk*, many Americans favored a change. They wanted education reform focused on rigorous academic standards for all core subjects including history. "The educational foundations of our society," the authors of *A Nation at Risk* noted, "are being eroded by a rising tide of mediocrity that threatens our very future as a Nation and a people...If any unfriendly power had attempted to impose on America the mediocre educational performance that exists today, we might well have viewed it as an act of war."[29]

Soon after the release of *A Nation at Risk,* a group of noted historians and educators including William McNeill, C. Vann Woodward, Gordon Craig, Diane Ravitch, and Paul Gagnon created the Bradley Commission to call for a nation-wide commitment to the teaching and learning of history. Bradley Commission members noted that the nation-wide education crisis that was the focus of *A Nation at Risk* was in many cases worse for history. In the elementary grades, they pointed out, "history is typically a forgotten subject." It had been replaced by content-light "expanding horizons" classes where students spent time learning about their family and community, not on the amazing stories of famous Americans or the great turning points of American history. In the middle and high school grades, Bradley members continued, students received a vast sludge of social studies classes but little if any U.S. history and almost no world history. To remedy these problems the Bradley Commission called for radical changes at the elementary level—the replacement of a hazy social studies curriculum with a curriculum focused on actual historical content as well as biography, literature, and geography. At the secondary level the Commission called for students to study four years of history, including world history, Western history, and U.S. history. It was time, Commission members argued, to give history its proper place in American schools: "History answers not only the what, the when, the where, and the who about the course of human experience on our planet but more importantly, the why." Commission members also noted that history "provides the basis for understanding such other disciplines as philosophy, the arts, religion, literature, law, and government."[30]

National and State Standards, Round I

Momentum was clearly building for change. In his 1990 State of the Union Address and in his America 2000 plan, President George H.W. Bush insisted that by the year 2000 Americans students "must be first in the world in math and science achievement." Bush also declared that every school should "ensure that all students learn to use their minds well so they may be prepared for responsible citizenship, further learning, and productive employment in our modern economy." It is, Bush insisted, time to act. "Education," he declared, "is the one investment that means more for our future because it means the most for our children. Real improvement in our schools is not simply a matter of spending more: It's a matter of asking more—expecting more—of our schools, our teachers, of our kids, of our parents, and ourselves." Bush also recommended the writing of "world class" standards in all major subjects, including history.[31] In response to the rising tide of support for reform, educators at the national and state level set to work.

At the national level, the attempt to write history standards failed. Educators and members of Congress condemned the set of national history standards produced under the leadership of the National Center for History in Schools at the University of California in Los Angeles under the direction of Gary Nash as being one-sided and overly negative in its portrayal of American history. At the state level, however, the 1990s and 2000s witnessed much positive change. State after state began writing history standards and developing history assessments. Though many state standards were of poor quality (either because they lacked rigor, were not specific, or were politically biased), several states did develop strong, rigorous history standards. The state history standards produced by South Carolina, Alabama, California, Indiana, Massachusetts, and New York offered well-developed U.S. and world history standards that were academically sound, cohesive, and challenging.

For example, consider California's grade 11 standards on the Civil Rights movement. The standards require students to read and discuss the Supreme Court's *Brown v. Board of Education* decision; understand Martin Luther King Jr.'s "philosophical and religious dedication to nonviolence by reading documents such as his 'Letter from Birmingham Jail'"; and be familiar with many of the famous leaders and activists of the Civil Rights Movement as well as key turning points of the movement including King, Rosa Parks, the sit-ins, the attempt to integrate Little Rock, Arkansas's Central High School, the March on Washington in 1963, and the Selma to Montgomery marches in 1965. The California standards also call for readings of books related to the era, including *The Autobiography of Malcolm X* and Richard Wright's *Native Son*.[32]

The Progressive Counter-Attack and No Child Left Behind

But just as it appeared possible for genuine reform in the teaching and learning of history to take place, political and institutional support for serious academic reforms changed. The shift came from something old and something new. Progressive educators at schools of education had continued to fight against serious academic history standards in favor of amorphous social studies and thinking skills. Theodore Sizer, former dean of the Harvard Graduate School of Education, insisted that the "myriad, detailed and mandatory state 'curriculum frameworks,' no matter how scholarly

160

they were, are attacks on intellectual freedom."[33] Popular education writer Jonathan Kozol insisted that assessments based on the state standards smacked of memories of "another social order not so long ago that regimented all its children...to march with pedagogic uniformity, efficiency, and every competence one can conceive—except for independent will—right into Poland, Austria, and France, and World War II."[34]

Alongside the progressive educators came radical and multicultural historians who insisted that state standards needed to be more reflective of recent scholarship on race, class, and gender. In his popular 1995 book *Lies My Teacher Told Me*, James Loewen insisted that one of the reasons African Americans and Hispanic students do so poorly is because they never hear their history. "Black students," Loewen argued, "consider American history as usually taught 'white' and assimilative, so they resist learning it. This explains why research shows a bigger differential between poor and rich students and white students, in history than in other school subjects." The same, Loewen argued, is true for girls because "women and women's concerns and perceptions still go underrepresented in history classes."[35] Loewen's claims managed to be both wrong (by the time he wrote his book scholarship and teaching had been transformed by the views of New Left, radical, and multicultural historians for three decades) and insulting at the same time (as if people can comprehend only the history of their own race or gender and only when it is written by those of their own race or gender).

Added to these forces was something new—national legislation that took the wind out of the sails of history educators. The No Child Left Behind Act (NCLB), passed by Congress in 2001, required that all schools receiving public funding had to test students in mathematics and reading.[36] History had been omitted. States and districts took notice. Support for history, as is attested by the studies discussed in the introduction to this section, waned. A second major blow came with the arrival and adoption by many states of the Common Core standards, also for only mathematics and English language arts. As NCLB did, the Common Core is pushing states and districts to focus overwhelmingly on adjusting and revising their curriculum and professional development programs around the Common Core's two areas of focus. Its website proudly declares that "the [mathematics and English language arts] standards were created to ensure that all students graduate from high school with the skills and knowledge necessary to succeed in college, career, and life, regardless of where they live." If the father of our Constitution, James Madison, or the father of public education, Horace Mann, were alive today they would surely wonder about what happened to the importance of educating students to become self-governing citizens in a democratic society.[37]

In 2000, it appeared that the stars were aligned and genuine reform could take place. Today, it is quite clear that devoted teachers and educators will need, once again, to rally support for genuine change. The trends of the last several years have led our nation's schools into a position where the importance of historical knowledge—the knowledge necessary for citizenship in this country—is simply not valued. Madison's fears are becoming reality.

The Common Core

It may sounds excessive to say that Common Core's English language arts (ELA) standards threaten the study of history in K–12. After all, the study of history in K–12 has never been one of the great strengths of the American school curriculum. Apart from relatively rare moments of reform, history instruction has lagged many other subjects. But Common Core has made a not very good situation considerably worse. In the words of a high school teacher, "if implemented as their authors intend, the common core will damage history education."[38] The Common Core is not directed focused on history, but the study of history in K–12 is now entangled in the Common Core's ELA standards.

The entanglement begins with a document titled *Common Core Standards for English Language Arts and Literacy in History/Social Studies, Science, and Technical Subjects.*[39] The bulk of the document is on ELA standards. But the last seven pages (pp. 59–66), titled "Literacy in History/Social Studies, Science, and Technical Subjects," provide "literacy" standards for these subjects in grades 6–12. The introduction to the whole document explains:

> The standards establish guidelines for English language arts (ELA) as well as for literacy in history/social studies, science, and technical subjects. Because students must learn to read, write, speak, listen, and use language effectively in a variety of content areas, the standards promote the literacy skills and concepts required for college and career readiness in multiple disciplines...

> Beginning in grade 6, the literacy standards allow teachers of ELA, history/social studies, science, and technical subjects to use their content area expertise to help students meet the particular challenges of reading, writing, speaking, listening, and language in their respective fields.

> It is important to note that the grade 6–12 literacy standards in history/social studies, science, and technical subjects are meant to supplement content standards in those areas, not replace them. States determine how to incorporate these standards into their existing standards for those subjects or adopt them as content area literacy standards.

Common Core's literacy standards are justified on the grounds that college readiness means being able to read, write, and speak in all subject areas—a reasonable expectation if the "all" doesn't mean every subject taught in college or a level of proficiency beyond the level of the coursework in the subjects taught in a typical high school.

Common Core's ELA standards, nevertheless, expect English teachers to teach "informational" texts about 50 percent of their reading instructional time at every grade level. At least, that is what K–12 curriculum specialists nationwide see as the implications of 10 standards for reading "informational" texts and only 9 for reading literary texts at every grade level in the ELA part of the ELA document, even if "informational" texts are called "nonfiction."

Common Core's Literacy Standards

Common Core's literacy standards are not the content standards that the ELA document promised. They are instead directions for teaching reading and writing in various subjects. Here are three standards for History/Social Studies in grades 11/12 as examples:

Integration of Knowledge and Ideas

CCSS.ELA-Literacy.RH.11–12.7 - Integrate and evaluate multiple sources of information presented in diverse formats and media (e.g., visually, quantitatively, as well as in words) in order to address a question or solve a problem.

CCSS.ELA-Literacy.RH.11–12.8 - Evaluate an author's premises, claims, and evidence by corroborating or challenging them with other information.

CCSS.ELA-Literacy.RH.11–12.9 - Integrate information from diverse sources, both primary and secondary, into a coherent understanding of an idea or event, noting discrepancies among sources.

These may be skills worth cultivating in students but they bend away from teaching actual historical knowledge. "Integrating" sources of information, evaluating premises, and so on are conceptual goals that make sense only if the student has already acquired a solid and reasonably detailed knowledge of historical events and chronology. At best, the Common Core assumes that other knowledge has somehow been gained, but by refocusing the teacher's effort on "premises, claims, and evidence," the basic historical content is eclipsed.

The new aim, enunciated in the Introduction of the document, is to use the subject at hand to teach students how to read, write, and talk about the subject. This reverses the traditional procedure in which teachers drew on what their students already knew about reading, writing, and speaking to teach the actual content of the subject. Secondary school learning had been turned on its head without any public murmur from history, science, or mathematics teachers or their professional organizations, probably because most subject teachers did not know they were being required to teach reading and writing in a document ostensibly designated for English and reading teachers. The National Council for the Social Studies apparently knew what the ELA standards writers intended, according to this article,[40] but, so far as we know, did not communicate any concerns to its members.

This stealth requirement should have sparked broad public discussion when the final version of the Common Core standards was released and before state boards of education voted to adopt them. But we have found no record of any attempt by a state board or commissioner of education to provide for robust commentary and input from teachers. Perhaps the shift was too subtle to register with the public officials charged with evaluating the new standards.

Repeating a Failed Experiment

A major attempt to get subject teachers to teach reading and writing skills called Writing across the Curriculum (WAC) or Reading and Writing across the Curriculum (RAWAC) took place in the 1960s and 1970s at the college level and in K–12, and it had gradually fizzled out with little to show for it. There was no explanation in the Common Core document of how Common Core's effort was different, if in fact it was. Perhaps the standards writers simply didn't know about these movements and why they failed. The National Council of Teachers of English's (NCTE) 2011 policy research brief did not reference even one study after boldly declaring that the "research is clear: discipline-based instruction in reading and writing enhances student achievement in all subjects."[41] RAWAC failed for many reasons. These are the most obvious:

No systematic information available: Ostensibly, it is good and desirable to make the teachers of secondary subjects assign more reading and to teach students how to read their assignments. But there was no systematic information on what average students

165

read, how much they read, or why they were not doing much reading, if that were the case. Why assign more reading if there were no good reasons to assign much heavy reading loads to begin with (e.g., no textbooks available, students couldn't read the available texts, students wouldn't do their homework)?

Misunderstanding of what history teachers do: The demise of RAWAC in K–12, at least in part, is attributable to a misunderstanding of how history teachers actually teach history. After giving students a range of documents to read, teachers might ask them, for example, to describe and document Lincoln's evolving political position on how best to preserve the Union from the beginning to the end of the Civil War. Such a directive requires the application of CCSS.ELA-Literacy.RH.11–12.7 to a history lesson: integrate and evaluate multiple sources of information presented in diverse formats and media in order to address a question or solve a problem. This is how general skills get developed. But in doing so history teachers are not trying to teach a literacy skill; they are aiming to expand students' knowledge.

Another possible example: a lesson on totalitarianism. History teachers might assign and discuss a reading on how a totalitarian state in the 20th century controls resources and people's behavior. They might then ask: "According to this reading, what is a totalitarian state like? What does it try to do? What were the weaknesses of the Soviet Union as an example of a totalitarian state?" History teachers are unlikely to talk about (or think in terms of) "main idea" or "supporting details" in discussing what students have read about a totalitarian state, but they are clearly talking about a main idea and supporting details when they raise specific questions for discussion about a specific topic. They are asking students to apply these general skills in topic-related language for the classroom lesson and thereby develop the skills.

History teachers (like science teachers) use the specific content of their discipline in ways that require students to apply their intellectual processes and their prior knowledge to what they have been assigned to read or do. If students cannot answer the questions on the grounds that they couldn't read the assignment, other issues (such as the student's placement or possible learning disabilities) need to be explored.

Less and less reading outside of school: The demise of RAWAC in K–12 can also be traced to the diminishing amount of reading and writing done outside of school hours. How much reading have students been doing on the topic under discussion? In other words, do they have any prior knowledge? Are they familiar with the vocabulary related to the topic? The two are related. Students can absorb some of the discipline-related vocabulary of a discipline-based topic by reading and re-reading the material carefully (as in history) or by working carefully with material named by these words (as in a science lab) without constantly consulting a glossary. But how to get students to do more reading or re-reading is not the purpose of a standard. Getting students to address questions about particular topics in a discipline with adequate and sufficient information (i.e., to develop their conscious understanding of the topics) is one purpose of a standard.

Reading and writing as homework is the student's responsibility, not the teacher's. This responsibility is not shaped by the words in an academic standard. It is dependent on a student's self-discipline and motivation, elements of the student's character beyond the teacher's control. Teachers can set up incentives and disincentives, but these must be reinforced by policies set by a school board, parents, and school administrators. They are not governed by academic objectives.

History teachers' self-image: The demise of RAWAC in K–12 can in part be traced to the self-image of those who teach discipline-specific content, such as history teaches. This is an issue highlighted in research on the subject. The need for writing in subject-based classrooms makes sense to most teachers, but RAWAC did not spur significantly more writing activities in secondary schools because content teachers did not see themselves as writing teachers. They continue to see English teachers as teachers of writing (and literature), and themselves as teachers of specific subjects like math, science, or history.

Stress on autobiographical, narrative, or informal writing: An emphasis on non-text-based writing in the ELA class began in the 1970s. Advocates of this writing process tended to stress autobiographical narrative writing, not informational or expository writing. Students were also encouraged to do free "journal" writing because it was shapeless and needed no correction. This undercuts the skills required for subject-based writing which flows from knowledge of content that exists outside of the student writer.

Professional development on different history content, not discipline-based reading: There is little in-depth research on this issue, and for good reason. We know little about the quality of the professional development individual teachers have received. At the time RAWAC was being promoted, professional development programs heavily emphasized critical pedagogy and multiculturalism. The workshops described in The Stealth Curriculum: Manipulating America's History Teachers[42] have a decided focus on manipulating teachers and their students into a certain understanding of U.S. and world history rather than on how to read and write in a history class. Reading and writing activities were included in these workshops, but the development of "literacy" skills was not their goal.

Providing professional development is a huge and very profitable industry because most of it is mandated by local, state, or federal authorities. But it has almost no track record of effectiveness in significantly increasing students' knowledge of the subject. This was the conclusion of a remarkably thorough review of the research on professional development for mathematics teachers undertaken by the National Mathematics Advisory Panel (NMAP) in 2008.[43] There is no reason to consider the situation different for history teachers. Furthermore, we are not even talking about professional development for history teachers seeking to teach reading and writing in their own subjects; these were workshops to prepare teachers to teach the content of their own subjects.

No information on qualifications of workshop providers: Professional development to teach history teachers how to teach students to read and write in their disciplines presents an even bleaker picture. Not one study showing the effectiveness of the practice is cited in the NCTE report in 2011 or in an IES report in 2008 despite both reports lauding its benefits. None of the studies reviewed by the NMAP for its task group report on professional development looked at the adequacy of the academic qualifications of the professional development providers in the reviewed studies. Yet the qualifications of professional development providers was such a serious issue in implementing the state's Education Reform Act of 1993 that the Massachusetts Department of Education required the involvement of historians in the "content" workshops for history teachers it funded even though it could not establish criteria for the organizers of these workshops.

How Common Core Damages the K–12 History Curriculum

The "exemplars" used by the authors of the ELA standards demonstrate that their limited understanding of high school curricula. The quality and complexity of the informational reading is generally inappropriate.

Inappropriate exemplars for informational reading: We find a few appropriate exemplars on the history of indigenous and African Americans. Among them, however, we find puzzling ones, such as E.H. Gombrich's *The Story of Art,* 16th Edition, Mark Kurlansky's *Cod: A Biography of the Fish That Changed the World,* and Wendy Thompson's *The Illustrated Book of Great Composers.* It's hard to see any high school history teacher comfortably tackling excerpts from those books in the middle of a grade 9 or 10 world history or a U.S. history course.

The informational exemplars in Appendix B for history teachers in grades 11–12 are even more bizarre. Along with a suitable text, Tocqueville's *Democracy in America,* we find Julian Bell's *Mirror of the World: A New History of Art* and *FedViews,* issued in 2009 by the Federal Reserve Bank of San Francisco. These two titles clearly don't fit into a standard grade 11 U.S. history course or a standard grade 12 U.S. government course. These exemplars are out of place not just in a typical high school history class but in a typical high school curriculum.

The standards writers wanted to make teachers across the curriculum as responsible as the English teacher for teaching "literacy." This at first sounds fair, almost noble. But to judge from the sample titles they offer for increasing and teaching informational reading in other subjects, informational literacy seems to be something teachers are to cultivate and students to acquire independent of a coherent, sequential, and substantive curriculum in the topic at hand.[44] Weak readers end up deprived of class time better spent immersed in the content of their courses.

Inappropriate literacy strategies—a nonhistorical approach to historical texts: Perhaps the oddest aspect of Common Core's approach to literary study is the advice given to teachers by its chief writer David Coleman, now president of the College Board, on the supposed value of "cold" or "close" (non-contextualized) reading of historical documents like the "Gettysburg Address." Doing so "levels the playing field," according to Coleman. History teachers believe doing so contributes to historical illiteracy.

No history or English teacher before the advent of Common Core would approach the study of a seminal historical document by withholding its historical context: why it was created at that particular time, by whom, and for what purpose. Likewise, they would save some preparation time for instruction in the language archaisms. Nor would they keep such information from being considered in interpreting Lincoln's speech. Yet, David Coleman has categorically declared: "This close reading approach forces students to rely exclusively on the text instead of privileging background knowledge, and levels the playing field for all students."

As high school teacher Craig Thurtell states: "This approach also permits the allocation of historical texts to English teachers, most of whom are untrained in the study of history, and leads to history standards [Common Core's literacy standards for history] that neglect the distinctiveness of the discipline."[45] Thurtell goes on to say that the "study of history requires the use of specific concepts and cognitive skills that characterize the discipline—concepts like evidence and causation and skills like contextualization, sourcing, and corroboration. These concepts and skills are largely distinct from those employed in literary analysis. Both disciplines engage in close readings of texts, for example, but with different purposes. The object of the literary critic is the text, or more broadly, the genre; for the historian it is, however limited or defined, a wider narrative of human history, which textual analysis serves."

Causes of Poor Reading in High School

Not only did the writers of the Common Core English language arts standards profoundly misunderstand how reading in a history class differs from reading in a literature class, they misunderstood the causes of the educational problem they sought to remedy. They set out to solve two problems. First, large numbers of high school graduates need remedial coursework in reading and writing as college freshmen. Second, large numbers of students fail to graduate from high school and go on to a post-secondary educational institution.

The architects of Common Core assumed that the major cause of these educational problems is that English teachers have given low-achieving students too heavy a diet of literary works and that teachers in other subjects have deliberately or unwittingly not taught them how to read complex texts in these other subjects. These assumptions don't hold up.

High school teachers will readily acknowledge that low-performing students have not been assigned complex textbooks because, generally speaking, they can't read them and, in fact, don't read much of anything with academic content. As a result, they have not acquired the knowledge and the vocabulary needed for reading complex history textbooks. Educational publishers and teachers have made intensive and expensive efforts to develop curriculum materials that accommodate students who are not interested in reading much. These accommodations in K–8 have gotten low-performing students into high school, but they can't be made at the college level. College-level materials are written at an adult level, often by those who teach college courses.

Unsolved

The problem addressed in this essay is larger than the Common Core and may be endemic to American society. Thomas Jefferson explained, "civil government is the sole object of forming societies." According to him, instruction in the history of that formation must sit at the center of the education of those who are, under the Constitution, to "transact together" the public business. To fail to do this, he warned, was to risk the citizenry of the nation becoming "a heterogeneous, incoherent, distracted mass,"[46] rather than the public-spirited body good republican government required.

But the United States has a spotty record of rising to the challenge of educating K–12 students in the nation's own history. We can do it well when we try, but reforms typically are not sustained for more than a generation before they give way to some new emphasis. The Common Core is the latest diversion of educational attention and energy away from the fundamental need to create a citizenry that has a fair knowledge of where our republic came from and how it has struggled to live up to its ideals. The motives of the writers of the Common Core ELA standards in trying to harness history to the goal of improvements in reading and writing may be at some level commendable, but the result is one more turning away from the essential content of history instruction.

Author Biographies

Ralph Ketcham is Maxwell Professor Emeritus of Citizenship and Public Affairs, Syracuse University. He specializes in American political thought, the era of American Revolution, public policy, and comparative political cultures. He is the author of *James Madison, A Biography* (1971, 1991).

Anders Lewis is a history teacher and art and history department head at the Advanced Math and Science Academy Charter School in Marlborough, Massachusetts. He holds a Ph.D. in American history from the University of Florida.

Sandra Stotsky is professor emerita of the University of Arkansas Department of Education Reform. Unlike many of the testing experts who drafted the Common Core, she had significant experience, prior to being on Common Core's validation committee, writing content standards, having helped to develop Massachusetts' highly regarded English content standards during her time as Senior Associate Commissioner at the Massachusetts Department of Education from 1999 to 2003. Stotsky has taught elementary school, French and German at the high school level, and undergraduate and graduate courses in reading, children's literature, and writing pedagogy. She has written numerous books, including *The Death and Resurrection of a Coherent Literature Curriculum* and *Losing our Language*. She earned an Ed.D. from Harvard Graduate School of Education.

Endnotes

1. Gayle Theiman, Joseph O'Brien, Patrice Preston-Grimes, John Broome, and Thomas Barker, "From the Field: What Social Studies Teachers Do in the Classroom," in Jeff Pass and Paul Fitchett, ed, *The Status of Social Studies: Views from the Field* (Charlotte: Information Age Publishing, 2013), pp. 47–48. The Social Studies Professional: Newsletter for Members of National Council for the Social Studies, October, 2013. http://www.socialstudies.org/publications/tssp.

2. All Together Now: Collaboration and Innovation for Youth Engagement: The Report of the Commission on Youth Voting and Civic Knowledge: http://www.civicyouth.org/wp-content/uploads/2013/09/CIRCLE-youthvoting-individualPages.pdf

3. Surbhi Godsay, Whitney Henderson, Peter Levine, and Josh Littenberg Tobias, "State Civic Education Requirements," pp.1–2. http://files.eric.ed.gov/fulltext/ED536256.pdf

4. For a summary of NAEP history scores, see Anders Lewis and Sandra Stotsky, 2012, The Rise and Fall of American History in Massachusetts: Pioneer Institute White Paper, p. 4. http://pioneer-institute.org/education/study-calls-for-reinstating-passage-of-u-s-history-test-as-graduation-requirement/

5. *Christian Science Monitor,* September 17, 2008.

6. The Daily Beast, July 1, 2011.

7. The Nation's Report Card: Civics 2010: National Assessment of Education Progress at Grades 4, 8, 12. http://www.nationsreportcard.gov/civics_2010/.

8. The Nation's Report Card: U.S. History 2010: National Assessment of Education Progress at Grades 4, 8, 12. http://nces.ed.gov/pubsearch/pubsinfo.asp?pubid=2011468.

9. Stotsky and Lewis, The Rise and Fall of the Study of American History in Massachusetts.

10. Madison to William T. Barry, Aug. 4, 1822; in R. Ketcham, ed., Selected Writings of James Madison (Indianapolis, 2009), p. 310.

11. Plutarch's Lives, trans. Sir Thomas North, London, 1579; reprinted NY, 1941, 8 volumes; VI, 374.

12. Madison to Washington, April 17, 1787.

13. Mondale, *School,* p. 29.

14. Quoted in E.D. Hirsch, *The Making of Americans.*

15. Tyack, *Seeking Common Ground,* p. 41

16. Salma Hale, *History of the United States from Their First Settlement as Colonies to the Close of the War with Great Britain in 1815* (New York: Charles Wiley, 1825), pp. 335–336.

17. Diane Ravitch, "The Plight of History in Schools" in Paul Gagnon, ed., *Historical Literacy: The Case for History in American Education* (Boston: Houghton Mifflin, 1989), p. 61.

18. Diane Ravitch, "A Brief History of Social Studies," in James Leming, Lucien Ellington, and Kathleen Porter, ed., *Where did Social Studies Go Wrong?* (Marlboro: Thomas Fordham Foundation, 2003), pp. 2–3.

19. Diane Ravitch, *Left Back: A Century of Failed School Reforms* (New York: Simon and Schuster), pp. 123–127. Gagnon, *Historical Literacy,* p. 4. Also see E.D. Hirsch, *The Making of Americans.*

20. Mondale, *School,* p. 98.

21. Ravitch, *Left Back,* pp. 241–243.

22. Mondale, *School,* pp. 63–64. Also see Patricia Albjerg Graham, "Assimilation, Adjustment, and Access: An Antiquarian View of American Education," in Diane Ravitch and Maris Vinovkis ed., *Learning from the Past: What History Teaches Us About School Reform* (Baltimore and London: Johns Hopkins University Press, 1995), p. 6.

23. Ravitch, *Left Back,* p. 345.

24. Ravitch, *Left Back,* p. 348.

25. Gagnon, Historical Literacy, p. 5.

26. Hirsch, *The Making of Americans. Ravitch, Left Back,* p. 345.

27. Peter Novick, The *Noble Dream: The "Objectivity Question" and the American Historical Profession* (Cambridge: Cambridge University Press), p.431. Howard Zinn, *A People's History of the United States: 1492–Present* (New York: HarperPerennial), p. 686.

28. Ravitch, *Left Back,* p. 410. In an extensive study in 2003, Abigail and Stephan Thernstrom wrote that the "average black and Hispanic student at the end of high school has academic skills that are at

about the eighth-grade level; in fact, on most of the NAEP tests, the majority of black students in twelfth grade have scores Below Basic, while those of Hispanics look only slightly better." See Abigail and Stephan Thernstrom, *No Excuses: Closing the Racial Gap in Learning* (New York: Simon and Schuster, 2003), p.22.

29. Quoted in David Angus and Jeffrey Mirel, "Rhetoric and Reality: The High School Curriculum," in Ravitch and Vinoviskis, *Learning from the Past*, p. 300.

30. Gagnon, *Historical Literacy*, p.10.

31. George H.W. Bush, State of the Union Address, January 31, 1990 at http://millercenter.org/president/speeches/detail/3423. Gary Nash, Charlotte Crabtree, and Ross Dunn, *History on Trial: Culture Wars and the Teaching of the Past* (New York: Alfred Knopf), pp. 150–152.

32. My review of state standards relies on work by Sheldon and Jeremy Stern. See http://edexcellence.net/publications/the-state-of-state-us.html. California's standards can be accessed at: http://www.cde.ca.gov/ci/hs/cf/.

33. Quoted in Thernstrom and Thernstrom, *No Excuses*, p.25.

34. Quoted in Thernstrom and Thernstrom, *No Excuses*, p.25.

35. James Loewen, *Lies My Teacher Told Me: Everything Your History Textbook Got Wrong* (New York: Simon and Schuster), 301–302.

36. Congress did establish, in 2001, the Teaching American History (TAH) program. The TAH program has provided millions of dollars in grants to recipients in every state to promote the professional development of teachers of American history. But the results, according to the U.S. Department of Education, have been lackluster. In a 2011 report, the Department of Education noted that with fewer and fewer states providing state-wide history assessments to students it was difficult to measure if students were doing any better because of the TAH program. The Department of Education report noted that "Grantee evaluations that were reviewed lacked rigorous designs, and could not support a meta-analysis to assess the impact of TAH on student achievement or teacher knowledge." The report also found that "Teaching American History grants often lacked support from district or school administrators and were not well integrated at the school level. Grantees struggled to recruit a diverse range of teachers, particularly less experienced teachers and those most in need of support." See U.S. Department of Education, Teach-

ing American History Evaluation, Final Report at: http://www2.
ed.gov/rschstat/eval/teaching/us-history/tah-report-9-9-11.pdf

37. The Common Core website is: http://www.corestandards.org/
about-the-standards/

38. See http://hnn.us/article/151479

39. http://www.corestandards.org/wp-content/uploads/ELA_Standards.pdf

40. http://hnn.us/article/151479

41. http://www.ncte.org/library/nctefiles/resources/journals/cc/0203-mar2011/cc0203policy.pdf

42. http://edexcellence.net/publications/stealth.html

43. http://www2.ed.gov/about/bdscomm/list/mathpanel/report/teachers.pdf

44. Sandra Stotsky. (2013). Literature or technical manuals: Who should be teaching what, where, and why? Nonpartisan Education Review/Essays, 9 (1). http://nonpartisaneducation.org/Review/Essays/v9n1.htm

45. http://hnn.us/article/151479

3

The Fate of Poetry in a Curriculum for the Proletariat

Anthony Esolen, Jamie Highfill, and Sandra Stotsky

We are concerned about the future of poetry in the face of the Common Core's English language arts standards and the Common Core's drive to prepare students for "college and career." The fate of poetry in the Common Core has occasioned little comment from the National Council of Teachers of English, International Reading Association, Association of Supervisors and Curriculum Developers or higher education bodies such as the American Academy of Arts and Sciences and the Modern Language Association. But there is a significant problem.

When these standards were adopted by state boards of education and governors in 2010, there were no reports of expressed concerns about changes in the balance between literary and non-literary content in the English curriculum. Thus, it falls upon those few organizations with a consistent history of interest in the humanizing mission of public school curriculum to explore what is happening with the nation's poetry curriculum.

Poetry study and recitation belongs prominently in the K–12 curriculum, despite the Common Core's workforce-oriented goals. In part I, Anthony Esolen discusses why students should read poetry at all, the kind of reading that poetry demands from us, and what poetry has to do with a child's developing imagination. In part II, Jamie Highfill explains how poetry has traditionally been taught in the public schools. In part III, Sandra Stotsky traces what we know from large-scale studies about the poetry curriculum in this country's public schools. In part IV, the authors discuss how Common Core's English language arts standards seem to be influencing the poetry curriculum in our public schools. In part V, the authors suggest what they see as the fate of poetry in school curriculum so long as Common Core's standards and any tests based on them legally shape K–12 education and teacher training.

Freedom and Poetry
Anthony Esolen

Where are the songs of Spring? Ay, where are they?
Think not of them, thou hast thy music too,—
While barred clouds bloom the soft-dying day,
And touch the stubble-plains with rosy hue;
Then in a wailful choir the small gnats mourn
Among the river sallows, borne aloft
Or sinking as the light wind lives or dies;
And full-grown lambs loud bleat from hilly bourn;
Hedge-crickets sing; and now with treble soft
The red-breast whistles from a garden-croft;
And gathering swallows twitter in the skies.

— John Keats, the final stanza of "Ode to Autumn"

Why should a young person read a poem? Why should he read those lines from "Ode to Autumn"? We cannot answer that question without asking some more fundamental ones. What is a child? What is a child for? He shares life with all the other living creatures upon the earth. He eats and drinks, he moves about, he grows, he may bring others of his kind into the world. All these things he shares in common with cattle, dogs, birds of the air, fish of the sea. Yet we perceive that his life is more than food and drink and raiment. His cup runneth over. What is the life of his life?

It would seem odd, even mad, if someone were to say, "I have a new and improved method of raising horses," without having first ascertained what horses are. It would hardly be sufficient if such a person, or a committee, or a bureaucracy flush with billions of dollars, were to assure us that they could tell the difference between a horse and a camel, that they once rode upon a horse in a parade, that they could spell the word, that they knew how much horse-meat they could sell by the pound, and that they had received bids from a glue factory for so much tonnage of equine bones. We would be even more wary, and more ready to call the men from the home for the insane, if they should assure us that their single centrally-directed method must be applied to ponies on the Orkney Islands as well as to wild mustangs in the American plains and draft-horses on the steppes of Mongolia.

Yet what the madmen would do with, or to, that patient dumb animal with the slow sad eyes, the ideologues of education today would do with children all over America. They would strap them all onto the same treadmill, subjecting their teachers to the same overseers with the same conforming textbooks, computer files, databases, and standardized tests, now and forevermore. And they would do so without troubling to ask the questions we are asking. What is a child? What is a child for? What is the life of his life?

We shall make three interrelated assertions. The child, as well as the fully realized human person to which his education should aim, is meant to be free; that he is meant to behold what is good and beautiful and true; and that he is meant to love it because it is so.

None of these assertions is original to us. They are the common wisdom of men and women who have thought and written about education from ancient Greece to the present day. They are to be found, expressed in a variety of ways but true to the central vision nonetheless, in the pagan Plato and the Christian Newman, in the metaphysical Aquinas and the artistic Leonardo, in poets as diverse as the faithful Dante and the skeptical Arnold, and in educational reformers of our own age, such as Maria Montessori, John Senior, and Stratford Caldecott. Let us examine each assertion to see how a poetic education bears upon it, remembering always that to speak of one assertion is to speak also of the others.

Raising Children to be Free

The first assertion, that education should lead the child into the freedom of the human person, might appear uncontroversial. Everyone, it is assumed, desires freedom; but freedom, as modern man conceives it, is strangely extrinsic to the person. A man is free if he is guaranteed by the polity in which he lives the license to choose among an array of socially acceptable objects. These objects are presented to him by marketers, campaigners, and celebrities as desirable for this or that purpose, usually for fulfilling a physical or psychological appetite. The appetites are taken as brute givens, not to be evaluated, much less to be curbed, denied, or redirected.[1] At best, modern man might say that freedom demands as its price the exercise of some lesser virtue, such as self-reliance (not burdening others needlessly) or tolerance (not feeling oneself burdened in turn). Neither those who call themselves conservative nor those who call themselves liberal recognize anything that freedom is for. It is apparently for nothing but what an individual wants.

That is essentially a materialistic and atomistic view of man, and one that reduces freedom to consumption. Man is cast as a consumer of products because he is himself a product, a thing. He is a unit in the masses, an atom in a welter of human stuff, and that human stuff, if it is to be managed, must be predictable. Hence we have seen in politics an obsession with the poll, essentially a machine for the manipulation of psychic things, silencing any deep concern for truth, even in the simple sense of a man's clear and forthright statement of his intent. "Is it true, or good, or beautiful?" No one asks. Rather the question is, "Will it work upon the electoral mass for gaining this immediate end?"[2]

If we wish to talk about human freedom, we must talk about that which resists reduction, or the statistical tactics of marketers and bureaucrats. We must put substance back into our notion of freedom. The body needs blood. The mind and heart and soul need love.

If we are talking about freedom but not about love and beauty, then we have reduced freedom to a political license, defined by what the authorities cannot tell us we cannot have. Such a freedom by definition cannot be the goal of education because it has no content or meaning. But a freedom for what is good and beautiful does have content and meaning. Such a freedom is won not by labor or techniques or the acquisition of marketable skills, but by a habit of mind that the philosopher Josef Pieper calls "leisure."

Compared with the exclusive ideal of work as activity, leisure implies (in the first place) an attitude of non-activity, of inward calm, of silence; it means not being "busy," but letting things happen. Leisure is a form of silence, of that silence which is the prerequisite of the apprehension of reality: only the silent hear and those who do not remain silent do not hear.[3]

Keats could not have written "Ode to Autumn" unless he too had listened to its silence and heard, with the ear and the heart and the mind, its sad and lovely songs. The poem is not a text to be manipulated by various techniques, so that the student may say clever things about it, to win admission to a prestigious school, for the satisfaction of physical and psychological lusts. It is too free for that.

Is such freedom—the inner freedom of a human soul, not the extrinsic license to indulge oneself in compulsions—really what school is for? Indeed, Pieper insists that it is above all what school is for. "One of the foundations of Western culture," he says, "is leisure," and "even the history of the word attests the fact; for leisure in Greek is *schole*, and in Latin *schola*, the English 'school.' The word used to designate the place where we educate and teach is derived from a word which means 'leisure.' 'School' does not, properly speaking, mean school but leisure."[4]

School is a haven for knowing—not just knowing about, in order to, but sheer and beautiful knowing. The aim of a liberal education is not skill, for, as Pieper says, "a functionary is trained," and training is concerned "with some one side or aspect of man," for some utility to be gained.[5] So we train electricians and carpenters, but only as electricians and carpenters, not as whole human beings. But if we believe that human beings are meant to be free, and if we intuit, however vaguely in our ill-bred and ill-educated world, that a free soul aims to know what is true and good and to love it, then we will see that the "use" of the liberal or free arts is precisely that they transcend the category of the useful.

We do not read poetry so that we can write better office memoranda later on. That gets things exactly backwards. We must never reduce human art to laboratory objects, for writing essays on standardized tests or in college courses, extending the compulsions and feeding the cancer. We want instead fully realized human beings who will read poetry because it is beautiful and because it brings us knowledge of what is true, even if it is knowledge that can no more be used than a sunset or a kiss can be used.

We want human beings who will read good and great books, not burn them or grind them to intellectual pulp. For there is more than one way to destroy a book. Ray Bradbury, in his renowned dystopian novel *Fahrenheit 451*, gives us a society in which books and the houses that hide them are burned by "firemen," with most people reduced to the inanities of television and Fun Parks and incessant music on the radio. Bradbury wrote the novel during the height of the McCarthy investigations into the activities of communists, alleged and real, in the State Department and Hollywood; but the novel has very little to do with political censorship. It does not so much predict that, in the future, the Bible, Shakespeare, Johnson, and Keats will not be read as it notices that right now they are not being read. The liberal arts have been dismissed as productive of strife—since they cannot be reduced to scientific consensus—and as economically useless. Thus it is no accident that the first person who brings the hero Montag out from the unreal world of machines and television is a young girl who resists the all-devouring claims of cradle-to-adulthood schooling:

> They want to know what I do with all my time. I tell them that sometimes I just sit and think. But I won't tell them what. I've got them running. And sometimes, I tell them, I like to put my head back, like this, and let the rain fall in my mouth. It tastes just like wine. Have you ever tried it?[6]

The girl thinks as she pleases, away from group projects and extra-curricular activities and the staggering demands of work. We're never told for certain that she reads books. But Bradbury presents her as very like people who read books. Montag will seek out an old professor who reads books, and who tells him that one of the three things necessary for true reading is leisure. That is not the same as time off. It is essentially a spiritual condition, keeping the real things of the world in their rightful place of honor, as do the hobos whom Montag meets in the end. These men preserve books by committing chapters of them to memory:

> There was a silence gathered all about that fire and the silence was in the men's faces, and time was there, time enough to sit by this rusting track under the trees, and look at the world and turn it over with the eyes.[7]

We want to raise children, fully human, whose hearts will be stirred by the heroism and the sanity of the true readers of books and cherishers of the world. They alone will be able to do what the formulas of the technocrat can never capture. They may or may not, as their inclinations lead them, pick through the staggering amount of information readily available today. But they will understand the difference between what is worth knowing and what is worth-less. They will not be staggered by the avalanche of sludge because they need not be on that slope to begin with. They need not wade through a thousand digitalized articles on the poetry of Keats. For the poetry of Keats is not a thing about which they gather information, as one would investigate the action of carotene in October leaves, or the effect of the earth's tilt upon weather patterns in the north Atlantic. They have first the autumn itself, and the poem. These are the mysterious things they cherish.

The Free Arts are for All

Someone may object that such poetry may be for the well-to-do, but not for ordinary people who have to sweat and strain to make a living. It is a frill, a luxury which we can indulge only if we can afford it, but the "global economy," that lumbering colossus, looms; and poetry will not help the prematurely aged college graduate make his way on the Exchange, or climb the slippery pole of Political or Managerial Ambition. So much less will it assist the plumber or the miner.

But that objection bespeaks an utter loss of hope and youth. It is tantamount to saying that we are not free. We must race "to the top"—the top of what, is never specified—or we will be cast adrift by the tides of some inexorable historical movement. In the midst of wealth that generations past would have considered princely, we race away from freedom and towards compulsions, and we assuage our consciences by telling ourselves that we have no choice.

But poetry, like music, like peaceful reflection, has always been for everyone. It has been man's common heritage of song. It unites the old and the young; it binds across the generations, even the centuries. In *Doorways to Poetry,* Louis Untermeyer, writing to young people in praise of that most exalted of human arts, says that from the beginning of mankind to the present day the pulse of poetry has never left us; it beats as strongly in the modern child as in the European cave-man and the prairie Indian. Long before they were written down, songs had the power to stir the senses of the listeners; and when today the lines leap from the printed page, our hearts are stirred and our pulses quicken with the same elemental excitement.[8]

A strange predicament indeed: when modern man with all his labor-saving machinery is less free for poetry than was the man who had to forage for his food every day, and poorer than our country poet Whittier, who cobbled shoes for mere cents, and wandered the flinty hills of New England, and wrote that a bare-foot boy in those hills enjoyed a royal freedom:

> Prince thou art—the grown-up man
> Only is republican.[9]

But is such freedom fit for children? Don't children have to be warehoused and worked over until they are ready for the supposed "real world," a world of wage-earning, political noise, and sexual release? On the contrary, children are almost the only human creatures remaining who stand a chance of enjoying that freedom. It is especially for them.

When Untermeyer sees a child, he sees a free human being, free to love the wonders about him. He also sees a poet, for "no one is without imagination, emotion, taste, and a response to the world's beauties and terrors, its actualities and its dreams."[10] When he sees a poet, he sees someone who has kept that youthful fire especially bright and lively.[11]

Beauty, the Common Desire of Man

Singing is what the lover does, said Saint Augustine,[12] the lover who beholds a thing of beauty. In all systems that reduce man to a proletarian, beauty must be reduced to decoration which only the rich can afford. Beauty is not serious; its appreciation is not rigorous. Poetry won't earn you a job, and therefore it is dispensable. Pieper thus lays bare the spiritual disease of such utilitarians:

> The inmost significance of the exaggerated value which is set upon hard work appears to be this: man seems to mistrust everything that is effortless; he can only enjoy, with a good conscience, what he has acquired with toil and trouble; he refuses to have anything as a gift.[13]

To put it another way, beauty is the splendor of an inner goodness or truth, and must be so received, or not received at all. But man as mere producer and consumer knows no such gift. He thinks of quantity only, and of "consumer demand," reducing his masters to "those at the top of a hierarchy of consumption."[14]

But the idea that poetry, or any of the arts, was a prerogative of the wealthy alone is historical nonsense. Visit an antique store or curiosity shop, and you will see that ordinary people used to surround themselves with objects of beauty. Even things they put to practical use, like chairs, bed-warmers, butter churns, and stirrups, were touched by the playful spirit of poetic creation. Poor miners, farmers, herdsmen, and quarrymen did not build flat gray boxes to live in; the flat gray box was visited upon the urban poor by their "betters" among modern architects. Poor fishermen, lumbermen, and trappers did not build hulking containers for children; they built schools that are sweet to behold, that looked something like chapels, or meeting halls, or homes. The hulking containers were visited upon us all by our "betters" among modern educational bureaucrats, supposedly to save money; and one lone parent stands as much chance of weighing upon what transpires within those containers as a dry leaf against a brick wall.

The aim of a liberal public education in literature used to be to bring beauty even to the poor. That was not so difficult after all, since many of the poets too had been poor; Herman Melville, our great epic poet in prose, wrote in the person of Ishmael that the whaling vessels were his Yale College and Harvard.[15] And the poor man, like his rich cousin, played a musical instrument, by training or by ear or both, or knew plenty of people who did so; he knew by heart a hundred songs secular and sacred; and he no more relished ugliness or brutality for its own sake than he daubed his own kitchen with filth.

We might turn the question around and ask why we should be so hardhearted as to deny the poor their best chance, these days perhaps their only chance, of encountering the beauty of poetry? Man is that peculiar creature who needs most what as an animal he does not need at all. He needs what he cannot put to use. He needs beauty.

But beauty is not the result of mass production. Nor is an appreciation of beauty the result of methods or actions upon the pedagogical assembly line. You cannot turn a poem over to a committee of students doing "group work" and expect anything so private, even so shy, as that appreciation. It cannot be forced or commanded. It must be waited upon. Its quiet utterance must be heard.

Such hearing—not labored at or screwed out of a human brain by educational technology—is well illustrated by a charming anecdote that Untermeyer tells, of a senior whose turn came round to recite to the class some work he had committed to memory. The lad—a football player—took the stage, and, with real feeling and much poise, recited the first eight stanzas of Gray's "Elegy."[16] When the boy took his seat, the teacher called for criticism. She asked one boy in particular, a boy who happened to be third baseman on the school team and who had inclined to be rather a "smart Alec." This time he was strangely silent. When the teacher pressed him, he became embarrassed, and then he stammered: "I can't criticize him. I think it was fine. That's my truly favorite poem, and I can't say anything about it. I like it too well."

The boy's reverent silence before the thing of beauty, Gray's poem, is at once childlike and mature and wholly opposed to the noise of our vast educational machine.

An Education in Love

And that brings us to our third assertion. The boy who loved Gray's "Elegy," though he was usually garrulous, could not speak when the teacher asked him to comment upon the recitation. He did not merely reply that he had nothing to say. He replied that he could not possibly have anything to say because he loved the poem too much to sully it with commentary.

Untermeyer did not write his textbook simply to help students to understand poetry. He wrote it so that they would learn to love poetry because it was beautiful and true and worthy of their love. That is not sentimentality. It is a fully human response, and, in our world of mass phenomena, with ugliness, banality, uniformity, and slovenliness everywhere, it is a response that teachers have a duty to foster, and never to embitter or squelch.

It has grown by now to be a long and tiresome habit, our assuming that all good educators must arm their students against appeals to beauty. That is why we batter them with the ugly. There may be a less "noble" reason, too. Scorn is easier than devotion, and flippancy, the cadaver of mirth, is easier still. But that is to betray our charge as teachers. Says C. S. Lewis:

> For every one pupil who needs to be guarded from a weak excess of sensibility there are three who need to be awakened from the slumber of cold vulgarity. The task of the modern educator is not to cut down jungles but to irrigate deserts. The right defense against false sentiments is to inculcate just sentiments. By starving the sensibility of our pupils we only make them easier prey to the propagandist when he comes. For famished nature will be avenged and a hard heart is no infallible protection against a soft head.[17]

Lewis' words are truer than ever. If the study of literature is only labor, for acquiring certain linguistic skills, then far from irrigating deserts, the teacher will be choking up with sand what few and trickling streams of humanity remain.

And again we ask, "What is a child?" Why should a child read the poem? What in the poem is true, and presented in beauty, worthy of our reverence and love?

For love is the key. Love will show us what is not a good reason for reading the poem. Suppose a child has a grandfather who lives a good bicycle's ride away. Grandfather has, scattered about his old house, flags from the Civil War, old coins, part of a harpoon, and a thousand books tumbled together by a principle of organization he alone knows, *The Sea-Hawk* next to *The City of God*. If you go there, he might be dozing in the sun, or playing cribbage with the neighbor next door. He might be scribbling a line or two of poetry. He might be turning a spindle on a lathe. With the grandfather, you never know. He might be doing nothing at all, which he reserves for the best of times, when he is most alert, and most content.

Why should the child visit his grandfather? The question makes no sense. Even to ask the question is to suggest that one has drifted some distance into madness or robotics.

Now suppose that the child's father, with an eye to the main chance, wishing to stuff his son's resume for enrolling him in the "best" high school, should say, "Son, here is a pad and pen. Go to grandfather's house and take inventory of the shelves, one at a time. You will organize them according to the following method, adapted from Dewey." Or, "Son, here is a recording device. Go visit your grandfather and engage him in meaningful conversation about a topic of current public import, so that you can write a report upon it, comparing what he has to say with the statements of various sources you will locate in print or digitally, organizing the whole into an exhibition of wide, deep, and thoughtful engagement. And be back before supper, or you'll catch it."

The point is not simply that it would be rude to the good grandfather and might hurt his feelings. It is that you cannot really visit the old man that way. You will have made him into an object for analysis and dissection. The encounter will be functional, not human. You may pick up plenty of information from it; you may jot down the dates of all his coins. You will gain no knowledge; for genuine human knowledge is to mere information as information is to chaos, or nothingness. You will surely gain no wisdom, which soars far beyond even knowledge. It would be better for you if you did not visit the grandfather at all if you are going to reduce yourself to a toiler in the traces and the grandfather to the object to be worked. It would be better for you to play the truant and turn aside to see if the wild grapes down the dead-end street are purple yet. It would be better for children never to read a poem at all, than to read it on the treadmill, as just a thing to be worked over, for acquiring some "skill," for a resume, for money, for stuff to buy, for death. It would be better to do nothing than to betray what ought to be loved.

It is true that one has to learn how to read a poem, and the old textbooks are full of helpful pointers for doing that. Untermeyer spends more than four hundred pages coaching his youthful readers in the art. He does not overburden them with technical terms. He wishes instead that the reader will be still and observe the art with the same heightened feeling and imagination with which the poet observes the world. Here he describes Tennyson's famous Eagle:

We see not only an eagle grasping the sheer rock of a high cliff, a lone black speck between the immense sweep of sky and ocean, but we see the world through his eyes: the sun is close and of a terrible brilliance, the entire universe is of an intense blue, and the tumultuous waves below him are slow-moving ripples. Therefore, the wave-lined ocean is a wrinkled sea, and when he shoots from his heights to strike at his prey, he falls like a 'thunderbolt'.[18]

One does not read poems to learn about poetic techniques. That again is backwards. One learns about poetic techniques, if one learns about them at all, the better to read poems; and one reads poems for their own sake—that is, because they are beautiful and wise. Tennyson's lyric shows us something about the eagle that is true, and it excites us, it captivates the imagination because his art presents that truth to us with the splendor of a grave and noble music.

A youth reads Dante's line describing Beatrice's first appearance to Virgil in the *Inferno: lucevan gli occhi suoi piu che la stella*, "Her eyes were shining brighter than the star." What is he to make of that? If he is taught that it is only a traditional metaphor and a bit of poetic exaggeration, he might as well never read a poem again. It is only by the exercise of his imagination, an exercise that is less like labor than like play, that is blessedly impractical, that receives both the beauty of a woman and the beauty of Dante's poetry as a gift, that he can enter into the spirit of the line and say, "Yes, that is true, I have seen it." Should someone then inquire as to whether seeing a heavenly beauty in the eyes of a virtuous young woman will assist the youth in his competition in a global economy, or in his private deliberation on tax rates, we must reply that Dante himself implicitly answers that question, by sending those who ask it down to their proper place several grades of the infernal funnel below. In other words, if you do not love, you should not read Dante.

The Love that Moves the Sun and the Other Stars

But perhaps, with our glance toward Dante, we have arrived at the real danger that poetry poses to the secular worshiper of work for work's sake, and the vast totalizing secular system that such work props up. It is this: poetry and devotion spring from the same fount. Poetry at its most sublime—the epics of Homer and Virgil, *The Divine Comedy, Paradise Lost,* Wordsworth's "Prelude"—is a record of man's encounter with what is more than man.

That is because there is a deep harmony that unites love with celebration—and that unites celebration, in all its boisterous energy, with the effortless enjoyment of what is beautiful and true for its own sake. To reduce all things to utility is to banish the feast. No one can ask what use can be made of a feast without destroying the spirit of festivity. And there can be no feast unless the soul is ushered into the precincts of the divine. It is as Pieper puts it, thinking of all the cultures that have ever graced the earth:

> There is no such thing as a festival "without gods"—whether it be a carnival or a marriage. That is not a demand, or a requirement; it does not mean that that is how things ought to be. Rather, it is meant as a simple statement of fact: however dim the recollection of the association may have become in men's minds, a feast "without gods," and unrelated to worship, is quite simply unknown.[19]

That does not mean that we must bind the festivity of poetry in our public schools to the seasons of any particular religious faith. It does mean, however, that poetry, and all of the arts properly approached, is like what Pieper describes as a Temple, whose space "is not used, is withdrawn from all merely utilitarian ends."[19] It is why the one book that Bradbury's hero commits to memory is *Ecclesiastes,* full of the sad poetry of The Preacher, along with chapters from the exalted visions of the apostle John, in *Revelation.* To use poetry as a field for gaining linguistic skills, or to neglect it altogether, is to dismantle the Temple and leave not one stone upon another. It is to banish the feast and to stifle in the souls of students the natural human spirit that wishes to celebrate the beauty and goodness of a truth beheld and received in gratitude. Again we turn to Keats:

> *A thing of beauty is a joy for ever:*
> *Its loveliness increases; it will never*
> *Pass into nothingness, but still will keep*
> *A bower quiet for us, and a sleep*
> *Full of sweet dreams, and health, and quiet breathing.*[21]

"We murder to dissect," says Wordsworth. One can no more teach poetry by poetry-dissolving means than one can devise a strategy for joy, or force inspiration, or demand love, for "the spirit blows where it will" (John 3:8), and one can only rejoice in gratitude when it comes, and follow where it leads.

We can make a safe bet on where twenty pages of reading about the Spanish Flu will lead you. Perhaps you may become interested in disease, perhaps not. But there will be no open door of a temple, beckoning you to leave the world of total work. We can make no safe bet on where reading *Paradise Lost* will lead you if you read it in the spirit of the feast, receiving it as a gift you cannot earn, its beauty ever gratuitous and overflowing beyond the cramped world of utility. If you enter that temple, you may be changed forever. You may learn to take the shoes from off your feet and to shuck the bridle from your back. You may see things your masters do not want you to see because then they would be your masters no more. You may incline your ear and heart to a music they have tried to drown out. You may even catch a fleeting intimation, like a still small voice on a mountaintop, of the Love that moves the sun and the other stars.

How Poetry Has Been Taught in the Schools
Jamie Highfill

Traditionally, the teaching of poetry has followed a three-pronged approach: (1) working out the meaning of a piece of poetry; (2) developing poetry-reading skills through studying tone, structure, diction, themes, rhythm and rhyme, figurative language, and style; and (3) having students write about poetry and write their own poems.

Poetry has been taught as enhancement, as reinforcement, and in isolation. Poetry has been taught by historical periods, by themes, and by subgenres. There are as many ways to organize poetry in literature curricula as there are types of poetry. In traditional literature anthologies, poetry has enjoyed its own section, whether as American poetry, English poetry, world poetry, or a combination. Textbook authors have reinforced what teachers have always known—that poetry is a distinct study in the great variety of literary choices, just as short stories, speeches, and novels are.

Young children love poetry. Songs like "Old MacDonald" and "I'm a Little Teapot" help students to hear and find rhythm. Even the alphabet is made into a song that rhymes to help children learn it more easily. In this way, poetry is a kinesthetic experience, engaging not just the mind but the body as well. Many children's stories are written in verse. Dr. Seuss is ubiquitous in classrooms for young students, as he should be. His poetry plays with sound, helping students hear the lilt and cadence of our language, while also telling imaginative stories. Shel Silverstein's whimsical poems similarly delight the ear and the mind.

Anthologies for older students have always included the great names of American and English literature: Robert Frost, Emily Dickinson, Walt Whitman, Anne Bradstreet, Theodore Roethke, Anne Sexton, William Carlos Williams, Shakespeare, Lewis Carroll, and Thomas Hardy. The list is extensive, but the fact that these same authors continue to appear is no accident. Their works speak to, indeed, are the stuff of English and American literary culture and history. The implicit if not explicit charge to educators is to initiate our students into the culture in which they will someday work and raise families. The literature of our culture reflects where we come from as much as does our history.

Working out the Meaning of a Poem

The first prong of traditional literary instruction might include questions about what the author wrote. A 1987 McDougal, Littel anthology of American literature asks these kinds of questions of students reading Emily Dickinson's poem "Some Keep the Sabbath Going to Church." For instance, "According to the poem, how does Dickinson like to celebrate the Sabbath? What is her favorite church?" These are fairly literal reading comprehension questions, designed to check students' understanding of what they have read.

A skilled teacher may then springboard from these questions to ask students to connect the poem's meaning to their own experiences in order to give the poem some personal context. The larger purpose is to foster the students' own thinking about the poem's meaning—to deepen their introspection by sharing the poet's feelings. As Robert Frost wrote, "No tears for the writer, no tears for the reader," a sentiment he echoed from the Roman lyric poet Horace.[22]

Teachers of poetry help students to build bridges among the scattered bits of knowledge with which they come into their classrooms, to hold up mirrors in front of them, and to help them understand that although literature, especially poetry, is an escape, it is also how we connect to each other as human beings. But as Archibald MacLeish wrote in the last line of his own poem "Ars Poetica:" "A poem should not mean/But be." And a good teacher knows when to leave the poem alone and not, as Billy Collins put it, "torture a confession out of it".[23]

How a Poem Is Put Together

In poetry especially, form and meaning are interwoven. Take Dylan Thomas' "Do Not Go Gentle Into That Good Night":

> *Do not go gentle into that good night,*
> *Old age should burn and rave at close of day;*
> *Rage, rage against the dying of the light.*
>
> *Though wise men at their end know dark is right,*
> *Because their words had forked no lightning they*
> *Do not go gentle into that good night.*

Good men, the last wave by, crying how bright
Their frail deeds might have danced in a green bay,
Rage, rage against the dying of the light.

Wild men who caught and sang the sun in flight,
And learn, too late, they grieved it on its way,
Do not go gentle into that good night.

Grave men, near death, who see with blinding sight
Blind eyes could blaze like meteors and be gay,
Rage, rage against the dying of the light.

And you, my father, there on that sad height,
Curse, bless, me now with your fierce tears, I pray.
Do not go gentle into that good night.
Rage, rage against the dying of the light.[24]

The metaphors of light for life and night for death help readers or listeners to understand that the speaker of the poem is begging someone to fight the approach of death. One can sense the almost desperate tone in the speaker's voice from the repetition of the first and third lines of the first stanza throughout the poem—a feature of the structure of a villanelle.[25]

Metaphor and allusion are universal in poetry and help readers or listeners to see the world in a new way. The allusion to the myth of Daedalus and Icarus in Thomas' poem does so:

Wild men who caught and sang the sun in flight,
And learn, too late, they grieved it on its way,

It implies that a son should have listened to what his father taught while he had the chance, just as Icarus should have listened to his father when he was told not to fly too high. Understanding the allusion personalizes as well as deepens the meaning of the poem.

As we see in Thomas' poem, rhyme scheme and rhythm also contribute to a poem's pleasing and sometimes not so pleasing sound. Surely there is value in that which is merely pleasing.[26] To again quote Keats:

A thing of beauty is a joy for ever[27]

Music may help to teach poetry too. Whether a teacher uses classical or contemporary music doesn't matter. When a poem has been set to music, the music often clarifies its meaning. William Sharp's operatic recording of Lewis Carroll's poem "Jabberwocky" makes evident that the poem, although written with many nonsense words, is a quest poem that tells the story of a boy leaving home and searching for, battling, and overcoming a monster. The boy returns home a hero with the head of the beast.

Sharp's music rises as the suspense grows, he stretches out the notes during the words "long time," and during the heat of the battle the piano music sounds almost scattered and frenzied. In the last stanza, the music resumes the slow, even tone it started with, and we know that life has returned to "normal." Students are able to "hear" the story even though half of the words are nonsense, just as they hear the desperation in the speaker's voice when Thomas repeats lines in his poem.

Traditional methods of teaching students to read poetry have usually included memorization. Memorization and recitation do not take place only in students' heads. There is a kinesthetic dimension to the practice of memorizing and reciting. Every teacher has seen students who seem to have memorized a poem well but who freeze when they have to stand up in front of a class of fellow students. Students do not understand why they can say their poems perfectly in their heads, but not in front of the class. As in any public speaking act, speakers must practice what they will say in the manner in which they will say it. It isn't enough for a student to memorize a poem in his head. He must practice reciting it aloud because the mind remembers what the body does. Kindergarten teachers know that hand motions with "Itsy Bitsy Spider" help elementary age children remember. Developing students' skills in reading is thus related to their own physical development.

Writing about Poetry and Writing Poetry

When a teacher teaches poetry, students must read an enormous amount. Not just one poem about love, but five, ten poems about love. In this way students learn subtleties not only about love but

198

also about form and structure. Likewise, students must write a great deal about the poems they read. They might write about the irony in Dickinson's line about God being "a noted clergyman." Or characterize Dickinson's attitude toward Nature, so prevalent in her poetry. Or parody Carroll's "Jabberwocky," following his rhythm, rhyme scheme, and theme.

By writing about poetry and then writing their own poems, students internalize an iterative composing process. Choice of words, length of lines, concision, metaphor—it's all part of learning to write, as in "Liking this, rejecting that, cautious and precise/ Weaving words together, you'll speak most happily/When skilled juxtaposition renews a common word."[28]

The group learning so popular in today's climate of education reform does not work for poetry instruction. Writing is a solitary activity. It requires reflection and the time to wade through the messiness of one's mind and to figure out what one thinks, and why one thinks it. E.M. Forster is credited with having said "How do I know what I think until I see what I say?"[29] If writing is the inking of our thinking, students must have the space to do so. And it is at these times that deeper learning takes place.

Reading and writing about poetry as well as writing poetry encourages students to find that inner world of their own and a place where they can be contemplative. A poem is not to be digested like a quick meal. It is to be savored, enjoyed, and appreciated. A school's poetry curriculum is not designed to teach skills that help students get jobs. Rather, it is to "make minds, not careers."[30] And when a mind is strengthened, so is the ability to secure employment.

What Was the Poetry Curriculum in America's Public Schools?
Sandra Stotsky

Once upon a time, poetry was a substantial part of the English curriculum. Several large-scale studies in the past century suggest its contours, always shaped by what English educators saw as its purpose in the schools.

Post World War II Studies

Possibly the most exhaustive examination of what was available in high school literature anthologies, the textbooks used for over a century in most secondary English classrooms, was reported in a 1963 book titled *High School English Textbooks*. James Lynch and Bertrand Evans, both professors of English at the University of California, Berkeley, scrutinized the contents of the 72 most frequently used anthologies for grades 9 to 12 in the 1950s, detailing by genre what they found.

Lynch and Evans viewed literature anthologies as "repositories of the very best ever thought and written in the spirit of the humanistic tradition and the Anglo-American heritage."[31] Because they considered poetry as the "literary heart" of an anthology, they calculated by grade level the number of different poems available across anthologies and listed the poets represented by these numbers.

Among their conclusions, Lynch and Evans suggest: (1) It is at least questionable "whether a high school student inadequately read in the poetry of his own culture is prepared to undertake the study of another." (2) "With lyric poetry particularly, the problem of finding poems with suitable translations is a serious one..." And (3) It is doubtful that "single short poems" by authors from various South American countries "cover" Latin American poetry or that "short poems" by authors across the world adequately "cover" world poetry.

In light of the many poems from outside that tradition in school anthologies, they questioned whether "world literature" should be included, given the "neglect by several anthologies of numerous major authors in the Anglo-American tradition." We shall note the continuing relevance of their concern.

While Lynch and Evans saw "literary importance" as the criterion for selection, for a subject they believed students should see as a "serious and important body of matter for study,"[32] George Norvell had a different view of the purpose for a school's English curriculum. He published in 1973 a major study of secondary students' interests in the texts they read in English class or independently.[33] His own interest in the topic had been sparked by his position as a state supervisor of English education in New York State for almost 30 years. By telling us what secondary students enjoyed reading in class or on their own, his report at the same time tells us what literary and non-literary texts they were assigned. Norvell's purpose was to be able to recommend to English teachers titles that students would enjoy reading, with the hope that if teachers assigned them students would develop a life-long love of reading, which he believed to be a major, if not the major, purpose of the school's English curriculum.

Norvell's information came from thousands of students across New York State. Not surprisingly, we learn from his study that students did not enjoy many of the selections they were assigned in English. The factor that most correlated with enjoyment was gender, not literary artistry or reading ability (with their teachers' assistance, students in his study were classified as superior, average, or weak readers). In fact, he found that "the reading materials commonly used in literature classes are better liked by girls than boys in a ratio of more than two to one." With respect to enjoyment by genre, "girls place essays and poems definitely higher than do boys...."[34] Even among types of poems, there were differences between the sexes. Although girls liked both lyric and narrative poetry equally well, boys liked lyric poetry significantly less than narrative poetry. Norvell concluded that "content is the touchstone of popularity," and that the vast majority of poems selected for study by their English teachers "deal with themes and ideas which young people would reject if offered to them in prose."[35]

In a sense, Norvell was partly paraphrasing the findings of one of the earliest studies of children's poetry preferences, a 1924 study by Helen Macintosh.[36] She had found that students like poems that are funny, tell a good story, have adventure and excitement, have romantic and dramatic qualities, deal with understandable and interesting material, and have rhythm and rhyme. We see these qualities in some of the poems in Norvell's study that high school boys said they liked best.

Although poetry and plays were boys' least favorite genres, nevertheless, boys did have some favorites among the poems studied in their English classes. Those with the highest ratings by boys in grades 10, 11, and 12 were: "Ballad of Billy the Kid" (Knibbs); "Casey at the Bat" (Thayer); "Dorlan's Home Walk" (Guiterman); "Cremation of Sam McGee" (Service); "Da Greata Stronga Man" (Daly); "Deacon's Masterpiece" (Holmes); "George Washington" (Kirk); and "Old Ironsides" (Holmes).[37] Poems with the highest ratings by girls in grades 10, 11, and 12 (in that same table) included: "Between Two Loves" (Daly); "Da Younga 'Merican" (Daly); "Dorlan's Home Walk" (Guiterman); "House with Nobody in It" (Kilmer); "How the Great Guest Came" (Markham); "O Captain! My Captain!" (Whitman); "Twins" (Leigh); and "George Washington" (Kirk). In general, girls liked the poems rated highly by boys more than the converse.

Core Knowledge Sequence

It is doubtful that many English teachers changed the poems they assigned to accord with the enjoyment ratings Norvell obtained. But, interestingly, use of a different criterion for selection turned up some of the same poets. In the late 1980s, the Core Knowledge Foundation, established by literary scholar E.D. Hirsch, issued the Core Knowledge Sequence, a set of content guidelines for grades K–8. Not surprisingly, many of the highly rated poems or authors assigned in grades 10, 11, and 12 in George Norvell's study are in the Core Knowledge Sequence. Required in grade 7 are poems by Edgar Allan Poe, Emily Dickinson, Alfred Lord Tennyson, William Blake, Robert Service, Wilfred Owen, Robert Frost, Countee Cullen, T.S. Eliot, Langston Hughes, and William Carlos Williams. Required in grade 8 are poems by e.e. cummings, Carl Sandburg, Dylan Thomas, Elizabeth Barrett Browning, Robert Browning, Emily Dickinson, William Wordsworth, Robert Frost, Edwin Arlington Robinson, William Shakespeare, Percy Bysshe Shelley, Gerard Manley Hopkins, Allen Ginsberg, Langston Hughes, and Gwendolyn Brooks.

The author lists stimulate several observations. First, we are struck by the fact that what the Core Knowledge Sequence requires in grades 7 and 8 seems to be at a higher level of conceptual and/ or reading difficulty than what students in the upper high school grades in the 1950s and 1960s mentioned as enjoyable reading. The difference in reading level may reflect lower academic standards in secondary English classes in American public schools after World War II and/or a deliberate increase in the relative difficulty of the literary works selected for the elementary and middle school grades in the Core Knowledge Sequence.

The latter hypothesis received some confirmation from the results of an examination of the selections in reading instructional textbooks for the elementary and middle school curriculum in the early years of the twentieth century. The difficulty level of the required literary texts in grades 7 and 8 in the Core Knowledge Sequence is close to the level of what was once in the school curriculum for all students in those grades.[38] This impressionistic finding raises the question: To what extent are secondary teachers responding to lower student reading skills today in selecting the genres and poems for all students in mixed-ability classes to read?

Second, the corpus of poems in the Core Knowledge Sequence has both a more British and a more African-American flavor than do Norvell's lists. The authors of the Core Knowledge Sequence acknowledge that they sought to include what they considered multicultural texts, and E.D. Hirsch's own literary scholarship centered on British poets.

Third, required titles in the Sequence say much less about a poem's or poet's popularity than about the purpose for schooling, as it sees it. Norvell was interested in recommending what students seemed to enjoy reading so long as the poems were of high quality—as he put it, where "the lines of student popularity and critical approval converge."[39] He was thus indirectly hinting at the need to cater to the school population that secondary English teachers were teaching in mid-century America. On the other hand, the Core Knowledge Sequence was and remains centered on "cultural" literacy, on what students should be familiar with (literary work or author or both) to be considered educated—or as the Sequence itself states: to provide a "foundation for later learning" and "the common ground for communication in a diverse society."

National Survey of High School English Teachers' Poetry Assignments

Stotsky's survey in 2010 of the major titles English teachers assign in grades 9, 10, and 11 in honors or standards classes (i.e., not in the highest or lowest English classes in a school) found little overall difference in the profile of poets and/or poems between their assignments and those in the Sequence. Interviewers spoke with over 400 English teachers to obtain descriptions of what they assigned in over 800 courses at these grade levels (two courses per teacher in a nationally representative sample of teachers at these grade levels).[40] Table 1 below is taken from this survey. This table excludes the book-length plays or poems (such as *Julius Caesar* or *The Iliad*) also mentioned by teachers.

Table 1: Major Poets Mentioned 15 or More Times by Grade Level

Major Poets Assigned	Grade			Total
	9	10	11	
Robert Frost	87	80	96	263
Emily Dickinson	49	66	113	228
Edgar Allan Poe	74	42	53	169
Langston Hughes	59	45	57	161
Walt Whitman	19	23	105	147
William Shakespeare	67	55	18	140
Maya Angelou	31	13	19	63
e.e. cummings	16	28	17	61
Carl Sandburg	19	13	22	54
Henry Wadsworth Longfellow	4	8	31	43
Anne Bradstreet	2	6	27	35
T.S. Eliot	2	7	22	31

Major Poets Assigned	Grade			Total
	9	10	11	
William Wordsworth	7	7	11	25
Edgar Lee Masters	4	7	14	25
William Cullen Bryant	0	3	19	22
Nicki Giovanni	7	9	5	21
Sylvia Plath	3	6	12	21
Ralph Waldo Emerson	0	2	19	21
William Carlos Williams	1	4	16	21
Gwendolyn Brooks	2	11	6	19
Paul Dunbar	7	2	10	19
Pablo Neruda	2	14	2	18
Theodore Roethke	3	12	2	17
Ezra Pound	2	5	10	17
Edwin Arlington Robinson	0	1	15	16
Homer	10	4	1	15
Robert Browning	2	5	8	15
John Keats	2	6	7	15
Pat Mora	4	11	0	15
Other Poets	183	325	307	815

While the overall profile of poets mentioned in the 2010 survey is not very different from those required in the Core Knowledge Sequence (and it is possible that the list of required poems in the Sequence influenced the contents of the very large American and British/world literature anthologies used by most high school English teachers), what is very different are the frequencies at which they are mentioned at each of these three grade levels. Beyond the first half dozen names, the numbers are miniscule, indicating that few students nationally are reading these poets. Not only are students on average by 2010 reading few poems, they are reading few poems or poets in common.

Common Core's English Language Arts Standards
Anthony Esolen, Jamie Highfill, and Sandra Stotsky

Common Core's English language arts standards, released in June 2010, contribute to the decline of poetry curriculum in this country. They do so by focusing on skills apart from content, by reducing the time devoted to literary works, and by treating poetry (when they do treat it) as texts to be analyzed and dissected for information and for examples of literary form.

Content- and Culture-Free Skills

To begin with, readers need to understand that most of Common Core's ELA standards are actually content- and culture-free skills. Here is a grade 9/10 literature standard as an example: "Determine a theme or central idea of a text, and analyze in detail its development over the course of the text, including how it emerges and is shaped and refined by specific details; provide an objective summary of the text." This is a content- and culture-free skill, not an academic standard for grade 9/10, because it can be applied as easily to "The Three Little Pigs" as to *Moby-Dick*. There is nothing in the "standard" to suggest level of reading difficulty or complexity.

Common Core did recognize that the same skill set could in theory be the curricular objective at every single grade level and that the content of a K–12 reading curriculum needs to increase in difficulty through the grades. So it provided an appendix that is supposed to help teachers understand what level of reading difficulty should characterize the texts chosen to address its ELA standards at each grade level. But when we look at the poems listed for each span of grades in Appendix B, which lists exemplars of "complexity" and "quality" (not recommended or required texts) for each successive grade span, we find an incoherent group of poems representing a wide range of intellectual levels, literary movements, and literary traditions at every grade span. What an English teacher or school may infer as guidelines to complexity or quality from any one group of poems is totally unclear. For example, the following poems serve as exemplars of complexity and quality for grades 6 to 8:

Longfellow, Henry Wadsworth. "Paul Revere's Ride"
Whitman, Walt. "O Captain! My Captain!"
Carroll, Lewis. "Jabberwocky."
Navajo tradition. "Twelfth Song of Thunder."
Dickinson, Emily. "The Railway Train."
Yeats, William Butler. "The Song of Wandering Aengus."
Frost, Robert. "The Road Not Taken."
Sandburg, Carl. "Chicago."
Hughes, Langston. "I, Too, Sing America."
Neruda, Pablo. "The Book of Questions."
Soto, Gary. "Oranges."
Giovanni, Nikki. "A Poem for My Librarian, Mrs. Long."

Some of the poems on this list may at first seem impressive for grades 6 to 8. But let's take a closer look at Pablo Neruda's "Book of Questions," for example. Below are a number of excerpts from this work, translated from Spanish into English. As a commentator on Google explains: "These are translated short poems...and all their contents are philosophical conundrums about ordinary things in life." While you, the reader, read them, you might ask yourself: For what purpose would a middle school English or reading teacher teach Neruda's poems? How many meet the criteria for enjoyment mentioned by George Norvell or Helen Mackintosh? How many are familiar to a large body of Americans, whether or not Spanish-speaking?

Tell me, is the rose naked
or is that her only dress?

Why do trees conceal
the splendor of their roots?

Who hears the regrets
of the thieving automobile?

Is there anything in the world sadder
than a train standing in the rain?

If I have died and don't know it of whom do I ask the time?
Why do leaves commit suicide when they feel yellow?

Is it true that in an anthill dreams are a duty?
Love, love, his and hers, if they've gone, where did they go?

How many weeks are in a day and how many years in a
month?

Readers might want to try another one—William Butler Yeats' "The Song of the Wandering Aengus." (It is described in an overview of a college lecture in the following way: "Yeats' commitment to a poetry of symbol is explored in 'The Song of the Wandering Aengus,' a fable of poetic vocation."[41]) How about one more? Emily Dickinson's "The Railway Train."

What at first seemed impressive may now seem pretentious. Such exemplars raise two distinct sets of questions: Who was the real audience for Appendix B in Common Core's ELA document? Teachers, or potential advocates for Common Core (e.g., the editorial board of the *New York Times*)? Why were Neruda's "Book of Questions" and Yeats' and Dickinson's poems listed as exemplars of complexity and quality for grades 6 to 8? Why were they listed at all in Common Core's Appendix B? Are they more appropriate for an Advanced Placement course in literature or for a college course?

And why offer such a randomly selected group of poems to illustrate complexity or quality? Does such a scattered list of poems suggest disdain for coherence of any kind in a curriculum?

Poetry Skills Taught in Common Core

Now let's look at some of the middle school literature standards themselves to get a sense of what skills English teachers are to develop in their middle school students in order to read poetry. Here are the few that seem most applicable to poetry in grades 6 to 8.

> *Determine the meaning of words and phrases as they are used in a text, including figurative and connotative meanings; analyze the impact of a specific word choice on meaning and tone.*
>
> *[At a later grade] Analyze the impact of rhymes and other repetitions of sounds (e.g., alliteration) on a specific verse or stanza of a poem or section of a story or drama*
>
> *Analyze how a particular sentence, chapter, scene, or stanza fits into the overall structure of a text and contributes to the development of the theme, setting, or plot.*

Earlier, in grade 4, students have been expected to:

> *Explain major differences between poems, drama, and prose, and refer to the structural elements of poems (e.g., verse, rhythm, meter)..."*

Given the paucity of standards mentioning poetry at all, never mind the elements of poetry, it is not clear that poetry as a genre can be well addressed by English teachers in a Common Core-oriented classroom. Nor can they easily choose to do so in the reduced amount of time that English teachers are to spend on literary texts during an academic year.

Reduction of reading instructional time for literary study

This has been thoroughly covered in the prior two chapters, but it is worth recalling in light of the topic at hand. The reduction of literary-historical content in the standards is an inevitable consequence of Common Core's emphasis on informational reading, and, thus, so is the reduction of poetry.[42]

How Poetry Is To Be Taught under the Common Core: A Case Study

David Coleman, chief architect of Common Core's English language arts standards, has been quoted as saying that "As you grow up in this world, you realize people really don't give a [expletive] about what you feel or what you think." But as teachers and students both know, poetry is very much about thinking and feeling. While the Common Core document purports to be about the

English language arts, there seems to be little place for the arts in Coleman's philosophy. His diktat about the appropriate ratio of literature to nonfiction reading across the curriculum[43] buried in a footnote on page five of the ELA document, seems to have stimulated bizarre advice on the texts to use in the English curriculum.

Nor has Coleman or his co-writer Susan Pimentel made clear attempts to set the record straight about the misinterpretation of these percentages in Common Core's ELA document. They claim that the English class is to continue its focus on literature all the while insisting on the teaching of more "informational" or nonfiction texts in the English class, and they have never offered a set of new percentages in place of the implicit 50/50 mandate. Utility and numbers seem to be Common Core's major concern, so that the study of poetry for it its own sake may almost disappear in language arts classrooms.

We describe in the following pages the literature curriculum developed for grade 8 English classes in the Fayetteville, Arkansas, schools by an outside consultant hired at an exorbitant fee to align the district's curriculum with Coleman's recommended percentages.[44] The consultant repeatedly discouraged the inclusion of poetry on the grounds that it cannot be analyzed by Lexile measures. According to Lexile.com, a website that explains how to determine a text's complexity, "Texts such as lists, recipes, poetry, and song lyrics are not analyzed because they lack conventional punctuation." In addition to dismissing poetry, broadly speaking, in such a series of genres, we find the coup de grace for a Common Core-based reading program: "Non-prose books do not receive a Lexile measure."

It is thus not surprising that the consultant's approach to the inclusion of poetry in a Common Core-based literature curriculum went something like this. First create a unit theme for each quarter of the school year, then choose two major nonfiction texts for two of the quarters and two major works of fiction for the other two quarters, all addressing the theme. Then find some short stories and pieces of nonfiction to go with the theme. And then find a poem that "fits" the theme.

She first established "Do the right thing" as the theme for the first quarter of the school year. After the testing consortium to which Arkansas belonged indicated that a work of fiction was to be the major work studied during the first quarter, the consultant asked teachers at a planning meeting to decide on the spot a text that would fit her theme. They chose *A Separate Peace* by John Knowles because enough copies were available in the school. They also added several short stories to complement, and be completed before, study of the novel: "The Mustache" by Robert Cormier, "All Summer in a Day" by Ray Bradbury, and "The Scarlet Ibis" by James Hurst. To meet nonfiction requirements, they included Philip Stanhope's "Letter to His Son: Rules of Conduct in Polite Company" and Mark Twain's "Advice to Youth."

Clearly, students could make connections among them and find common ideas. Who couldn't? The theme had already been decided upon by a consultant with no background at all in teaching English. While the literature class should be a place for students to discuss ethical principles, do students engage in "deeper" thinking when they are only asked "Did this character do the right thing?" (That was the question teachers were given by the consultant.) The pieces ceased to become occasions for reflection on the part of the learner. Rather, they were used to "beat" students on the head with an idea that was repeated over and over and over, as in the "drill and practice" methods that reformers continually denigrate.

The only poetry selection included in the first quarter readings was Emily Dickinson's "I'm Nobody! Who Are You?"

I'm nobody! Who are you?
Are you nobody, too?
Then there's a pair of us—don't tell!
They'd banish—you know!

How dreary to be somebody!
How public like a frog
To tell one's name the livelong day
To an admiring bog!

While the speaker in this poem has something in common with the character of Gene in *A Separate Peace*, it is not clear what connections the poem has with the other texts in the themed unit. After being given the theme at the onset of study, students had little interest in analyzing the meaning of this poem. The Dickinson poem was simply an afterthought, a condescension, and it is not something students are likely to remember.

Selections for the second quarter's theme, "Do the right thing in the world," included Henry Wadsworth Longfellow's "The Midnight Ride of Paul Revere," but not for its delightful cadence and irregular rhyme, reminiscent of the sound of the horse's hoof beats. No, the poem was to be assigned after grade 8 English students had read the first chapter in Malcolm Gladwell's *The Tipping Point*.[45] But once students had read Gladwell's references to Paul Revere, what was the point of reading a poem about him? Students could not have analyzed the poem for Longfellow's historical inaccuracies. The poem was simply a place-filler, it seemed, and in effect a waste of the students' and the teachers' time. The "So what?" of the poem wasn't "discovered" by the students; it was a given. It thus became a boring experience for students and teachers.

No poetry was included in the third quarter, whose theme was "How the world affects our decision to do the right thing." For the fourth quarter, the major work to be read was *Truce*, a 116 page work of nonfiction about the Christmas truce of 1914 in which soldiers chose, against orders, to stop fighting in World War I (this text was also selected by the consultant).[46] Also included were: Walt Whitman's "I Hear America Singing," William Butler Yeats' "Politics," Robert Frost's "The Road Not Taken," and Polonius' advice to his son, Laertes, from *Hamlet*.

Poetry could be assigned to go beyond the consultant's vision for the unit. To develop student understanding of patriotism and the nature of war, Jamie Highfill gave students Stephen Crane's "War is Kind" and Wilfred Owen's "Dulce Et Decorum Est" to read. Students discussed the sarcastic nature of both poems and then compared what they believed the poets to be saying with how the soldiers in Truce stopped fighting—inferring that sometimes "the right thing" is more than patriotism and a love of one's country but a love of all humanity.

To work more poetry into the curriculum, Highfill assigned more poems as homework, directing particular poems to particular groups of students. These groups read Wilfred Owens' "The Send Off," Alfred, Lord Tennyson's "The Charge of the Light Brigade," Carl Sandburg's "Grass" and "Iron," Joy Gresham's "Snow in Madrid," and Alan Seeger's "I Have a Rendezvous With Death." After becoming familiar with many different war poems, students had more nuanced ideas about war (pageantry, lost innocence, violence, sacrifice, youth, idealism, chivalry, the idea of quest) than they would with only the three original poems assigned in the consultant-designed unit.

Disturbingly, few English teachers in this district raised objections about the ham-handed way that the original curriculum was designed. Nor were they vocal about the lack of poetry as a study in and of itself. Seven poems over the course of a school year let teachers know how important poetry is in a Common Core-based curriculum. In fact, one administrator indicated that because she didn't understand poetry, it was not important for use in the classroom. Her advice to the English teachers was to follow the "curriculum" as prescribed.

Nor were the consultant's credentials ever questioned. That she had never taught in an English classroom was never raised, and her focus on Lexile levels, without consideration of the difficulty or ease of the subject matter, was accepted at face value. English teachers' own classroom curricula honed over years of trial and error in teaching were discarded without a thought.

Poetry has become a "nobody" in Common Core. Why teach students how to read and write poetry if it doesn't follow conventional punctuation? If it can't be measured? If it's too subjective, like art? Common Core seems to be more about convention, about standardization, and about taking the "art" out of English language arts.

Why the Hostility to Poetry in Common Core?

The Common Core English language arts standards were intended to apply to all students indiscriminately to ensure that they would become efficient workers in a "global economy." In other words, the aim is precisely the reverse of that to which the old proponents of a humane education were committed. Those proponents knew well that common workers would have little opportunity from day to day to encounter the great works of human art and thought. They therefore sought to give them what they could, when they could—in school. The aim was to raise and ennoble them, to give them some of what their more fortunate neighbors would enjoy. But the aim here is to depress and level, not to ennoble. It is to make proletarians of us all.

But no one will buy a product with the label "proletarian" upon it. That is why we must mask the reality with slogans. According to the Common Corers, students trained to become workers will "actively seek the wide, deep, and thoughtful engagement with high-quality literary and informational texts that builds knowledge, enlarges experience, and broadens worldviews." That is the language of the marketer and the campaigner.

The designers of the Common Core, ideologues themselves, do not recognize this. In all their hundreds of clotted and ill-written pages of self-promotion, diktats, and appeals to statistics, they mention beauty only once, in the context of a "skill." But the greatest "skill" in reading is not a skill at all. It is something quite different. It is a virtue, a habit of peaceful reception. One cannot produce joy on an assembly line. One cannot manufacture gratitude. One cannot devise a formula for humble hearing.

So it is no surprise that the Common Corers gradually leach poetry out of the high school system. We see how the process takes place in the "task example" for one of the poems they left behind, Keats' poignant "Ode on a Grecian Urn." The poet is beholding an ancient urn, decorated with bands of sculpture, of gods and men and maidens dancing, of a lover trying to woo his beloved and ever "winning near the goal," of a town beyond the sculpture itself, dwelling in the imagination's distance, a town pouring forth her people on this feast day, while a priest leads the ribboned heifer to sacrifice. It is all youth, and strangely deathless; the feasters know no satiety; the lover will never feel "a burning forehead, and a parching tongue." And Keats, who though young was in poor health and was ever aware of the passage of time and the battering waves of change, ends his poem with these solemn words:

> *Thou, silent form, dost tease us out of thought*
> *As doth eternity: Cold Pastoral!*
> *When old age shall this generation waste,*
> *Thou shalt remain, in midst of other woe*
> *Than ours, a friend to man, to whom thou say'st,*
> *"Beauty is truth, truth beauty,"—that is all*
> *Ye know on earth, and all ye need to know.*

Here, for once, is a chance to talk about something as high as the heavens and as deep as the sea! The teacher could ask why we feel a strange sweet sadness when we behold a beautiful thing made by the hands of someone long since passed away. Or whether beauty does give us a vision of truth, even in the midst of sorrow and age and decay and death. Or whether the still silence of a work of art can speak more deeply to us than a month of words and flashing lights and noise. Or why Keats seems to say that the wiser we grow, the more we understand that beauty alone will show us the truth we need. Or perhaps we should not at first ask the poem any question at all, but listen to it, and listen again, and be silent.

We should treat Keats' ode with the same reverence with which Keats treats the urn. We should seek from the poetry the wisdom he seeks from the sculpture. Or we should not seek so much as accept. We should learn how to behold.

Here is the sum of what the Corers have to advise, in their banal and lifeless prose:

> Students cite strong and thorough textual evidence from John Keats's "Ode on a Grecian Urn" to support their analysis of what the poem says explicitly about the urn as well as what can be inferred about the urn from evidence in the poem. Based

on their close reading, students draw inferences from the text regarding what meanings the figures decorating the urn convey as well as noting where the poem leaves matters about the urn and its decoration uncertain.

But neither the urn nor the poem is a teacher. The poem is a crime scene, and the students are forensic investigators. Or the poem is a dreary piece of "text," and the students are to engage in a dreary, impersonal, mechanical piece of drudgery. If we want young people to hate poetry, here is the way to make sure of it.

To see what we mean by this dryness, this numbness, we shall now submit the great aim of the Common Core Standards in English Language Arts, as declared by its clumsy begetters:

> As a natural outgrowth of meeting the charge to define college and career readiness, the Standards also lay out a vision of what it means to be a literate person in the twenty-first century. Indeed, the skills and understandings students are expected to demonstrate have wide applicability outside the classroom or workplace. Students who meet the Standards readily undertake the close, attentive reading that is at the heart of understanding and enjoying complex works of literature. They habitually perform the critical reading necessary to pick carefully through the staggering amount of information available today in print and digitally. They actively seek the wide, deep, and thoughtful engagement with high-quality literary and informational texts that builds knowledge, enlarges experience, and broadens worldviews. They reflexively demonstrate the cogent reasoning and use of evidence that is essential to both private deliberation and responsible citizenship in a democratic republic. In short, students who meet the Standards develop the skills in reading, writing, speaking, and listening that are the foundation for any creative and purposeful expression in language.

No one who could write that excerpted paragraph above, with not the least touch of self-awareness, modesty, or wit, without any sense for what words mean (do we demonstrate cogent reasoning reflexively, as when somebody raps us on the knee with a hammer?), without any love of language, without any clear thought but only the aim to smother us under a barrage of verbiage, heaping one vague piety after another, one Great Insight after another, one dead cliché after another—no such person can possibly have really known the wonder of poetry, or can remember the wonder of childhood.

In all that heap of self-promotion and veiled threats, there is not one well-turned phrase, not one moment of tender regard for a child, or a parent, or a mill-stream, or a fading autumn day, or a poem. There is no life in it, but a gray death-in-life—work here, vote there, shop here, die there.

The Common Corers do not talk often of truth. Recall that their ideal student will "reflexively demonstrate the cogent reasoning and use of evidence that is essential to both private deliberation and responsible citizenship in a democratic republic." No one wishes to dismiss cogent reasoning and use of evidence, or private deliberation, or responsible citizenship. Evidence that can be used has its place. Far be it from us to decry criminal investigators. But what does "cogent reasoning" mean? If it means only that one examines things that one can measure, for participating in political or social machinery, then we deny most strenuously that one reads literature for those purposes.

We must not limit reason to what can be calculated or reduced to statistics or forensics. Perhaps that is why the Common Core has so little to say about poetry, and why, in all of the literary samples they include on their site, not one of them has anything to do with man's longing for the divine.

That omission cannot be the result of chance. The odds are overwhelmingly against it. It means that you have to avoid most of Chaucer, much of Shakespeare, and all of Spenser. You cannot include a single sacred lyric by Donne, Herbert, or Hopkins. Milton must be banished from the Common Core garden, his sin being that he writes about sin, his profanity that he writes about holiness. With him goes the greatest and most influential poem in English, *Paradise Lost*. Along with Milton goes much of Dryden and Pope and Johnson, much of the best of Wordsworth and Keats, almost all of Coleridge. The fact is that English literature until recently was quite steeped in Scripture and was often preoccupied with the great existential questions of human life, which could not even be posed without reference to faith. Out goes Tennyson's "In Memoriam." Out goes Browning's rascally theologian, Fra Lippo Lippi. Out goes Eliot's "Four Quartets." Out goes any real learning about Sidney's great sequence of sonnets, *Astrophil* and *Stella*. Open an old bound volume of *The Century*, a supposedly secular magazine, and you will see that more than half of the poems, many written by ordinary people whose names we have forgotten, have to do with God and man. All must go.

This is no coincidence. The whole thrust of their standards is away from poetry and toward "informational" texts. Not one of the high school essays which they include in their massive appendix has to do with poetry. It is not hard to see why. Information can be managed. But poetry cannot. Information for information's sake befits a soulless drudge in a soulless world. One may scour the hundreds of pages of the Common Core, including its appendices filled with samples of writing by students that the proponents commend, and not find one sentence steeped in wonder. Poetry for poetry's sake befits a fully mature human being, who is infinitely more than a worker or a voter. Common Core's English language arts standards reveal the grim irony of the misnomer "Common Core," for there is no core at all in any set of standards built around a negative: no heart, no shared objects of love, reverence, and memory.

Author Biographies

Anthony Esolen is professor of English at Providence College, where he has taught since 1990. He is the author of many books (both academic and popular), including *Ten Ways to Destroy the Imagination of Your Child* and a translation of Dante's *Divine Comedy* for Modern Library. Esolen earned an M.A. and Ph.D. in Renaissance English Literature from the University of North Carolina—Chapel Hill.

Jamie Highfill contributed a chapter, "Doing the Right Thing: Comedy and Political Satire in Grade 8," to *The Death and Resurrection of a Coherent Literature Curriculum*, by Sandra Stotsky. From 2005 to 2012, she served as co-director of the Northwest Arkansas Writing Project, an affiliate of the National Writing Project, at the University of Arkansas. She moved to northern Virginia at the end of the 2013 school year.

Sandra Stotsky is professor emerita of the University of Arkansas Department of Education Reform. Unlike many of the testing experts who drafted the Common Core, she had significant experience, prior to being on Common Core's validation committee, writing content standards, having helped to develop Massachusetts' highly regarded English content standards during her time as Senior Associate Commissioner at the Massachusetts Department of Education from 1999 to 2003. Stotsky has taught elementary school, French and German at the high school level, and undergraduate and graduate courses in reading, children's literature, and writing pedagogy. She has written numerous books, including *The Death and Resurrection of a Coherent Literature Curriculum* and *Losing our Language*. She earned an Ed.D. from Harvard Graduate School of Education.

Endnotes

1. Romano Guardini wrote, shortly after the misery of the Second World War, that only by asceticism could modern man recover his civilization and culture, for "only the freedom won through self-mastery can address itself with earnestness and gravity to those decisions which will affect all reality." See *The End of the Modern World* (Chicago: Henry Regnery Company, 1968), p. 113.

2. Gabriel Marcel, writing shortly after the Second World War, puts the issue to us as a challenge to revive the very possibility of a human civilization: "The more techniques advance, the more reflection is thrust into the background—and I believe that this cannot be a matter of mere chance... [T]he progress and above all the extreme diffusion of techniques tends to create a spiritual and intellectual atmosphere (or, more precisely, an anti-spiritual and anti-intellectual atmosphere) as unfavorable as possible to the exercise of reflection" (p. 5). For "techniques," read "skills;" not reflection, but reflex actions, like the predictable responses of a machine.

3. Josef Pieper, Leisure: The Basis of *Culture* trans. Alexander Dru (New York: New American Library, 1963), pp. 40–41.

4. Pieper, p. 20.

5. Pieper, p. 34.

6. Ray Bradbury, *Fahrenheit 451* (New York: Simon and Schuster, 2013), p. 20.

7. Bradbury, p. 139.

8. Louis Untermeyer, *Doorways to Poetry* (New York: Harcourt, Brace and Company, 1938), p. 21. Untermeyer wrote those words while America was still mired in economic depression.

9. John Greenleaf Whittier, "The Barefoot Boy," ll. 11–12. By contrast with that happy freedom, Pieper describes the urge to deny the liberality of the liberal arts as a kind of proletarianism, whether "occasioned by lack of property, State compulsion, or spiritual impoverishment."

10. Untermeyer, p. 495.

11. Untermeyer, p.13. Here is what he has to say: "Poetry has a special appeal for youth. This is so chiefly because life is new and the world's wonders are fresh and vivid when we are young. Poetry

and youth are made for each other. Although poets are caricatured in the comic papers, poetry is not written by queer creatures who know nothing about life and by retired scholars who remain in hiding behind their books and their beards. Youth is the time when ideas and emotions rise quickly to the surface; in spring every boy and every girl becomes a poet."

12. Augustine, Sermon 336, par. 1.

13. Pieper, pp. 32–33. "In the beginning there is always a gift," he goes on to say, recognizing that at the foundation of any person's true engagement with reality must lie the virtue of gratitude. For there is grace both in giving and receiving.

14. Richard Weaver, *Ideas Have Consequences* (University of Chicago, 1948), p. 77. Lacking any transcendent aim, says Weaver, "having become incapable of knowing," modern man "becomes incapable of working, in the sense that all work is a bringing of the ideal from potentiality to actuality," p. 73. Work for work's sake may be strenuous, but it is not truly human work. It may possess considerable rigor; so do corpses.

15. Melville, *Moby-Dick*, ch. 24 (New York: W. W. Norton, 1967), p. 101.

16. Thomas Gray, "Elegy Written in a Country Graveyard," 1751.

17. C. S. Lewis, *The Abolition of Man* (New York: Macmillan, 1965), p. 24.

18. Untermeyer, p. 190.

19. Pieper, pp. 56–57.

20. Pieper, p. 58.

21. Keats, "Endymion: A Poetic Romance," ll. 1-5, in Selected Poems and Letters, ed. Douglas Bush (Boston: Houghton Mifflin Company, 1959), p. 39.

22. A.S. Kline, trans. *Horace: Ars Poetica* (www.poetryintranslation. com), 2005, lines 99–104.

23. Billy Collins, "Introduction to Poetry," *The Apple That Astonished Paris* (Fayetteville, AR: The University of Arkansas Press, 1988), p. 58.

24. X.J. Kennedy and Dana Goia, Literature: *An Introduction to Fiction, Poetry, Drama, and Writing,* (New York: Pearson, Longman, 2009), p. 606.

25. A villanelle consists of five stanzas of three lines each and a sixth stanza with four lines. The rhyme scheme of "aba" is repeated through the first five stanzas, and then changes to "abaa" in the sixth. The first line of the poem is repeated at the end of the second and fourth stanzas, and as the third line in the sixth stanza. The last line of the first stanza is repeated at the end of the third, fifth and sixth stanzas of the poem.

26. Rene Wellek and Austin Warren discuss that very question in their *Theory of Literature* (New York: Harcourt, Brace & World, 1942), p. 32. "The pleasure of literature, we need to maintain, is not one preference among a long list of possible pleasures, but is a 'higher pleasure' because pleasure is in a higher kind of activity, i.e. non-acquisitive contemplation. And the utility—the seriousness, the instructiveness—of literature is a pleasurable seriousness, i.e. not the seriousness of a duty which must be done or of a lesson to be learned but an aesthetic seriousness, a seriousness of perception..., Now however, when history, like literature, appears a loose, ill-defined discipline, and when science rather is the impressive rival, it is contended rather that literature gives a knowledge of those particularities with which science and philosophy are not concerned."

27. Keats, "Endymion," p. 39.

28. Kline, 48–48.

29. E. M. Forster, *Aspects of the Novel* (New York: Harcourt, Inc., 1927).

30. Chris Hedges, *Empire of Illusion* (New York: Nation Books, 2009), p. 107.

31. James J. Lynch and Bertrand Evans, *High School English Textbooks: A Critical Examination* (Boston: Little, Brown, 1963), p. 5.

32. Lynch and Evans, p. 129.

33. George Norvell. *The Reading Interests of Young People* (East Lansing: Michigan State University Press, 1973).

34. Norvell, pp. 7–8.

35. Norvell, p. 53.

36. Helen Mackintosh. A study of children's choices in poetry. *The Elementary English Review* 1924: 1, 85–89.

37. Norvell. Reading Interests. From Table 22-1, pp. 125–127.

38. See Chapter 1 in Sandra Stotsky, *Losing Our Language* (The Free Press, 1999).

39. Norvell, p. 2.

40. FORUM 4: *Literary Study in Grades 9, 10, and 11: A National Survey.* (Boston: Association of Literary Scholars, Critics, and Writers, 2010). http://www.alscw.org/publications/forum/forum_4.pdf

41. English 310, Modern Poetry, Yale University. http://oyc.yale.edu/english/engl-310/lecture-4.

42. Mark Bauerlein and Sandra Stotsky. *How Common Core's ELA Standards Place College Readiness at Risk.* White Paper No. 89. Boston: Pioneer Institute, September 2012. http://pioneer-institute.org/download/how-common-cores-ela-standards-place-college-readiness-at-risk/

43. "Teachers of senior English classes, for example, are not required to devote 70 percent of reading to information texts. Rather, 70 percent of student reading across the grade should be informational."

44. Rose Ann Pearce, "Advisers Train Educators: Goal is to Improve Student Learning," *Northwest Arkansas Times* November 11, 2013. http://docs.newsbank.com/s/InfoWeb/aggdocs/NewsBank/14A02A8CB065B988/A48E7DF7EA354DD28BD81A193C-79B506?p_multi=NATF&s_lang=en-US

45. Malcolm Gladwell, *The Tipping Point* (New York: Little, Brown, and Company, 2002), p. 60.

46. Jim Murphy, Truce: *The Day the Soldiers Stopped Fighting* (NY: Scholastic Press, 2009), 116 pages. The book received many awards and was recommended for reading by YALSA, Best Books for Young Adults; Booklist Editors Choice; and Junior Library Guild. Its reading level according to ATOS for Books, a readability formula, was 8.2 (grade 8, second month).

4

Common Core's Mathematics Standards Still Don't Make the Grade

Ze'ev Wurman

Editor's Note

This report was published in July 2010, the third and final report of a series issued by the Pioneer Institute on the Common Core Mathematics Standards. The series tracked successive drafts of the Standards, and this third report addressed the final version. The authors of the Standards responded to the first two Pioneer reports by making some of the changes recommended, but Wurman writes in this final report that the changes were inadequate. He offers a side-by-side comparison of the Common Core Mathematics Standards in California and Massachusetts. Note that this is a critique of the content of the Common Core Mathematics Standards rather than the rationales put forward by its architects for taking their distinctive approach.

Review of Mathematics Standards

California's standards for K–12 mathematics, adopted in 1997, have been widely regarded as the best in the nation.[1] Massachusetts also offers well-regarded standards frequently credited with making Massachusetts the highest achieving state in the nation. How does the Common Core—supposedly an improvement on state standards—compare?

The Common Core leaves serious gaps in students' math education. That's the conclusion reached by applying the National Mathematics Advisory Panel's (NMAP) metrics. California's current mathematics standards and the 2010 draft standards in Massachusetts offer substantially better approaches. (Hereafter, for the sake of simplicity I will refer to these just as California's and Massachusetts' standards. Because both states have since adopted the Common Core, these references should be understood as historical.)

NMAP was established in 2006 to use the "best available scientific evidence" to recommend ways "to foster greater knowledge of and improved performance in mathematics among American students."[2] Its first charge was to outline "the critical skills and skill progressions for students to acquire competence in algebra and readiness for higher levels of mathematics." NMAP proposed three clusters of concepts and skills: Fluency with Whole Numbers, Fluency with Fractions, and Particular Aspects of Geometry and Measurement. This review analyzes how the Common Core, California, and Massachusetts standards address topics in terms of those clusters.

Fluency with Whole Numbers

NMAP's final report recommends two grade-level benchmarks for fluency with whole numbers (p. 20).

By the end of Grade 3, students should be proficient with the addition and subtraction of whole numbers.

By the end of Grade 5, students should be proficient with multiplication and division of whole numbers.

Massachusetts expects students to be fluent in addition and subtraction using the standard algorithms by grade 3, while both California and Common Core expect students to be fluent by grade 4.[3]

Both the California standards and the Massachusetts standards expect students to reach fluency with multiplication using the standard algorithm by grade 4, and fluency with division using the standard algorithm by grade 5. In contrast, Common Core expects fluency with multiplication using the standard algorithm by grade 5, and fluency with division using the standard algorithm by grade 6.

Standard algorithms require, among other things, memorizing addition and subtraction facts and the multiplication table. Both California and Massachusetts require memorization of addition facts to 20 in grade 1, while Common Core expects memorization to 18 by grade 2. California expects memorization of the multiplication table by grade 3, while both Massachusetts and Common Core expect it in grade 4.

All three sets of standards develop fluency with the arithmetic of integers by grade 5 as recommended by the NMAP, though Common Core notably defers division to grade 6, which is commonly the first year of middle school. This implies that K–5 elementary schools would no longer be fully responsible for teaching students operations with integers. More importantly, middle school mathematics focuses on ratios, rates, and percents, concepts that draw heavily on division skills. Under the Common Core scheme, students enter middle school without complete mastery of division, which may undermine their ability to learn the new concepts of ratio and proportional thinking.

Both Massachusetts and California introduce estimation skills alongside computation starting in kindergarten, to assist in estimating the expected result of computations and to verify answers.[4]

In contrast, Common Core defers estimation skills to grade 3, offering insufficient opportunity to develop the deep sense of numeracy that estimation instills.

Fluency with Fractions

The Common Core has received much praise for carefully and consistently developing students' skills with fractions. Its treatment of common fractions is lengthy and meticulous, even if steeped in a peculiar pedagogy, reminding us more of a lesson plan than of standards.[5] In grade three, the Common Core uses a number line as a helpful ordering visualization. But it persists in imposing this visual model far too long, until grade seven. The number line is a legitimate and helpful device for introducing the idea of fractions as numbers and for ordering them, but the Common Core's continued reliance on this device over the next several years of instruction is unprecented.[6] In contrast with its early and meticulous development of fractions, the Common Core starts developing decimal fractions only in grade 4, while California and Massachusetts start students working with decimals in grade 2. Even more disappointing is Common Core's failure to introduce decimals using dollar bills and coins, a well-established approach that builds on children's natural fascination with money.

The first two NMAP benchmarks for fractions expect students to recognize fractions and decimals in grade 4 and to develop fluency in conversions between the two. NMAP further specifies[7]:

> By the end of Grade 4, students should be able to identify and represent fractions and decimals, and compare them on a number line or with other common representations of fractions and decimals.

Both California (4NS1.9) and Massachusetts (4.N.5) meet this expectation in grade 4. Common Core, however, does not discuss conversion or relations between common fractions and decimals until grade 7. The NMAP benchmarks also expect that:

> *By the end of Grade 5, students should be proficient with comparing fractions and decimals and common percent and with the addition and subtraction of fractions and decimals.*

Both California (5NS1.2, 5NS1.5, 5NS2.1) and Massachusetts (5.N.2, 5.N.3, 5.N.7, 5.N.8) meet this expectation, with Massachusetts deferring study of percents to grade 6 (6.N.5). In contrast, Common Core defers serious work with percents to grade 7.

NMAP continues:

> *By the end of Grade 6, students should be proficient with all operations involving positive and negative integers.*

California meets this benchmark by grade 6 (6NS2.3), while Massachusetts meets most of it in grade 6 (6.N.5, 6.N.12, 6.NS.16), deferring fluency for multiplication and division with negative numbers to grade 7 (7.N.1, 7.N.4). The Common Core introduces the concept of a negative number only in grade 6 and it does not expect fluency with them until grade 7.[8]

In short, the Common Core has a well-developed learning progression for common fractions, but it fails to introduce decimal fractions early and neglects to build naturally on the concept of money. It completely neglects development of flexibility with fraction representations, a focus of NMAP, of the national Research Council's *Adding It Up*, and the National Council of Teachers of Mathematics' (NCTM) *Curriculum Focal Points*.[9]

Another surprising deficiency in Common Core's approach to fractions is the absence of any material on least common denominators beyond the simple multiplication of denominators. Students must then handle unwieldy numbers even when adding simple fractions such as $1/6 + 5/18 + 2/3$, a situation that bodes ill for their fluency later on with operations on fractions. Common Core also neglects teaching prime factorization[10] at any grade and thus develops only rudimentary skills in finding the least common multiple or greatest common factor. Both California and Massachusetts extensively develop these skills, which become critical in later grades for manipulating polynomial and rational expressions.

Finally, Common Core's coherent presentation of fractions is undermined by repeated use of visual fractions (number lines, area models, tape diagrams).[11] Some fractions, of course, lend themselves easily to visualization but others do not, and students are thus trained to rely on training wheels that prove unhelpful in the long run.

Particular Aspects of Geometry and Measurement

For geometry and measurement, NMAP has two recommended benchmarks for grades 5 and 6:

> *By the end of Grade 5, students should be able to solve problems involving perimeter and area of triangles and all quadrilaterals having at least one pair of parallel sides (i.e., trapezoids).*

> *By the end of Grade 6, students should be able to analyze the properties of two- dimensional shapes and solve problems involving perimeter and area, and analyze the properties of three-dimensional shapes and solve problems involving surface area and volume.*

California, Massachusetts, and the Common Core standards all deal with the geometry of two- and three-dimensional bodies in a disorganized and often unspecific way. California's standards are the clearest of the three. Common Core focuses on the relations between rectangular areas and multiplication throughout grade 6, while both California and Massachusetts connect the two during development of multiplication in the early grades before focusing on the geometrical nature of area. California is explicit about recognizing special triangles like isosceles, equilateral, and right angle in grade 3 and deriving the area of a triangle in grade 5, the sum of triangle angles in grade 5, and area and perimeter of a circle in grade 6. Massachusetts teaches special triangles in grade 4 but doesn't mention the derivation of the area of a triangle. It does expect students to calculate the surface area of a pyramid in grade

5, which implies students learn at least the formula by then. Massachusetts doesn't teach the sum of triangle angles, but does teach area and perimeter of a circle in grade 6. Common Core doesn't mention special triangles except right triangle in grade 4, doesn't teach how to calculate the area of a triangle at all (except possibly by a rote formula at some unspecified time), but expects triangles to be known in grade 6. It doesn't teach the sum of triangle angles until grade 8, and it teaches area and perimeter of circles as late as grade 7.

NMAP recommends as a benchmark for geometry and measurement in grade 7:

By the end of Grade 7, students should be familiar with the relationship between similar triangles and the concept of the slope of a line.

California teaches similarity in grade 6 (6NS1.3) but without explicit connection to slopes, a topic that is covered in its Framework instead. Massachusetts teaches similarity in grade 7, and it suggests the connection between similarity and the slope of a line:

7.G.3. Apply the geometric concepts of similarity and congruence; relate similarity to concepts of proportionality and scale factor, and use them in solutions of problems. For example, indirectly measure the height of a tree by using its shadow.

Common Core addresses this benchmark directly, but only in grade 8, a year later than NMAP recommends.

While both California and Massachusetts teach use of the straightedge and compass in K–8 (in grades 5 and 7 in California, and in grade 8 in Massachusetts), as well as some classical geometrical constructions to develop intuition and an esthetic sense about geometry, Common Core teaches use of only the ruler and protractor in K–8, which relegates geometry to just another facet of measurement.

Common Core's effort to replace the traditional foundations of school geometry is even more problematic. Common Core attempts to base congruency, covered in grade 8 and in high school, on the notion of rigid motions, and to derive the rest of geometry from this basis. This approach has not been widely used anywhere in the world, and in the few cases in which it has been used, it has met with failure. Thirty years ago, when Russia attempted a nation-wide experiment with a similar method to teaching geometry, the approach proved too difficult for students and was soon discontinued. Perhaps the best assessment of this new geometry is the testimony of R. James Milgram, a member of the Common Core Validation Committee, delivered to the California Academic Content Standards Commission in July 2010: "We are dealing with an experiment on a national scale."

Preparation for the Study of Algebra

One of NMAP's major recommendations called for more students to take an "authentic" Algebra 1 course in grade 8. "All school districts should ensure that all prepared students have access to an authentic algebra course—and should prepare more students than at present to enroll in such a course by Grade 8."[12] NMAP's Task Group on Conceptual Knowledge and Skills supported this recommendation. The group researched the importance of taking algebra early and found six studies that met NMAP's rigorous criteria for evidence. The Task Group concluded:

> It is important to note that these six studies drew on four [different] national data sets …The consistency of their findings is striking. The studies…provide some evidence that there are long-term benefits for Grade 7 or 8 students with the requisite mathematical background for algebra if they can take an authentic Algebra course in Grade 7 or 8: higher mathematics achievement in high school and the opportunity to take advanced mathematics course work in Grade 11 or 12.[13]

Of the three sets of standards, only California sequences its content to prepare all students for Algebra 1 in grade 8. Both Massachusetts and Common Core aim for only a little more than pre-algebra in grade 8.[14] But all high-achieving countries teach either the equivalent of Algebra 1 in grade 8 or a combination of Algebra 1 and Geometry in grades 8 and 9.[15] Common Core, on the other hand, does not prepare students to take Algebra 1 in grade 8. High achieving countries introduce preparatory material in the early grades. In Singapore, for example, grade 5 students solve rate problems involving motion at constant speed. Such problems cannot appear in Common Core before grade 6 because its standards on ratio are first taught in grade 6.

High-achieving countries, as well as California and Massachusetts, require students to solve simple linear equations in the early grades. For example, in grade 3, California asks students to:

> *Represent relationships of quantities in the form of mathematical expressions, equations, or inequalities.*
>
> *Express simple unit conversions in symbolic form (e.g., inches = feet × 12).*
>
> *Extend and recognize a linear pattern by its rules (e.g., the number of legs on a given number of horses may be calculated by counting by 4s or by multiplying the number of horses by 4).*

And in grade 4:

> *Use letters, boxes, or other symbols to stand for any number in simple expressions or equations (e.g., demonstrate an understanding and the use of the concept of a variable).*
>
> *Understand that an equation such as $y = 3x + 5$ is a prescription for determining a second number when a first number is given.*
>
> *Know and understand that equals added to equals are equal.*
>
> *Know and understand that equals multiplied by equals are equal.*

And in grade 5:

> *Know and use the distributive property in equations and expressions with variables.*
>
> *Solve problems involving linear functions with integer values; write the equation; and graph the resulting ordered pairs of integers on a grid.*

In contrast, some Common Core standards in grades 1 and 2, (e.g., 1.OA.(1) and 2.OA.(1)), appear to be related to this topic, but they are unclear. They seem to ask students to solve simple equations, but the language is ambiguous, particularly considering that a grade 6 standard calls for what seems like even a more basic concept:

Write expressions that record operations with numbers and with letters standing for numbers. For example, express the calculation "Subtract y from 5" as 5 − y. (6.EE.2.a.)

There is also a marked paucity of standards developing early algebraic skills. Unit conversion doesn't start until grade 4, and when it does, the standards are unclear:

4.MD.1. Know relative sizes of measurement units within one system of units including km, m, cm; kg, g; lb, oz.; l, ml; hr, min, sec. Within a single system of measurement, express measurements in a larger unit in terms of a smaller unit. Record measurement equivalents in a two-column table. For example, know that 1 ft is 12 times as long as 1 in. Express the length of a 4 ft snake as 48 in. Generate a conversion table for feet and inches listing the number pairs (1, 12), (2, 24), (3, 36)...

4.MD.2. Use the four operations to solve word problems involving distances, intervals of time, liquid volumes, masses of objects, and money, including problems involving simple fractions or decimals, and problems that require expressing measurements given in a larger unit in terms of a smaller unit. Represent measurement quantities using diagrams such as number line diagrams that feature a measurement scale.

It is hard to know whether these standards expect students to work with expressions or to fill up conversion tables. These standards are particularly difficult to interpret because the grade 5 standards seems less demanding.[16]

5. MD.1. Convert among different-sized standard measurement units within a given measurement system (e.g., convert 5 cm to 0.05 m), and use these conversions in solving multi-step, real world problems.

Common Core's grade 8 standards are also incoherent. The Common Core inserts four unrelated statistics standards meant to help prepare students for algebra. These standards can do little more than develop "statistics appreciation," because students have no foundation to address them mathematically. For example, students are asked to draw a best-fit line after "eyeballing" scatterplot data. They are also asked to form hypotheses about the relationships among disparate data sets without the mathematical means to support their guesses. These standards contradict Common Core's goal of "fewer, clearer, higher" standards.

Important Issues in Using Common Core's High School Mathematics Standards

Low academic expectations for college and career readiness

Common Core marks certain high school mathematics standards with a plus sign (+), explaining that, "all standards without a (+) symbol should be in the common mathematics curriculum for all college and career ready students." It immediately goes on to state that "standards with a (+) sign may also appear in courses intended for all students," thus leaving it unclear whether or not college readiness includes these standards, too. Common Core implies that the content of its standards is sufficient for about three years of high school mathematics— Algebra I, Geometry, and an additional year of mathematics somewhat similar to Algebra II.[17] But even with the "plus" standards, the content described in its high school mathematics standards lacks some of the content expected for students finishing a typical Algebra II course—the criterion for determining "college readiness" for most four-year colleges in this country.[18] Without the standards marked "plus," Common Core's content for college readiness is far below what is expected today for college eligibility.[19]

235

The Report of the Mathematics Review Panel on the Common Core and Massachusetts Standards (July 2010), written by seven mathematics educators chosen by the Commissioner of Elementary and Secondary Education, noted that the 2010 draft Massachusetts standards "have clearer expectations for linear functions and geometric proof while [Common Core's] include a good deal more statistics." The report expressed concern that Common Core's standards would generate "two tracks" of students and it noted that some of the standards marked (+) in Common Core are included in Massachusetts's draft Algebra, Geometry, and Algebra 2 courses: "logarithmic functions, inverse functions, and some aspects of complex numbers." Concerned that the (+) standards in Common Core "actually generate two tracks" and "that students may be excluded from advanced mathematics courses/ concepts through tracking," the panel suggested that the "Department of Elementary and Secondary Education consider each (+) standard individually and determine whether or not, for this state, each (+) standard be mandated for inclusion in the Algebra–Algebra 2 sequence." Clearly, Common Core's standards for "college readiness" in mathematics are far below Massachusetts' expectations.

Lack of organization in course form

When the first draft of Common Core's College and Career Readiness Standards was released in September 2009, many commented on its low aspirations, problematic wording, and poor organization. Even after substantial rewriting and reorganization, the standards are still difficult for teachers and textbook publishers to use.

Common Core's high school standards are currently grouped into so-called "conceptual categories." Originally there were six, but one, modeling, has since been distributed across the other five.[20] In contrast, the 2010 draft of Massachusetts's standards (and the 2000 standards document) organizes high school mathematical content by two-year grade spans (9–10 and 11–12) and also by course—Algebra 1, Geometry, Algebra 2, and Precalculus. California organizes all its high school mathematics standards by course, from Algebra to Calculus.

Negative consequences of the failure to organize high school standards by course

Common Core's high school standards were not written with the structure of high school courses in mind. The depth with which a topic should be treated depends on the course it is in. But in the Common Core, where the topic appears simply in a long list of topics in a conceptual category, the appropriate depth is not apparent. Further, many mathematical topics appear in multiple courses. Manipulation of polynomials, their factorization, and manipulation of rational expressions appear in Algebra 1, Algebra 2, trigonometry, and mathematics analysis. The general topic is the same—"the manipulation of X." But in order to write standards with course structure in mind, the writer must adjust the wording to the appropriate depth for a particular course, e.g., polynomials of second degree, polynomials of trigonometric functions, etc. But when the only goal is to simply generate a comprehensive list of topics as Common Core does, one ends up with a standard such as this one:

> *A-APR-7. (+) Understand that rational expressions form a system analogous to the rational numbers, closed under addition, subtraction, multiplication, and division by a nonzero rational expression; add, subtract, multiply, and divide rational expressions.*

This standard is potentially applicable to Algebra 1, Algebra 2, Trigonometry, or Mathematical Analysis. There is little here to guide teachers or textbook publishers. It all depends on its interpretation, which is absent. Consequently, states may end up replicating it verbatim in four different courses and supplementing it with an explanation, or relying on a teacher to interpret it properly. Neither is efficient or effective. And there are many other such examples in the Common Core.

Moreover, states could use Common Core's high school mathematics standards in varying ways to construct high school mathematics courses. Textbook publishers, too, could construct high school mathematics courses with varying content and at different depths. This would result in little uniformity, undermining the primary reason that the Common Core's advocates advanced for creating common standards.

A tendency to undervalue technical skills

Common Core's Standards mention "manipulation of polynomials and rational expressions," but the standards do not specify their complexity, or the level of fluency students need to develop with them. In fact, when California considered ways to strengthen Common Core's mathematics standards, it concluded that many of these skills needed to be added to create an Algebra 1 course comparable to its current one.

Missing standards

Common Core claims to provide content for about two years worth of high school mathematics beyond Algebra 1. Yet many topics typically included in such courses are conspicuously absent or barely addressed. For example, here is Common Core's standard on factoring, a key technical skill on which many other skills are based:

> *A-SSE-2. Use the structure of an expression to identify ways to rewrite it. For example, see $x4 - y4$ as $(x2)2 - (y2)2$, thus recognizing it as a difference of squares that can be factored as $(x2 - y2)(x2 + y2)$.*

The comparable California and Massachusetts standards are:

> *CA-A1-11. Students apply basic factoring techniques to second- and simple third-degree polynomials. These techniques include finding a common factor for all terms in a polynomial, recognizing the difference of two squares, and recognizing perfect squares of binomials.*

> *MA-10.A.9. Demonstrate facility in symbolic manipulation of polynomial and rational expressions by applying the commutative, associative and distributive principles. Include factoring,*

238

simplifying rational expressions, and applying the rules of positive integer exponents.

The differences are striking. Does Common Core address general factoring skills, or does it ask only for recognition of certain "well known" forms? What class of expressions is Common Core's standard intended to be applied to? Teachers will have to guess or let a test writer behind a closed door decide for the nation.

Logarithms and advanced topics are barely mentioned or missing

Mathematical induction is absent. Solving equations and problems with absolute values is missing. Parametric equations are omitted. Infinite geometric series are absent. Arithmetic series are simply forgotten. Conic sections are incompletely handled. Frequency and amplitude of periodic functions are mentioned, but their phase is left out. Double-angle formulas are mentioned, but half-angle formulas are missing. Polar coordinates are mentioned, but no work is expected with polar forms of functions. And the list goes on.

Summary

In K–8, all three sets of standards develop fluency with the arithmetic of integers by grade 5 as recommended by NMAP. The only notable exception is division, which Common Core defers to grade 6. Although Common Core has a well-developed learning progression for common fractions, it fails to use money to introduce decimal fractions early, neglects to develop students' flexibility with fraction representations, provides no material on teaching and using least common denominators beyond the simple multiplication of denominators, fails to teach prime factorization at any grade, and seriously misuses visual fractions.

In grades 9–12, Common Core replaces traditional Euclidean geometry with an approach that is based on the notion of rigid motions. This approach has not been widely used elsewhere, and has been considered ineffective where it was tried. It is at best a nationwide experiment. Common Core's preparation for Algebra 1 in grade 8 is weak compared to the standards in California and in high-achieving countries. And compared to California and Massachusetts standards for Algebra 1, Geometry, and Algebra 2, Common Core's standards show low academic expectations inadequate for a true college-readiness. Its high school standards are not organized into courses or by grade level, as they are everywhere else, thus providing schools and textbook publishers no clear and uniform guidance on course content.

Author Biography

Ze'ev Wurman is a Silicon Valley engineer and executive who spent two years in the United States Department of Education under George W. Bush as a senior policy adviser in the Office of Planning, Evaluation, and Policy Development. He also served on the 2010 California State Academic Content Standards Commission, which evaluated the Common Core against California's current standards. Wurman holds over 20 patents, has 30 years' experience developing algorithms, CAD software, and hardware and software architectures, and has published many technical papers in trade and professional journals. He has a B.Sc. and M.Sc. in electrical engineering from Technion, Israel Institute of Technology.

Endnotes

1. In detailed comparison of state standards in 2005, California's mathematics standards were rated as the best. See Klein, D., Braams, B.J., Parker, T., Quirk, W., Schmid, W., & Wilson, W.S. *The State of State Math Standards 2005* Washington, DC: Thomas B. Fordham Institute, 2005.

2. *Foundations for Success: The Final Report of the National Mathematics Advisory Panel.* U.S. Department of Education: Washington, D.C., 2008.

3. "Standard algorithm" is "an ordered sequence of steps followed to solve a specific class of math problems. An example of a class of problems would be adding two two-digit numbers or multiplying two digits by one digit. To be considered an algorithm the steps must always provide a correct answer for all problems in that class. A standard algorithm is the most efficient and universally practiced algorithm for a particular class." S. Ocken, *Algorithms, Algebra and Access* September 2001. The term "standard algorithm" is not common outside the United States. Standards elsewhere are typically couched simply as "addition and subtraction using formal algorithms" (Singapore, gr. 1)" or "addition/subtraction within 3 places" (Hong Kong, gr. 2) or "addition/subtraction of N-digit (N=2, 3, 4) numbers" (Japan, Korea, grades 1-2). The rise over the last 20-25 years in the United States of pedagogical approaches that call for non-standard algorithms has led to the need to distinguish "standard algorithms" from "algorithms" plain and simple.

4. Hong Kong starts teaching estimation of results in grade 1, and Korea in grade 2.

5. K-8 teachers have often had difficulty in teaching fractions. The Common Core begins with the important and valid premise that fractions are simply numbers, and it illustrates this point with the number line. But what begins as a helpful visual aid quickly becomes a crutch. The Common Core assumes the value of this number line approach without any evidence of its educational utility, and it defers developing students' fluency with the standard algorithmic approach until quite late in their intellectual growth. These steps differ substantially from instruction in other countries that have achieved excellent records in mathematics instruction. The number line is not routinely and pervasively used in any Far Eastern country.

6. Also observed by others, e.g., R. James Milgram, *Review of Final Draft Core Standards*, testimony submitted to the California Academic Content Standards Commission, July 7, 2010, p. 2.

7. *Common Core State Standards for Mathematics* page 46. http://www.corestandards.org/wp-content/uploads/Math_Standards.pdf

8. The exact point at which Common Core expects full fluency of arithmetic with integers is unclear. Grade 7 develops manipulation of positive and negative rational numbers but is unclear on expectations of fluency. Since there are no standards describing fluency with rational numbers beyond grade 7, we assume that fluency is achieved at that grade.

9. Jeremy Kilpatrick, Jane Swafford, and Bradford Findell, eds., *Adding It Up* National Research Council: Washington, D.C., 2001, p.233 ff; Curriculum Focal Points, NCTM, Reston, VA, 2006, grades 4 through 7, pp. 16-19. Known as the Fundamental Theorem of Arithmetic.

10. R. James Milgram, *Review of Final Draft Core Standards* testimony submitted to the California Academic Content Standards Commission, July 7, 2010, pp. 4-5.

11. Ibid.

12. *Foundations for Success: The Final Report of the National Mathematics Advisory Panel* U.S. Department of Education: Washington, D.C., 2008.

13. *Foundations for Success: The National Mathematics Advisory Panel, Reports of the Task Groups and Subcommittees* U.S. Department of Education: Washington, D.C., 2008. Chapter 3, p. 3-47

14. Milgram writes "[Common Core's] standards illustrate many serious flaws... Among these difficulties are that a large number of the arithmetic and operations, as well as the place value, standards are one, two, or even more years behind the corresponding standards for many if not all the high achieving countries" (R. James Milgram, July 2010 testimony, p. 3). Jonathan Goodman, another mathematician, writes: "The proposed Common Core standards are similar in earlier grades but have significantly lower expectations with respect to algebra and geometry than the published standards of other countries I examined." (Jonathan Goodman, "A Comparison of Proposed US Common Core Math Standards to Standards of Selected Asian Countries," *Education News* July 9, 2010.)

15. This combined approach should not be confused with so-called "integrated mathematics" approaches in the U.S. that attempt to teach units of study combining algebra and geometry content. High achieving countries alternate geometry and algebra units lasting a few weeks or months, with each unit taught independently and brought to closure.

16. See R. James Milgram's testimony, p.8

17. The intended scope of the content by course can be seen in a diagram in the March 2010 draft showing the content partitioned into courses.

18. To understand more clearly what California felt it needed to add to Common Core's standards in order to meet current California high school course expectations, see the strengthened standards at http://www.scoe.net/castandards/ agenda/2010/20100722_ccs_ recommendations. pdf on p. 127 ff.

19. The California Commission for Academic Content Standards recommended adding to Common Core's mathematics standards all of California's Calculus and Advanced Statistics standards, and supplemented the courses that students take before these two courses with numerous standards in geometry, algebra, and trigonometry.

20. Buried at the end of the final version of its mathematics standards document is an admission of the rushed and incomplete effort it represents (p. 84). Common Core promises that "sample high school pathways for mathematics" will be made available shortly after the release of the final document on June 2. However, such suggestions, whenever they come, will have no binding power. Common Core's writing committees have been disbanded and most states will have already adopted the standards.

5

Lowering the Bar: How Common Core Math Fails to Prepare High School Students for STEM

R. James Milgram and Sandra Stotsky

Introduction

The Common Core State Standards promise to make students "college-ready," but it is not clear what that promise means. The Standards do not define the term, nor do any of the Common Core's official documents. Professor Jason Zimba, a lead writer of the Common Core's mathematics standards, however, gives us some idea. At the March 2010 meeting of the Massachusetts Board of Elementary and Secondary Education, Zimba addressed the question of what kind of college the students will be prepared for. The minutes of the meeting record, "Mr. Zimba said that the concept of college readiness is minimal and focuses on non-selective colleges."[1]

Zimba's characterization of the standard of college readiness embedded in the Common Core has not attracted the attention it deserves. This "minimal" approach and focus on readiness for non-selective colleges has serious implications for the high school mathematics and science curriculum. It also bears on mathematics-dependent undergraduate majors and post-baccalaureate or graduate programs, and a wide range of post-graduate programs that require a high level of mathematical knowledge.

Zimba's definition of "college-readiness" nullifies the main reason the federal government provided over four billion dollars in Race to the Top (RttT) funds.[2] The federal government expected these new standards to improve students' preparation for science, technology, engineering, and math (STEM) fields.[3] If Zimba's explanation of the Common Core's actual approach is accurate, the Standards would push in the opposite direction—towards lower levels of preparation in STEM fields.

How should the dissonance between the minimal approach to college readiness and the rhetoric of STEM preparation in the RttT competition be understood? Though they contradict one another, both were part of an effort to sell the Common Core to the states. At one and the same time, the Common Core would deliver higher-than-ever academic achievement in STEM fields without threatening to impose daunting intellectual challenges on students. Common Core would somehow simultaneously offer low standards and high performance.

This doubletalk has succeeded partly because the two pitches have been addressed to different audiences. Those who care primarily about the nation achieving higher performance in STEM fields have heard one message. Those who worry about the stresses of teaching and learning a high standards curriculum have heard the other message. Another factor, however, is the generally low-level of understanding of mathematics among Americans. All too often we are ready to treat mathematics instruction as too technical or too difficult for the general public to assess and that it is therefore better left to the discretion of supposed experts. For both these reasons, proponents of the Common Core Mathematics Standards initially gained a great deal of public support without facing much in the way of critical scrutiny.

Were the Standards "Validated"?

The Common Core website's "About the Standards" page describes the Common Core's mathematics and English language arts standards as resulting from "collaboration with teachers, school administrators, and experts to provide a clear and consistent framework to prepare our children for college and the workforce."[4] The document claims: "These standards define the knowledge and skills students should have within their K–12 education careers so that they will graduate from high school able to succeed in entry-level, credit-bearing academic college courses and in workforce training programs." To assure the public that Common Core's standards reflect their definition, the National Governors Association (NGA) and the Council of Chief State School Officers (CCSSO)—the two organizations funded by the Bill and Melinda Gates Foundation to develop Common Core's standards—also created a Validation Committee (VC).

The VC consisted of about 30 members during 2009–2010. Some were ex officio, others were recommended by the governor or commissioner of education of an individual state. The official rationale for choosing members of the VC is not clear. R. James Milgram, one of the co-authors of this essay, was the only mathematician on the VC. Several other members of the VC were mathematics educators. The distinction between mathematicians and math teachers may not be self-apparent, but they are different professions which involve different kinds of preparation and different skills. Mathematicians work in the world of rigorous definitions and proofs. Math teachers must understand some of this but their expertise is conveying knowledge of number and technique to students. Some committee members held doctorates in mathematics education, academic appointments in schools of education or were engaged full-time in teacher training and professional development.

The other author of this essay, Sandra Stotsky, who developed the highly regarded Massachusetts state standards while working in the Massachusetts Department of Education from 1999–2003, was the only expert on K–12 English language arts standards.

Members of the VC signed an agreement restricting what they could tell the public about their work on the committee. One stipulation was they could never, then or in the future, indicate whether the VC discussed the meaning of college readiness or had any recommendations to offer on the matter. As a condition of membership, all VC members had to agree to ten conditions, among which were the following:

> Ownership of the Common Core State Standards, including all drafts, copies, reviews, comments, and non-final versions (collectively, Common Core State Standards), shall reside solely and exclusively with the Council of Chief State School Officers ("CCSSO") and the National Governors Association Center for Best Practices ("NGA Center").

> I agree to maintain the deliberations, discussions, and work of the Validation Committee, including the content of any draft or final documents, on a strictly confidential basis and shall not disclose or communicate any information related to the same, including in summary form, except within the membership of the Validation Committee and to CCSSO and the NGA Center.

The original charge to the VC in the summer of 2009, before the grade-level mathematics standards were developed, asked the members to evaluate the standards according to "college- and career-readiness":

> Review the process used to develop the college- and career-readiness standards and recommend improvements in that process. These recommendations will be used to inform the K–12 development process.

> Validate the sufficiency of the evidence supporting each college- and career-readiness standard. Each member is asked to determine whether each standard has sufficient evidence to warrant its inclusion.
>
> Add any standard that is not now included in the common core state standards that they feel should be included and provide the following evidence to support its inclusion: 1) evidence that the standard is essential to college and career success; and 2) evidence that the standard is internationally comparable.

This charge was later reduced for unknown reasons by unidentified individuals to just the first two and least important of the three points above. Culmination of participation on the committee was reduced to signing or not signing a letter in May 2010 asserting that the standards were:

1. Reflective of the core knowledge and skills in ELA and mathematics that students need to be college- and career-ready.

2. Appropriate in terms of their level of clarity and specificity.

3. Comparable to the expectations of other leading nations.

4. Informed by available research or evidence.

5. The result of processes that reflect best practices for standards development.

6. A solid starting point for adoption of cross-state Common Core standards.

7. A sound basis for eventual development of standards-based assessments.

The VC members who signed the letter were listed in the brief official report on the VC (since committee work was confidential, there was little the rapporteur could report), while the five members who did not sign off were not listed as such, nor their reasons mentioned. Stotsky's letter explaining why she could not sign off can be viewed here,[5] and Milgram's letter can be viewed here.[6]

Zimba and Stotsky's 2010 Exchange

The March 2010 meeting of the Massachusetts Board of Elementary and Secondary Education was meant to provide a forum for higher education faculty and high school mathematics and English teachers to discuss the academic meaning of Common Core's college-readiness standards. Commissioner of Education Mitchell Chester invited the Common Core authors, Jason Zimba and Susan Pimentel. Zimba had rarely spoken to the public since his appointment as a lead writer of Common Core's mathematics standards.

The meeting was video recorded. In Zimba's initial presentation he said, "We have agreement to the extent that it's a fuzzy definition, that the minimally college-ready student is a student who passed Algebra II." Stotsky (a member of the Massachusetts Board at the time) asked him to clarify what he meant. Zimba stated, "In my original remarks, I didn't make that point strongly enough or signal the agreement that we have on this—the definition of college readiness. I think it's a fair critique that it's a minimal definition of college readiness."

Stotsky remarked at this point "for some colleges," and Zimba responded by stating, "Well, for the colleges most kids go to, but not for the colleges most parents aspire to."

Stotsky then asked, "Not for STEM? Not for international competitiveness?" Zimba responded, "Not only not for STEM, it's also not for selective colleges. For example, for UC Berkeley, whether you are going to be an engineer or not, you'd better have precalculus to get into UC Berkeley."

Stotsky then said, "Right, but we have to think of the engineering colleges and the scientific pathway."

Zimba added "That's true, I think the third pathway [a pathway that does not exist in the final version] goes a lot towards that. But your issue is broader than that."[7]

Stotsky agreed, saying, "I'm not just thinking about selective colleges. There's a much broader question here." Zimba then added, "That's right. It's both, I think, in the sense of being clear about what this college readiness does and doesn't get you, and that's the big subject."

Stotsky then summarized her objections to this minimalist definition: if "college-readiness" applies only to a certain type of college and to a low level of mathematical expertise, then it will not command international respect in the areas of technology, economics, and business. Zimba appeared to agree as he then said, "OK. Thank you."

Unreadiness

What does Common Core mean when it says that by addressing its standards, "[students] will graduate from high school able to succeed in entry-level, credit-bearing academic college courses and in workforce training programs?"[8] Zimba's remarks in 2010 define college readiness as instruction that would let students attend a non-selective college without the need to take remedial courses in mathematics or English. It would not prepare students for any more demanding programs. To attain those, students would either have to prepare themselves outside the Common Core or take remedial courses once admitted to college.

"College readiness" in these terms apparently does not apply to the top 20-30% of high school students who are capable of entering a selective college or university.

State standards for high school students typically apply to all students. But the Common Core's mathematics standards, in the words of one of their three primary authors, do not match the needs or aspirations of the students best able to pursue STEM fields in college and beyond.

Zimba 2.0

Zimba later tried to retract his 2010 definition of "college-ready" and to claim that the Common Core standards prepare students for more rigorous academic work. On August 2, 2013, Common Core Watch at the Thomas B. Fordham Institute posted the first of two blogs by Zimba, in which he explained what he actually meant at the 2010 Massachusetts board of education meeting.[9] According to Zimba, college- and career-readiness means readiness for entry-level, credit-bearing courses in mathematics at all public four-year colleges, as well as courses at two-year colleges that transfer for credit at four-year colleges. This 2013 definition contradicted Zimba's comments in 2010. The new definition also applied to a weaker document than the one referred to in 2010.

The 2013 version of the Common Core is less rigorous than the draft as it stood in 2010. When Zimba spoke at the Massachusetts Board meeting, his comments could have referred to either of two documents: the "public comment draft" released on March 10, or the draft as it would stand after further work on the mathematics standards during the next two weeks of March. The difference between the two drafts is significant and bears on the controversy since.

The March 10 public comment draft indicates (via subheadings but not actual content) more rigorous math standards than those that appear in the final version. Pages 51–52 of the March 10 draft show the following place-markers (commonly called "stubs") for standards that the writers intended to fill in later:

Limits and Continuity	F–LC
Differential Calculus	F–DC
Application of Derivatives	F–AD
Integral Calculus	F–IC
Applications of Integration	F–AI
Infinite Series	F–IS

These topics are consistent with Zimba's March 2010 comments. They are the major topics for a one-year calculus course.

But the March 10 draft did not indicate how the standards writers intended to reach these topics. The March 10 draft itself ended its substantive detail at the algebra II level. The draft included no precalculus material, and only partially described the necessary material in trigonometry. Apart from some trigonometry, none of the seven stubs (listed above) or any precalculus material appears in Common Core's final mathematics standards. The deletion of the higher level material represented by the March 10 stubs was not explained in any official Common Core documents.

A few months earlier, however, the other lead writer for Common Core's mathematics standards, William McCallum, was quoted on a foundation website as saying: "The overall standards would not be too high, certainly not in comparison [to] other nations, including East Asia, where math education excels."[10]

No high school topics were added to the March 10 draft to strengthen the final version or to create the "third high school pathway." The final version is weaker than the March 10 version in other respects as well. In response to public comments, the standards writers introduced "corrections," some of which included mathematical errors and weakened lower grade standards. For instance:

> *6.RP1 Understand the concept of a ratio and use ratio language to describe a ratio relationship between two quantities. For example, "The ratio of wings to beaks in the bird house at the zoo was 2:1, because for every 2 wings there was 1 beak." "For every vote candidate A received, candidate C received nearly three votes."*

[Comment: "nearly" does not correspond to ratio or rate in any way. At best it corresponds to a range of ratios, but the tools for handling such objects are not covered until college and require advanced calculus.]

> *6.RP3(b). Solve unit rate problems including those involving unit pricing and constant speed. For example, if it took 7 hours to mow 4 lawns, then at that rate, how many lawns could be mowed in 35 hours? At what rate were lawns being mowed?*

[Comment: There is no indication of the size of the lawns or the amount of time it takes to mow each. Rather, the hidden assumption is that they all take the same time to mow.]

Academic Implications of Race to the Top (RttT) Agreements

The judging criteria for Race to the Top require state colleges and universities to alter their definitions of "remedial education" and to concede significant authority to state boards of K–12 education. Yet when states decided to apply for RttT awards, they did not consult the state boards of higher education or trustees or regents of public universities—or at least there is no record that any did.

The federal government published the conditions for RttT awards in the Federal Register on Friday, April 9, 2010 (vol. 75, no. 68, pages 18172–18185). The introduction notes:

> We intend to promote collaboration and better alignment between public elementary, secondary, and postsecondary education systems by establishing a competitive preference priority for applications that include commitments from public IHEs [Institution of Higher Education] or IHE systems to participate in the design and development of the consortium's final high school summative assessments and to implement policies that exempt from remedial courses and place into credit-bearing college courses students who meet the consortium-adopted achievement standard (as defined in this notice) for those assessments...

> Eligible applicants addressing this priority must provide, for each IHE or IHE system, a letter of intent that: (a) commits the IHE or IHE system to participate with the consortium in the design and development of the consortium's final high school summative assessments in mathematics and English language arts in order to ensure that the assessments measure college readiness; (b) commits the IHE or IHE system to implement policies, once the final high school summative assessments are implemented, that exempt from remedial courses and place into credit-bearing college courses any student who meets the consortium-adopted achievement standard (as defined in this notice) for each assessment and any other placement requirement established by the IHE or IHE system; and (c) is signed

by the State's higher education executive officer (if the State has one) and the president or head of each participating IHE or IHE system.

Although colleges and universities (IHEs) clearly have a role in designing the assessments, the two consortia in charge of the tests—PARCC and SBAC—will not be able to test the material required at selective public or private colleges. Common Core tests cannot address topics that are not in the Common Core standards. Thus major topics in trigonometry and precalculus that do not appear in these standards will not appear on the tests. Moreover, the tests cannot address even the few slightly more advanced standards in the Common Core, identified as (+) standards.

These omissions will have genuine consequences. The RttT agreement requires public state colleges and universities to place students into credit-bearing mathematics (and English) courses if these students have (1) passed a Common Core-based "college readiness" test and (2) been admitted to a public college or university. The agreement in other words mandates that under-prepared students be exempted from remedial courses that they would need to take in order to succeed in standard college-level courses. The only option left to the colleges will be to lower the level of rigor of their credit-bearing academic courses. This, of course, will have a domino effect on the whole undergraduate curriculum. The possibly unforeseen but entirely foreseeable consequence of the Common Core's omissions combined with the RttT stipulations is that public colleges will have to lower their academic standards but private colleges and universities will be under no such constraints.

A possible argument against this conclusion is that colleges don't have to admit students who pass the Common Core tests but fail to meet their institutional standards. That objection, however, is hollow. Few colleges and universities can afford to shut their doors to the very large cohort of students who will be prepared up to the Common Core "college readiness" standard but no further. Moreover, in many states, including California, public colleges and universities are required by law to admit the top 30 percent of students graduating from high schools in the state.

Faculty members at these colleges may well be taken by surprise at the deterioration of admissions standards. The members of college faculties typically have little say in setting admissions standards and are unaware of the changes that Common Core will bring.

The Common Core college admissions requirements apply to all kinds of public colleges and universities, not just to community colleges for which the "minimal definition of college readiness" might be appropriate. The Common Core-forced lowering of admissions standards will alter the way even non-selective colleges operate. Currently, non-selective colleges often place new students into remedial "Intermediate Algebra" courses. This will have to end. The Common Core will also force changes in the way colleges handle transfer students. Currently, many colleges treat some for-credit courses at non-selective institutions as merely remedial and require students to start over with entry-level courses. The Common Core procedures will require new "articulation agreements" between two- and four-year public colleges that will entail granting transfer credit for these courses.

Another huge concern is the fact that community colleges often require a very high percentage of their entering students take remedial courses in mathematics and English even though many of them passed high school level courses in these subjects. But under Common Core, if students pass the PARCC or SBAC high school exams these colleges will be required to admit them to credit-bearing courses whether or not they are ready. And there is every reason to expect that these two exams will not be designed to verify that the levels of expertise of these students will match up to college expectations because, otherwise, it is likely that the failure rates on PARCC and SBAC will be unacceptably high.

Educational Significance of Common Core's College Readiness Standards in Mathematics

Two major academic consequences loom in these federal conditions for an RttT award. First, these conditions will likely lower the level of introductory mathematics courses at selective public colleges and universities.

Students who are admitted to a selective public institution would, under this agreement, be able to take a credit-bearing mathematics course if they had passed the PARCC or SBAC algebra II test. However, students with just this background would probably fail a regular calculus course or even a precalculus course. Public colleges and universities would then be compelled to provide lower-level (but credit-bearing) introductory mathematics courses in order to avoid high failure rates.

Second, the federal conditions for a RttT award effectively give a state board and a state department of elementary and secondary education control of the content of entry courses in all public colleges and universities. A significant gap has already grown between the entry-level expectations of colleges and universities and the typical academic preparedness of high school graduates. High schools insist that college expectations are too high and that current high school preparation should be sufficient. Colleges insist that high schools are falling short and leaving students ill-prepared for college-level academic work.

The Common Core will widen this gap. It gives greatly increased leverage to the side that favors setting the standards low so as to maximize the number of students who can be declared "college ready." The lever in this case is the power ceded to state boards of education, departments of education, and education schools, which under RttT play an outsized role in setting college entry expectations. PARCC's definition of "college readiness" is:

> Students who earn the status of "college- and career-ready" in mathematics will have demonstrated the academic knowledge, skills, and practices necessary to enter directly into, and succeed in, entry-level, credit-bearing courses in college algebra, introductory college statistics, or technical courses requiring an equivalent level of mathematics.[11]

Most (46) state boards and departments of elementary and secondary education have adopted Common Core's college- and career-ready standards, some (such as Pennsylvania and Alaska) with a few minor changes. All 46 adopted the standards without consulting the faculty who teach freshman mathematics courses in these states.

The government data for STEM are compelling. It is extremely rare for students who begin their undergraduate years with coursework in precalculus or an even lower level of mathematical knowledge to achieve a bachelor's degree in a STEM area.[12] Even worse, students whose last high school mathematics course was Algebra II have less than a 40 percent chance of obtaining a four-year college degree in *any* subject area.[13] The National Center for Education Statistics (NCES) publication STEM in Postsecondary Education shows that only 2.1 percent of STEM-intending students who had to take pre-college mathematics coursework in their freshman year graduated with a STEM degree *(see Table 7 in the NCES report)*.[14]

Significance of Common Core's Standards in Mathematics for High School Science

Any set of educational standards aims to establish a basic threshold for what all students should achieve in their studies. But standards also typically point to aspirations well above the threshold for students who are more capable and more highly motivated. A key problem with the Common Core Standards is that they establish a (fairly low) threshold but offer next to nothing in the realm of aspirations beyond this. The lack of aspirational standards—or supplemental standards— has particular bearing on the education of students in the sciences.

The traditional 19th and 20th century high school science curriculum consisted of very basic and low level biology, chemistry, and physics. The mathematical requirements for these courses were relatively simple; they involve only part of the material in Algebra I, Geometry, and Algebra II. The Common Core mathematics requirements are arguably adequate to prepare students for yesterday's science courses.

Today, however, high school science also includes attempts to prepare students in basic engineering, computer science, robotics, and other burgeoning fields that feed growing sectors of our economy. These courses require much deeper mathematics preparation. Basic engineering, for example, requires linear algebra, familiarity with partial fraction decompositions of rational functions, and more trigonometry than was previously required. In robotics, students must be able to work with polynomials where the variables are the basic elementary trigonometry functions sin(t) and cos(t). If high schools want to offer molecular biology, students will need significant preparation in statistics and probability, as well as in discrete mathematics.

Of course, only a minority of high school students are capable of pursuing these topics. The Common Core, however, will impose a new obstacle in their path by lowering the quality of their general preparation and orienting school curricula away from the mathematical skills they will need to achieve. This threatens to have a profound effect on our ability to compete in today's world.

Unanswered Questions

The Common Core's college and career readiness standards aim for admission to non-selective community colleges. This can be confirmed by the May 2013 report issued by the National Center on Education and the Economy: *What Does It Really Mean to Be College and Work Ready?* The mathematics panel for this report was co-chaired by Phil Daro, who is described on page 44 of the report as having chaired the Common Core State Standards Mathematics Workgroup. The report pursued the question, "What is required to be successful in our nation's colleges and workplaces?" It sought to find the answer in the "requirements of community colleges, because, by doing so, we can provide a very concrete image of what it means to be 'college and career ready.'" The report's conclusion suggests an even lower standard than what Zimba proposed: "Based on our data, one cannot make the case that high school graduates must be proficient in Algebra II to be ready for college and careers."

In September 2013, a Hechinger Institute writer reported Zimba acknowledging that students who do not go beyond Common Core's high school standards could be precluded from attending selective colleges, and that these standards are not aligned with expectations of many colleges. Zimba said, "If you want to take calculus your freshman year in college, you will need to take more mathematics than is in the Common Core."[15]

Why is the mismatch between college expectations and the Common Core's definition of "college-readiness" not indicated in the Common Core document? Neither advocates of Common Core's standards nor the many organizations endorsing the Common Core have publicized the Common Core's implications for higher education.

Why didn't those who recognized the shortcomings of the Common Core's standards suggest an additional set of standards that would fill in Common Core's deficiencies? Adding supplemental standards would prepare students for the freshman mathematics course required for most majors in science, mathematics, engineering, finance, and economics.

Who was responsible for informing local and state educators in charge of secondary school curricula about the deficiencies in Common Core's standards? Who was responsible for outlining the additional standards pathways that would prepare students for admission to selective colleges and universities?

Whose responsibility is it now to ensure that American high school students will be eligible for admission to selective academic institutions? Admission to these institutions is important, since their faculty and students have propelled this nation's economic, scientific, and industrial development for over a century.

Proponents of the Common Core standards have had very little to say about "college-readiness" other than to declare that the standards will somehow ensure that it happens. We see strong reasons to doubt these assurances.

Author Biographies

R. James Milgram, along with Sandra Stotsky, was one of twenty-five members of the Common Core's validation committee, and the only mathematics content expert among the group. Milgram declined to endorse the new standards because of their poor structure and slow pace, which would leave students years behind their international peers and in some cases unprepared for college. Milgram is professor emeritus of algebraic topology at Stanford University, where he has taught since 1970. He has authored more than 100 published mathematics papers and four books. Milgram simultaneously received his bachelor's and master's degrees in mathematics from the University of Chicago, and three years later completed his Ph.D. in mathematics at the University of Minnesota.

Sandra Stotsky is professor emerita of the University of Arkansas Department of Education Reform. Unlike many of the testing experts who drafted the Common Core, she had significant experience, prior to being on Common Core's validation committee, writing content standards, having helped to develop Massachusetts' highly regarded English content standards during her time as Senior Associate Commissioner at the Massachusetts Department of Education from 1999 to 2003. Stotsky has taught elementary school, French and German at the high school level, and undergraduate and graduate courses in reading, children's literature, and writing pedagogy. She has written numerous books, including *The Death and Resurrection of a Coherent Literature Curriculum* and *Losing our Language*. She earned an Ed.D. from Harvard Graduate School of Education.

Endnotes

1. "Minutes of the Regular Meeting of the Massachusetts Board of Elementary and Secondary Education." March 23, 2013. http://www.doe.mass.edu/boe/minutes/10/0323reg.pdf.

2. "Knowledge and Skills for the Jobs of the Future," The White House. http://www.whitehouse.gov/issues/education/reform.

3. "Race to the Top Fund." http://www2.ed.gov/programs/racetothetop/index.html.

4. "About the Core." http://www.corestandards.org/about-the-standards.

5. "Stotsky's Letter on Common Core." http://nyceye.blogspot.com/2013/08/mass-standards-czar-stotskys-letter-on.html.

6. "Review of Final Draft Core Standards." ftp://math.stanford.edu/pub/papers/milgram/final-report-for-validation-committee.pdf.

7. See Appendix A of the version of the Common Core Mathematics Standards posted in the late summer of 2010, after the release of the final version on June 2, 2010. There is a third pathway, and it is the "calculus pathway." But since this pathway uses mathematics standards that were in the original version and, as Zimba pointed out in 2013, these standards are insufficient for reaching precalculus in high school, what was gained by listing them again?

8. "About the Core." http://www.corestandards.org/about-the-standards.

9. Jason Zimba, August 2, 2013, "Critics' Math Doesn't Add Up." *Common Core Watch.* Thomas B. Fordham Institute. http://www.edexcellence.net/commentary/education-gadfly-daily/common-core- watch/2013/critics-math-doesnt-add-up.html; Jason Zimba, August 8, 2013, "What I Learned About the Opposition to the Common Core State Standards when I Testified in Indiana," *Common Core Watch,* Thomas B. Fordham Institute. http://www.edexcellence.net/commentary/education-gadfly-daily/common-core-watch/2013/what-i-learned-about-the-common-core-state-standards-when-i-testified-in-indiana.html.

10. John Fensterwald, "Common-Core Standards Under Fire," Thoughts on Public Education, Silicon Valley Education Foundation. January 17, 2010. http://toped.svefoundation.org/2010/01/17/common-core-standards-under-fire/.

11. http://www.isbe.net/assessment/pdfs/2013/parcc/PARCC-FAA-Spring13.pdf.

12. *Statement on Competencies in Mathematics Expected of Entering College Students* (2013), http://icas-ca.org/Websites/icasca/images/ICAS-Statement-Math-Competencies-2013.pdf. See pps. 13-16 for details of minimal mathematics expectations for STEM.

13. C. Adelman. *The Toolbox Revisited: Paths to Degree Completion from High School through College*, U.S. Dept. of Education, 2006, Table 5

14. *STEM in Postsecondary Education*, 2012, NCES 2013152 (see, especially, Tables 2, 4, 7, and 12).

15. Sarah Carr, "Teachers Feel Urgency of Common Core Standards." *The Advocate*. September 4, 2013. http://theadvocate.com/home/6914390-125/common-core

6

The Revenge of K–12: How Common Core and the New SAT Lower College Standards in the U.S.

Richard P. Phelps and R. James Milgram

Editor's Introduction

The original essay, including an appendix titled Chinese Mathematics Standards for Lower Secondary School, is available on the Pioneer Institute website and in hard copy. Presented below are sections 5 through 8 and 10 of the original study.

Introduction

The promise that the Common Core Mathematics Standards (CCMS) would anchor K–12 education to higher education and backmap from the upper grades down to the primary grades has proven hollow. Higher education has scarcely been involved with CCMS except that many institutions have agreed to place high school students who pass a Common Core-based high school examination directly into credit-bearing freshman coursework (without remediation) in return for their states receiving "Race to the Top" grant funds.

Because the CCMS are low standards, topping out at about the level of a weak Algebra II course, many students will reach college unprepared for serious work in the STEM disciplines. This situation is the result of several contributing factors. The Common Core's supporters present the CCMS as equivalent to "college readiness." Many students will rely on that assurance and forgo whatever opportunities they have to take more advanced high school courses in mathematics. Many high schools will also rely on that assurance and cease to offer more advanced mathematics courses. But in this paper, we focus on another way in which CCMS will hurt students as they pursue college degrees: the "alignment" of the SAT to Common Core's high school standards.

Colleges will be harmed in three ways by that alignment of the SAT (and other) college admission tests to the lower level of high school mathematics coursework set by the CCMS. First, the alignment of major college admission tests down to the level of the Common Core Standards (CCS) cements the low CCMS high school standards in place for a long time. Second, SAT scores will become less informative to college admission directors as they are less correlated with aptitude for college work and more correlated with measures that are already available, such as high school grade-point average, class rank, and the new "college ready" estimates of the two Common Core testing consortia. Third, the SAT will abandon its role in locating students with high STEM potential in high schools with a weak mathematics and science curriculum.

The SAT-ACT Convergence: More Marketing, Less Rigor

On March 5, 2014, David Coleman, president of the College Board, announced planned changes in the Mathematics SAT.[1] He explained that there would be three areas of focus: problem solving and data analysis (which will include ratios and percentages and other mathematical reasoning used to solve problems in the real world); the "heart of algebra" (which will test how well students can work with linear equations "a powerful set of tools that echo throughout many fields of study"); and what will be called the "passport to advanced math" (which will focus on the student's familiarity with complex equations and their applications in science and social science). It is worth noting that the promised changes in the Mathematics SAT appear to be close to what the 1989 and 2000 National Council of Teachers of Mathematics standards were asking for, a move away from assessing mathematical skills and techniques to assessing ideas *about* mathematics from a philosophical perspective.[2]

Prior to Coleman's arrival, competent and experienced testing experts suffused the College Board's staff. But, rather than rely on them, Coleman appointed Cyndie Schmeiser, previously president of rival ACT's education division, as College Board's Director of Assessments.[3] Schmeiser brought along her own trusted advisors to supervise the College Board's psychometric staff.[4] Many of the "college readiness" measures and conventions for CCS-aligned tests sound exactly like ACT's.

Ironically, while ACT criticized low U.S. education standards, the company steadily lowered standards for its flagship product, the ACT college admission test. In contrast to test administrations 20 years ago, current students taking the ACT more than once can choose which session's scores will be sent off to college; the writing test is optional; and scores are no longer flagged when tests are administered with accommodations.

As high school students learned that the ACT was more flexible in its administration standards than College Board was with the SAT's, ACT's business grew. To compete, College Board also changed its score-reporting policy so students could take the test as many times as they pleased but only report to colleges scores (one would assume the highest) from the particular testing session the student chose.

Since Coleman and Schmeiser arrived at College Board, they have adopted other ACT innovations: elimination of the penalty for guessing and making the writing test optional.

The key driver of growth in ACT testing over the past decade, however, has been statewide administration of the ACT. Several states now administer the ACT to all of their high school juniors and seniors. There are benefits for the states. Some high schoolers who had not planned on applying to college change their minds after receiving a surprisingly high ACT test score. But, the benefits to ACT are even greater. The state pays the student test fee, and the state's schools administer the test, saving ACT enormous effort and expense. The SAT and the ACT in other states are administered in controlled, highly secure environments by SAT or ACT proctors. In ACT statewide administrations, the level of security is not yet clear.

The ACT test's competitor, the SAT, began as an acronym for Scholastic Aptitude Test. The original SAT was developed in the late 1930s to give students from less socially and financially advantaged backgrounds a chance to show their eligibility for this country's most demanding institutions of higher learning.[5] James B. Conant, president of Harvard College, and others encouraged development of such a test to find "diamonds in the rough"—students with high academic potential who did not come from well-to-do or socially-connected families and had not been exposed to the fine arts, other cultures through travel, libraries filled with great literature, or advanced science and mathematics coursework in their public high schools.

Aptitude testing's name provokes resentment. To some, "aptitude" implies a genetic inheritance or native intelligence–an intellectual superiority that some people simply have and others don't. It sounds unfair and undemocratic. Some critics argue that achievement tests promote equality of opportunity and aptitude tests stifle it. The stigma is unfortunate and stymies better understanding and wider use of a useful psychometric tool. The College Board, aware of the stigma, in 1994 changed the words SAT stood for to Scholastic Assessment Test. Then in 1997 it announced that the letters SAT stood for nothing at all.

Apitude is to Achievment as Prediction is to Review

The key difference between achievement and aptitude tests, however, has nothing to do with native intelligence. Achievement tests are retrospective. They measure knowledge already learned, whereas aptitude tests are predictive, measuring readiness for future activities. A high quality achievement test is highly aligned with a curriculum students have taken and validated by how well it summarizes the student's accumulated knowledge. Such a test might be entirely appropriate for college admission if college coursework were just like high school coursework. But, it's not.[6]

A high quality predictive test is highly aligned with desirable future outcomes and validated by the correlation between test performance and those outcomes—predictive validity. Predictive tests are widely used in business, industry, and government when organizations wish to estimate how well new employees will perform in new situations.

The best predictive tests are perfected over time. In the beginning, one incorporates the best available expertise for an initial version that represents a best guess at prediction. Then one tests the test by administering it, either in field tests or actual operational administrations. Afterwards, one calculates the correlation of individual test items with the desired outcomes. Highly correlated items will be used again; poorly correlated items will be tossed, and replaced by new draft items ready for try-out.

If one were to try to replicate from scratch what other countries with more successful education systems do—*require high quality retrospective achievement tests for secondary school exit and separate, predictive tests for university entrance*—how would one do it? One would develop a best-guess initial test with items intended to be retrospective and others intended to be predictive, and try it out on a representative student population. Afterwards, the items highly correlated with the mastery of the school curriculum would be kept in one pile and items most predictive of future success kept in another. Poorly correlated items would be tossed. Then, one would write more items and run the process again.

Ultimately, the test items in the two piles would be different, but probably not entirely. Some good retrospective test items can also be highly predictive. The retrospective test would have items highly aligned with the past curriculum and focused on measuring mastery of content and skills. The predictive test would demand less mastery of content and instead include "common knowledge" facts or present commonplace situations in order to measure one's readiness to acquire new knowledge or skills or reason through problems. Predictive tests are sometimes called "readiness" or "reasoning" tests.[7]

The key differences between retrospective and predictive tests for college admission are:

- Predictive tests can be periodically adjusted to optimize their predictive validity (tossing poorly predictive test items and drafting new ones); retrospective tests are less flexible—their test items must cover the high school content domain, whether or not they are predictive. Further, in the case of the major test consortia for the Common Core Standards, the PARCC and SBAC, they are required to test the material listed in the non-plus (required) standards, but are not allowed to test the material in the CC (+)-standards (more demanding optional standards), which almost certainly have more to do with college readiness than the non-plus standards.

- Considering all the information about applicants available to college admission counselors, predictive tests tell them more. A retrospective test covering the high school curriculum largely duplicates information in other available measures, such as the high school grade point average (GPA) and class ranking.

- A predictive test can identify a unique population of students who can succeed in college but who otherwise would not go to college, or would enroll in postsecondary programs that do not tap their full potential. This population of students includes those who may be:

  - bored by the rigidity of a particular high school curriculum but who nonetheless learn much on their own by studying what interests them;

  - not well adapted to the social environment of a particular high school but who may be comfortable with the social environment of a college; or

  - of high ability or motivation but enrolled in a dysfunctional high school.

This population can be rather sizeable, but it is not organized and has no lobbying power. Indeed, most students in this population do not know that they belong to it.

With a new CCS-aligned SAT, we come full circle. Those who have criticized the SAT as socio-economically biased still do not understand that retrospective achievement tests, even if academically less demanding—strengthen instead of weaken the influence of parents' income and education.[8,9] Perfection over time will not be possible with a CCS-aligned SAT even after the new tests are administered several times, the test items are analyzed, and it is discovered, as is inevitable, that some of them are not predictive. The College Board will be stuck with a limited test that they will be powerless to improve.

With a predictive test, one would toss the non-predictive items—as they are providing no useful information—and try out some new ones. With an aligned SAT, thorough, representative coverage of the CCS standards will be necessary to maintain alignment. Test items representing all the standards must remain, whether or not they predict anything useful. The available test item set for a CCS-aligned SAT will remain basically static, even after the new, lower predictive validity of the test becomes known.

David Coleman also hinted at possible changes in the Advanced Placement (AP) exams when he announced planned changes in the Mathematics SAT in March 2014.[10] They would, first, be aligned with the CCMS and second, be changed in emphasis in the direction of more "problem solving." The College Board has since issued drastically revised and highly controversial Advanced Placement U.S. History Standards, but has not yet revised the Advanced Placement mathematics standards.

One Test, Many Purposes: The Chilean Experiment

Those promoting the new SAT do not concede that it will be less predictive, but they assert that it will be aligned to the allegedly high, "rigorous" standards of the Common Core. In fact, the two goals are, to a large extent, mutually exclusive.

A test promising to address multiple measurement needs with a single measurement instrument can be quite tempting to policy makers. It saves time and money and reduces disruption. But what happened in Chile can serve as a warning.[11,12]

Prior to 2002, higher education institutions in Chile employed a predictive test modeled on the College Board's SAT for college admission, the *Prueba de Aptitud Académica* (PAA). Some faculty in some disciplines (e.g., engineering) added their own specialized content tests to admission requirements, but most relied on PAA scores and high school grades to evaluate applicants. Chile's system was not unlike what one found in most of the United States at that time: most students taking the SAT and some students taking one or more Advanced Placement (AP) tests in their best subjects and/or SAT achievement tests.

Then, in 2000, a small group of academics, with no testing experts among them, proposed replacing the PAA with a test that could also monitor the implementation of a new high school curriculum. Called the *Prueba de Selección Universitaria* (PSU),[13] in a typically Panglossian way it was described simultaneously as a high school exit test, as a university entrance examination, as a way to monitor implementation of the new high school curriculum, and as a way to increase opportunities for students from low socioeconomic backgrounds.[14] Authorities in Chile and at the World Bank also argued that the test would fairly measure mastery of two very different national curricula, incentivize high schools to implement the new curriculum, incentivize high school students to study more, predict success in university generally, and predict success across very different types of university programs.

The PSU was sold as a test that could do anything one might like a test to do, but it actually does nothing well.[15] In fact, the PSU is a retrospective achievement test that covers only one of Chile's two high school curricula, but it is not used as a high school exit exam (if it were, the majority of students would not graduate). Instead, it is used as a university entrance exam, although its predictive validity coefficients are much lower than those for the current ACT or SAT in the United States[16] and, so far as we can tell from a single study,[17] much lower than those for the prior Chilean exams, the PAA and associated subject tests.[18]

The 40 percent of Chilean high school students who follow the vocational-technical track stand almost no chance of succeeding on the PSU; they are not even exposed to the last two years of the curriculum it covers. (Moreover, in some rural areas, the vocational-technical track is the only one available.) Unlike current SAT and ACT exams, the content base of the PSU is very specific and coachable, advantaging wealthier parents who can pay to have their children coached. Over time, the PSU score disparity across

275

socio-economic groups has widened.[19] Children of wealthier parents have taken places in elite universities that once were available to poorer students with good grades and potential.[20]

With audits and evaluations bringing only bad news,[21] the Council of Rectors, the group of university heads responsible for the PSU, has closed ranks. The effect is that an assessment program with little transparency grows ever-thicker walls around its "black box."[22] Unfortunately, the PSU will continue to be used for the foreseeable future.

The Chilean college admission system seems to work well for well-to-do parents—their children arrive in the primary grades ready for school, attend private schools with advanced curricula, follow the college track (the *científico-humanista* track) in high school, and receive four full years of that curriculum. The PSU is less than ideal for the majority of students—students who follow the vocational-technical track in high school, or start from behind in the early grades, or never see all four years of the college-track curriculum in high school. Given the similarities of the Chilean system with what is being proposed for the new Core Standards, it seems legitimate to worry that the outcomes here will be similar to those in Chile.

Multi-Level and Multi-Targeted Testing

The best testing systems, such as those in many European and East Asian countries, are multi-level and multi-targeted. A multi-level testing system administers tests at more than one educational level (i.e., primary, intermediate, lower secondary, and upper secondary). European and Asian students typically face high-stakes tests at the beginning or the end (or both) of at least two educational levels.[23]

A multi-target testing system gives every student, regardless of achievement level or choice of curriculum, a high-stakes test with a challenging but attainable goal. In some systems, tests are set at differing levels of difficulty related to different certifications (e.g., a "regular" diploma and an "honors" diploma). In other systems, tests cover different subject matter. For example, the French *baccalauréat*–the secondary level exit exam for their academic track–is subdivided, first, by three *séries* (literature, economics and social science, science), and then, by *spécialités, options,* and *travaux personnel encadrés* (personal project work). Ultimately, one French student might take just one from among a spectrum of dozens of possible exit exams, as well as a completely different higher education entrance exam from among variety of them.

In the United States, high-stakes tests for students are uncommon at any but the high school level. Moreover, with few exceptions, they are single-target tests—meaning that every student, regardless of achievement level, course selection, curricular preference, or school quality must meet the same standard of performance to pass.

Ironically, European and East Asian societies with smaller disparities in income and academic achievement than the U.S. have acknowledged their children's differences by offering a range of academic options and achievement targets.[24] The U.S. has for decades been pushing most children[25] toward the same path—college—and is now setting a single academic achievement target.

A single academic achievement target must of necessity be low, otherwise, politically unacceptable numbers of students will fail. School systems with low targets have typically concentrated on bringing the lowest-achieving students up to the target level. This means that average- and high-achieving students are apt to be neglected or deliberately held back. Schools judged on overall student performance can increase average scores, for instance, either by retaining high-achieving students with their age-level peers rather than letting them advance a grade or by making these same students take courses in subject matter they have already mastered. These artificially restrained students all too often lose motivation, suffer from extreme boredom, act out, and/or drop out.[26]

The single-target problem has two solutions, one passive and one active. The passive solution lets individual students take a minimum-competency test early in their school careers; once students pass it they are allowed to move on.[27] If the test is high stakes only for individual students, then no one has an incentive to hold higher-achieving students back, that is, to prevent them from taking accelerated course work afterward, based solely on the test results.

The active solution to the single-target problem, and the solution that promises greater overall benefits, is to offer multiple targets. New York stands out historically as the one state that employed a multiple-target examination system, with a Regents "Competency" exam required for high school graduation with a "regular" diploma, and a Regents "Honors" exam required for graduation with an "honors" diploma.[28]

European and East Asian testing systems reflect their educational programs. Students are differentiated by curricular emphasis and achievement level, and so are their high-stakes examinations. Differentiation, which starts at the lower secondary or middle school level in many countries, exists in virtually all of them by the upper-secondary level. Students attend schools with vastly different orientations: advanced academic schools to prepare for university, general schools for the working world or for advanced technical training, and vocational-technical schools for direct entry into the skilled trades. Typically, all three types of school require exit tests for a diploma.

Supporters of the one-size-fits-all U.S. system often label European and East Asian education systems as "elitist" and our system as a more "democratic," "second chance" system. That contrast may have been valid 60 years ago but is no longer. It is now easier to enter upper-academic levels in current European systems, and most countries now offer bridge programs for, say, a dissatisfied vocational-track graduate to enter a university or an advanced technical program. Typically, bridge programs are free of charge.[29]

Our public education system is neither less elitist nor more conducive to "second chances." In typical European or East Asian systems, multiple programs and tracks offer multiple opportunities for students to attain high achievement in something. A student in the high achieving countries who enters a vocational-technical program at the lower-secondary level and finishes by passing the industry-guild certification examination as a machinist enters an elite of the world's most skilled and highly remunerated craftsmen. By contrast, a high school student in a career-technical program in the United States may be perceived as attending a "dumping ground" school and may receive only low-quality training with out-of-date equipment. The typical solution to problems with secondary-level vocational-technical training in the high-achieving countries has been continuous improvement; the solution in most states is to pass off responsibility to community colleges.

Lip service was paid in the early days of selling CCS to a sequence of standards for career-technical programs.[30] In the final CCS documents, however, the word "career" appears only with "college," as in "college and career readiness." Any original intention with respect to curricular diversity, in this case to technical/occupational standards for career readiness, was abandoned as career readiness was assumed to be equivalent to readiness for college without clear evidence to support the equivalence.

The best examination systems make sense as integrated wholes. To be fair to all students, a testing system should offer opportunities and incentives to all students, and students are not all the same.

Other Countries, Other Tests

Test requirements in the No Child Left Behind (NCLB) Act—mostly retained in the Race to the Top (RttT), SBAC, and PARCC initiatives—lead to low *student* scores. For U.S. students, already among the least stressed in the world, NCLB made school life even easier. Because the testing component of NCLB included no consequences for students, the message sent to them was that they need not work very hard. In this way, the largest potential benefit of testing—increased student motivation to work to pass the test—never accrued.[31]

When schools are held accountable for students' test performance, classroom teachers and school administrators, who should be the major supporters of a testing program, are put into the demeaning position of cajoling students to cooperate. Such a dynamic is unheard of in other countries where, unambiguously, it is the students who are tested and held accountable, not their teachers.

For example, the *abitur*, the exit test for German academic high schools, consists each year of test questions submitted by subject area teachers and university professors. Teachers also take part in scoring the test. Indeed, one of the arguments for adding constructed-response test items (i.e., open-ended essay questions) to high-stakes state tests in the U.S. was the opportunity for further involving teachers in the testing process in addition to having them serve on test item review committees during test development.[32] Perhaps holding students accountable for their own test performance is what lies behind the fact that when students in high-achieving countries do not score as well as they expect, they say it is because they did not work hard enough. U.S. students tend to blame their teachers for poor scores instead.[33]

The origin of the U.S. focus on making *teachers* accountable for student test scores appears to lie with education researchers.[34] There is no reason to disbelieve the researchers' primary assertion: of the within-school factors that are quantified and available in the databases they analyze, teacher quality has the single largest effect on student achievement. The fallacy occurs something like this: because education policymakers have no direct control over what happens outside the schoolhouse door, they focus their scarce resources on "within-school" factors, e.g. teachers.

Note that students are not generally considered "within-school" factors. After all, their legal guardians live at home; school officials only have them on loan several hours each weekday for about nine months a year. Nonetheless, students are sentient, willful creatures with agendas of their own who bring a lot of baggage with them from home to school. That baggage and their wills have more control over their performance—which is the performance being measured on the tests—than teachers do. Applying stakes to the test-takers has a more direct and stronger motivating effect on student achievement. The stakes need not be very high to be effective, but there must be some.[35] Who knows how well students try to perform on state NCLB tests?

In most countries, prospective university students must pass a retrospective achievement test to obtain a high school diploma and then sit for a completely separate university entrance test. In many countries each university administers its own entrance exam or leaves it up to each of its discipline-based departments to administer its own entrance exam (see Table 1). The original College Board and SAT tests were efforts to facilitate the process for potential applicants: instead of traveling and sitting for different college entrance exams, they could sit for just one test each and send their scores to multiple colleges.

Table 1. Requirements for admission to higher education, by method and country

	Completion of secondary/degree or certificate	Upper secondary exit exam	Separate entrance exam	Additional course work	Experience	Academic standards	Late or re-entry options for adults and dropouts
Australia	■	□	■		◎	■	Yes
Canada	■	□	◎	□			Yes
France	■	■	◎	◎	◎	■	Yes
Germany	◎	■	◎				Yes
Italy	■	■				■	Yes
Japan	■	■	◎, ■				Yes
Russia	◎		◎			■	Yes
Spain	■		■	■		■	
Sweden	■	■	◎		◎	■	Yes
Switzerland	■	□	■		◎		
United Kingdom	■	■	◎			■	Yes
United States	□		○			○	Yes

■ Uniform national requirement; □ Only some jurisdictions require; ◎ Each institution has its own exams or requirements;
○ Only some institutions require SOURCE: updated from Phelps, et al., *Higher education: An international perspective*, chapter 2

Other advanced countries that require both high-stakes retrospective secondary school exit exams and separate high-stakes predictive college entrance exams include the Czech Republic, Denmark, Iceland, Korea, and the Netherlands. Southeast Asian countries include Brunei, Cambodia, Indonesia, Malaysia, Myanmar, the Philippines, Singapore, and Vietnam.[36]

Then there is Finland. Testing critics have encouraged us to examine its education and testing system, learn from it, and copy it.[37] Why look at Korea, Japan, China, Singapore, the Netherlands, or other countries with strong testing and accountability programs that tend to score consistently high on a variety of international assessments when one can instead focus on the single anomalous country with an apparently mild testing and accountability program that scored highly just once on just one international assessment and, otherwise, tends to score below the world average?

Finnish students excelled on a single administration of the Programme for International Student Assessment (PISA), a test of low middle school mathematics skills given to 15-year olds. PISA de-emphasizes the fundamentals of mathematics in favor of routine examples of "mathematical literacy" from everyday life and has been characterized by U.S. mathematicians as "shopping cart" math, and criticized by Finnish mathematicians for the misleading signal it gave of Finnish students' mathematical performance. Finland's scores on more recent PISA tests have declined.[38] Its students have scored consistently lower on the more mathematics-intensive Trends in International Mathematics and Science Study (TIMSS).[39]

The two testing consortia, PARCC and SBAC, are designing tests covering a mathematics sequence that tops out with a weak Algebra II course. Until the Bill & Melinda Gates Foundation and the U.S. Education Department open their minds to a wider pool of information sources and more intellectual diversity, they will continue to produce education policy white elephants.[40] It is unfortunate that the designers of CCS did not investigate what other countries with better functioning education systems do, beyond the single aspect of content standards.

Advanced High School Math Predicts College Success

Even in the absence of multi-level and multi-targeted standards in the U.S., ambitious students find ways to distinguish themselves. Advanced Placement exams have been one such avenue, but an even more important one has been to take the most advanced mathematics courses the high school offers.

Table 2 correlates the highest mathematics course taken in high school with the percentage of those obtaining a four-year college degree.

Table 2. Relationship of bachelor's degree attainment to highest level of high school mathematics coursework in 1982 and 1992

Level of math	Class of 1982		Class of 1992	
	% reaching this level of math	Earned bachelor's degree	% reaching this level of math	Earned bachelor's degree
Calculus	5.2	82.1	9.7	83.3
Pre-calculus	4.8	75.9	10.8	74.6
Trigonometry	9.3	64.7	12.1	60.0
Algebra II	24.6	46.4	30.0	39.3
Geometry	16.3	31.0	14.2	16.7
Algebra I	21.8	13.4	16.5	7.0
Pre-algebra	18.0	5.4	6.7	3.9

SOURCE: C. Adelman, *The Tool Box Revisited*, Table 5, p. 62.[41]

Clifford Adelman found that *the highest level of mathematics course taken in high school is the single strongest predictor of success in college, stronger than socioeconomic status, high school grade point average, or college admission test scores.*[42]

Table 2 shows that for students whose highest high school mathematics course was Algebra I, only 7 percent obtained a four-year degree in 1992. Table 2 also shows that for the class of 1982, a student who entered college with only Algebra II had a 46 percent chance of obtaining a four-year degree. For the class of 1992, this probability dropped to 39 percent. We estimate that the odds for the class of 2012 will be about 31 percent to 33 percent due to larger numbers of students taking Algebra II and the weakening of high school mathematics coursework due to course title inflation and the adoption of CCMS. Algebra II was already becoming an increasingly lower standard for college preparation and will continue to decline.

Thus, it is not surprising that a student who completed a mathematics course beyond Algebra II in 1992 had at least a 60 percent chance at finishing a four-year college degree program.

There are several points to draw from this data. First, the lower standard set by CCMS that culminates in a weak Algebra II course as the summit of the mathematics curriculum will sentence a great many students to a higher risk of not completing college. Second, because the SATs are aligned to this lower mathematical standard, high schools will feel less urgency in offering more advanced courses. Third, the students will also understand that the material in these courses will not appear on the SATs and they will also feel less urgency in taking such courses. Fourth, colleges will be harmed as they find few and fewer American students matriculating with the mathematical skills needed for college-level work in the STEM fields. Fifth, defining college readiness as mastering weak algebra II content disadvantages students whose school districts do not have high socio-economic status.

Table 3 shows that the availability of advanced mathematics courses is strongly related to the socio-economic status (SES) of the school district the student attends. A student attending a high school in the lowest SES quintile has only three/fifths the likelihood of access to calculus when compared with a student in the highest SES quintile; the data are similar for trigonometry and statistics. But if the math required in high school stops with algebra II because of CCMS, the opportunities for students of lower socio-economic status will decline further.

Table 3. Relationship of availability of coursework in statistics, trigonometry, or calculus to school district's socio-economic status for high school graduates in 1992

School district's socio-economic status	Percent attending high schools that offered...		
	Calculus	Trigonometry	Statistics
Highest quintile	71.6	83.1	34.0
Second highest quintile	56.2	73.2	27.1
Middle quintile	54.1	71.4	24.9
Second lowest quintile	49.3	70.3	20.3
Lowest quintile	43.5	63.7	18.5

SOURCES: National Center for Education Statistics: NELS:88/94 (NCES 96-130), and NELS:88/2000 Postsecondary Transcript Files (NCES 2003-402)

The gap between what colleges need from students and what the Common Core will supply is not limited to pre calculus. Common Core Algebra II, for example, does not cover logarithms or conic sections adequately, or analysis of rational functions and preparation for the partial fraction decomposition of rational functions. All of these were standard high school topics in a traditional Algebra II course, and are essential for STEM and related majors in college.

The end of the CCMS mathematics sequence at the level of a weak algebra II course will dramatically reduce the U.S. STEM pipeline. Data from the National Center for Education Statistics indicates that only two percent of STEM-intending students whose first college course is pre-calculus or lower ever graduate with a major in STEM areas today.[43]

Unready and Unwilling

The Common Core movement began with the noble goal of fixing our underperforming K–12 education system by shaping it to serve our first-class higher education system in mathematics and science. The results, however, are trending closer to the converse. Common Core Mathematics has emerged as a force that seems likely to reshape our college and university STEM programs for the worse by making them adjust downwards to an underperforming K–12 pipeline.

After the CCS had been written, one of the two CCS-based testing consortia, PARCC, publicized an effort to include some higher education officials in test development and implementation.[44] According to PARCC's chairman, Mitchell Chester, "The PARCC Governing Board has made a commitment to work with a broad group of stakeholders…" But, the higher education representatives were chosen by the PARCC board, making it easy to pick friends and sycophants.

The CCS assessment and evaluation system as a whole does not even remotely resemble those of the world's best education systems. PARCC and SBAC are mostly building replacements for the NCLB tests, which will be administered under the same rules and conventions as current NCLB tests (but at several more grade levels). Scores on SBAC and PARCC high school examinations, however, will also be used to determine college readiness, as they define it. As currently proposed, those who achieve a score that statistically predicts a 75 percent probability of achieving at least a "C" in beginning college algebra or introductory statistics at a two- or four-year college will be designated "college ready".[45]

Are the PARCC and SBAC high school examinations needed for this purpose? Arguably not, as there already exist national community-college level admission tests—COMPASS (ACT), and ACCUPLACER (College Board). PARCC and SBAC are using hundreds of millions of dollars of public funds to re-create the wheel and displace solutions that had already been developed (and extensively tested and refined) in the private sector. The "college readiness" measure based on SBAC and PARCC high school tests will be graded on a 1 to 5 scale, with a "4" (sound familiar?) representing a pass out of remedial coursework.

The College Board is converting the SAT into a secondary school exit exam, but it will be used, inappropriately, as a college entrance exam. The U.S. seems to be preparing to replicate Chile's illogical and dysfunctional assessment system.

When states applied for a Race to the Top grant, they agreed to a stipulation that state institutions of higher education "exempt from remedial courses and place into credit-bearing college courses students who meet the consortium-adopted achievement standard for those assessments."[46] (These stipulations have been carried over into the PARCC and SBAC rules and regulations.)

In other words, the many higher education administrators who agreed to participate in their state's application for RttT funds relinquished their prerogative to place in remedial courses admitted students who have passed a Common Core-based high school test. That agreement has been expanded to include all public two- and four-year institutions in PARCC and SBAC consortia states.[47] The PARCC "college ready" target courses are beginning college algebra or introductory statistics at a two- or four-year college, courses that students in high-achieving countries take in middle school.[48] The CCMS-based assessment can replace the colleges' own placement exams, or currently available commercial exams (e.g., COMPASS, ACCUPLACER). A failed K–12 system for which the CCS were developed will determine the standards of entry to our currently internationally dominant higher education system in mathematics and science.

Moreover, once the SAT's alignment to the CCMS is completed, we can declare the end of aptitude testing in college admissions.[49]

Is the end of an SAT designed specifically to be predictive of college work a good thing? Emphatically no. Aligning the SAT to the CCMS will lower its predictive validity—because it will be less correlated with college outcomes.[50] It will also lower its "incremental predictive validity"—the proportion of the prediction estimate unique to the SAT (after all other factors are controlled)—because it will be more correlated with other measures already available to college admission officers, such as high school grade point average, class rank, *and* the new "college ready" estimate from SBAC or PARCC.

Clearly, the new SAT will reduce the amount of useful information the College Board provides colleges. Aligning the college admission test to the CCMS will decrease its correlation with *real* college work. This means less information for matching student abilities to colleges' missions and resources. Moreover, students will bear the consequences when schools do not teach the CCMS adequately or sufficiently. Furthermore, students in private schools and states choosing not to adopt the CCMS may be disadvantaged by a CCMS-aligned SAT.

Finally, a CCMS-aligned SAT will diminish opportunities for a substantial population of students that would benefit from a less retrospective and more predictive test, especially academically able low-income students attending high schools with inadequate math and science curriculum and instruction.

Below the Bench

CCS proponents frequently assert that the standards are "internationally benchmarked." This is at best misleading. By international benchmarks, the CC Mathematics Standards rate very poor. The education systems of most of the highest-achieving countries— our economic competitors— have one aspect in common: multiple sets of secondary standards, or "pathways." Just a few states excepted, our country does not. Most European and East Asian countries have much smaller disparities in income and narrower "achievement gaps" across demographic groups than we have in the U.S. Nevertheless, by high school and in some countries by middle school, they provide for differences in curriculum preferences, in academic achievement, and in long-term goals.

Although lip service was paid to building career-tech and advanced "pathways" in the development of the CCS, only a single set of standards was finally offered for the PARCC and SBAC high school tests in the final version for both ELA and mathematics. Accordingly, all students are to be educated by age-based grade levels in a slow-moving train on a single track heading to colleges with low standards. *When there is just one set of standards*, standards, test items, and passing scores must be low enough to avoid having a politically unacceptable number of students fail.

Moreover, higher education institutions signing on to their state's Race to the Top application had to agree to place all high school students they accept who have passed a Common Core-based college readiness test directly into credit-bearing courses, i.e., *without remediation*. Many of these students will fail in current credit-bearing courses for freshmen until those courses too are watered down.

Unless our high schools provide the coursework they need, mathematically capable students will no longer be able to prepare for careers in science, technology, engineering, and mathematics (STEM).

While the CCS initiative lowers standards for advanced students in all grades, it will harm one group of students the most: low-income students with high academic potential. High schools with predominantly low-income students will likely drop their advanced mathematics and science courses, leaving low-income students with high academic potential without the opportunity to take these courses.

These students will also be harmed by the conversion of the SAT from a predictive (aptitude) test to a retrospective (achievement) test. Such a conversion makes it more susceptible to coaching and tutoring. This means, as we saw in the case of Chile, that high-income parents will be able to buy greater access to demanding colleges and ultimately to higher-paying jobs for their children. Conversion of the SAT test from a test validated by its predictive quality—its alignment to knowledge and skills useful in college—

to a test validated by its retrospective quality—its alignment to the level of CCS-determined high school coursework—also means that the SAT will lose its ability entirely to find the "diamonds in the rough"—students with high academic potential in high schools with a weak mathematics and science curriculum.

PARCC and SBAC, the two testing consortia, are not developing assessment systems that will look like those in the world's highest-performing school systems. To a certain extent their tests will resemble some tests other countries use for *some* of their students. But, even so, they are not being developed the way that high-performing countries develop tests.

If the SAT and ACT developers stubbornly continue down their current (and we believe) unfortunate paths, lowering test administration standards and reducing predictive validity, colleges serious about maintaining high academic standards could well create a group like the original College Entrance Examination Board[51]—run by higher education institutions to serve higher education institutions—to sponsor the development of a predictive college admission test that enlightened institutions may use in place of the SAT and ACT examinations they will want to drop. This new organization could issue a request for proposals with the overarching goal "to develop a test with the highest predictive validity attainable." There should be no shortage of bidders; many large test developers, with expertise in large-scale educational testing, predictive testing, or both, are capable of challenging the SAT and ACT duopoly with a superior alternative.

If we seriously wish to emulate countries with high-performing education systems, we must consider more than just a single secondary curriculum track and a single testing target. High-performing countries offer their students a wide variety of curricular choices and tests, at different educational levels, and with different targets. Our students, too, have different goals and interests. It is long past time that we recognized that.

Author Biographies

Richard P. Phelps is editor or author of four books—*Correcting Fallacies about Educational and Psychological Testing* (APA, 2008/2009); *Standardized Testing Primer* (Peter Lang, 2007); *Defending Standardized Testing* (Psychology Press, 2005); and *Kill the Messenger* (Transaction, 2003, 2005)—and founder of the Nonpartisan Education Review (http://nonpartisaneducation.org).

R. James Milgram, along with Sandra Stotsky, was one of twenty-five members of the Common Core's validation committee, and the only mathematics content expert among the group. Milgram declined to endorse the new standards because of their poor structure and slow pace, which would leave students years behind their international peers and in some cases unprepared for college. Milgram is professor emeritus of algebraic topology at Stanford University, where he has taught since 1970. He has authored more than 100 published mathematics papers and four books. Milgram simultaneously received his bachelor's and master's degrees in mathematics from the University of Chicago, and three years later completed his Ph.D. in mathematics at the University of Minnesota.

Endnotes

1. For details see the press release, College Board. (2014, March 5). "The College Board Announces Bold Plans to Expand Access to Opportunity; Redesign of the SAT." Author. https://www.college-board.org/releases/2014/expand-opportunity-redesign-sat

2. See http://www.fayar.net/east/teacher.web/math/Standards/Previous/CurrEvStds/currstand5-8.htm

3. The longtime director of research at the College Board, Wayne Camara, left shortly thereafter and now works at ACT.

4. For example, check out the testing and measurement expertise of Schmeiser confidants Ranjit Sidhu and Craig Jerald, now senior executives at College Board.

5. Rebecca Zwick. (2007). *College admission testing.* Washington, D.C.: National Association of College Admission Counselors.

6. For an extended discussion of the different histories and character of achievement and aptitude tests, see Richard P. Phelps, (2007). Aptitude or achievement: Two separate historical paths, chapter 2 in *Standardized Testing Primer*, New York: Peter Lang.

7. David Lohman. (2005, Summer). Is ability separate from achievement? *Cognitively Speaking, 4,* University of Iowa, Belin-Blank Center; David Lohman. (2006). "Beliefs about differences between ability and accomplishment: From folk theories to cognitive science." *Roeper Review, 29,* 32–40; David Lohman. (2009). Identifying academically talented students: Some general principles, two specific procedures. In Larisa Shavinina (Ed.) *International Handbook on Giftedness.* (pp. 971–998). Dordrecht, Netherlands: Springer.

8. See G. M. Lavergne. (2007, November 9). College admissions as conspiracy theory. *The Chronicle of Higher Education*, B9–B13; Wayne Camara. (2008). College admission testing: Myths and realities in an age of admissions hype. In R. P. Phelps, (Ed.), *Correcting fallacies about educational and psychological testing* (pp. 147–180), Washington, DC: American Psychological Association.

9. David Lohman. (2004). Aptitude for college: The importance of reasoning tests for minority admissions. In R. Zwick (Ed.), *Rethinking the SAT: The future of standardized testing in university admissions,* (pp. 41–56). New York: Routledge; J. S. Wyner, J. M. Bridgeland, & J. J. DiIulio, Jr. (n. d.) *Achievement trap: How America is*

failing millions of high-achieving students from lower-income families. Lansdowne, VA & Washington, DC: Jack Kent Cooke Foundation & Civic Enterprises. See also Rebecca Zwick. (2004). Is the SAT a "wealth test"? The link between educational achievement and socioeconomic status. In R. Zwick (Ed.) *Rethinking the SAT*, pp. 203–216. Mahwah, NJ: Psychology Press.

10. College Board. (2014, March 5). "The College Board Announces Bold Plans to Expand Access to Opportunity; Redesign of the SAT." Author. https://www.collegeboard.org/releases/2014/expand-opportunity-redesign-sat

11. For another example, see Iasonas Lamprianou (2012) Unintended consequences of forced policymaking in high stakes examinations: the case of the Republic of Cyprus, *Assessment in Education: Principles, Policy & Practice*, 19:1, 27-44, DOI: 10.1080/0969594X.2011.608348. Cyprus, too, replaced separate secondary exit and postsecondary entrance exams with a single test, with unfortunate results.

12. In addition, some US-based critics of high school exit exams provide abundant evidence that they are not predictive of college work and argue for their elimination on that basis. (Not being psychometricians, they do not seem to realize that they are not designed to be predictive; they are designed to summarize mastery of the high school curriculum, something society considers important.) See, for example, Sean F. Reardon, Nicole Arshan, Allison Atteberry, & Michal Kurlaender. (2008, September). High stakes, no effects: Effects of failing the California High School Exit Exam, Paper prepared for the International Sociological Association Forum of Sociology, Barcelona, Spain, September 5–8; and John Robert Warren and Eric Grodsky, Exit Exams Harm Students Who Fail Them - and Don't Benefit Students Who Pass Them, *Phi Delta Kappan*, Vol. 90, No. 09, May 2009, p.p. 645-649.

13. For an overview of this issue, see Stephan Heyneman. (1987). *Uses of examinations in developing countries: Selection, research, and education sector management.* Seminar paper No. 36, Economic Development Institute, The World Bank, Washington, DC. "Where school inputs vary widely...academic achievement tests are likely to measure the opportunity to learn more than the ability to learn. [Developing] nations concerned about picking their future talent

must consider the possibility that an aptitude test…may be more able to overcome the local differences in school quality" (p. 253)

14. They cited the change of affairs in California when Richard Atkinson was president of the university system as justifying precedent. Atkinson changed the admission requirements to deemphasize the SAT I (the standard SAT with Critical Reading and Mathematics) and emphasize SAT II subject tests. In other words, Atkinson replaced aptitude testing with achievement testing. The result: to reach the same levels of predictive validity required more than an hour's worth of additional testing. Shortly after Richard Atkinson retired, the University of California system resumed the previous admission regime.

15. N. Brandt. (2010) *Chile: Climbing on giants' shoulders: Better schools for all Chilean children*, Economics Department Working Papers No. 784, Washington, DC: World Bank; MIDE-UC. (2000). *Reformulacion de las Pruebas de Selección a la Educación Superior*, Proyecto FONDEF; Ministerio de Educación. (2000, Nov. 22). Comisión Nuevo Currículum de la Enseñanza Media y Pruebas del Sistema de Admisión a la Educación Superior, Santiago, Chile: Author; Organisation for Economic Co-operation and Development, and World Bank. (2009). *Tertiary Education in Chile*, Paris: OECD; World Bank. (2001, October 19). *Implementation Completion Report* (CPL-38830; SCL 38836); World Bank. (2005, December). Implementation Completion Report (TF-25378 SCL-44040 PPFB-P3360).

16. J. L. Kobrin, B. F. Patterson, E. J. Shaw, K. D. Mattern, & S. M. Barbuti. (2008). *Validity of the SAT for predicting first-year college grade point average*. (College Board Research Report No. 2008-5). New York: College Board; Richard P Phelps. (2014, Jan. 7). "Large-scale testing: Uses and abuses", Presentation at Universidad Finis Terrae, Santiago, Chile. http://www.finisterrae.cl/portada/item/ richard-phelps-dictara-charla-sobre-pruebas-estandarizadas; Willingham, W. W., Lewis, C., Morgan, R., & Ramist, L. (1990). Implications of using freshman GPA as the criterion for the predictive validity of the SAT. *Predicting college grades: An analysis of institutional trends over two decades*. Princeton, NJ: Educational Testing Service; ACT Research Services. (n.d.). Research Services summary tables: Based on institutions in the 1997–98 prediction. Iowa City, IA: ACT.

17. A. M. Prado Salces. (2008). *Estudio de validez predictive de la PSU y comparacion con el sistema PAA*, Tesis para optar al grado de magister en economia aplicada, Memoria para optar al titulo de ingeniero civil industrial. Santiago, Chile: Universidad de Chile.

18. S. Prado. (2008, August 19). "Predicción y PSU". Carta al Editor. *El Mercurio*.

19. For a general overview of this issue, see Stephan Heyneman. (2004). Education and Corruption. *International Journal of Educational Development, 24*(6), pp. 637–648.

20. See, for example, Mladen Koljatic, & Mónica Silva. (2011, October). Acceso y Equidad en las Demandas Estudiantiles. *Revista de Administración y Economía*. Número Especial de Educación, pp. 24-29; Mladen Koljatic, & Mónica Silva. (2011, December 5). Acceso a la información y sistemas de medición en educación en Chile: El caso de las pruebas de admission. Seminario Educación y Transparencia organizado por Fundación ProAcceso; Mónica Silva. (2013, May 16). La pertinencia de la PSU y las necesidades de cambio en el sistema de selección universitaria. Paper presented at INACAP; Mónica Silva. (2013, August 23). Sistemas y Procesos de Selección y Admisión Universitaria. Paper presented for class in higher education administration, Pontificia Universidad Católica de Chile.

21. Educational Testing Service. (2004, December). *Suggestions for improving the comparability of scores on the PSU Prueba de Ciencias* (draft), Princeton: Author; Educational Testing Service. (2005, January). Evaluación Externa de las Pruebas de Selección Universitaria (PSU). Princeton: Author; Harald Beyer. (2007, January 17). "Equidad en PSU". Carta al Editor. El Mercurio; Pearson Measurement. (2013, January), Final Report: Evaluation of the Chile PSU.

22. Richard P. Phelps. (2014, Feb. 2). Evaluaciones educacionales de gran escala en Chile: Son necesarias? *CIPER*. http://ciper-chile.cl/2014/02/06/evaluaciones-educacionales-de-gran-escala-en-chile-%C2%BFson-necesarias/

23. See chapters 1 & 7, Richard P Phelps (2005). *Kill the messenger: The war on standardized testing*. New Brunswick, NJ: Transaction; and Richard P. Phelps. (2001, August). Benchmarking to the world's best in Mathematics: Quality control in curriculum and instruction

among the top performers in the TIMSS. *Evaluation Review*. 25(4), 391–439.

24. See for example this figure from the Trends in Mathematics and Science Study (TIMSS); the key indicator is the spread of the squares in each country's bar: http://nces.ed.gov/timss/figure11_4.asp

25. I.e., all children, but for some with certain disabilities.

26. Clifford Adelman. (1999). *Answers in the Toolbox*. Washington, DC.: U.S. Department of Education; http://www2.ed.gov/pubs/Toolbox/toolbox.html; Clifford Adelman. (2006). *The Toolbox Revisited: Paths to Degree Completion from High School Through College*. Washington, DC: U.S. Department of Education. http://www2.ed.gov/rschstat/research/pubs/toolboxrevisit/toolbox.pdf

27. A minimum competency test is a high-stakes test that requires performance at or above a single threshold test score before a certain attainment (e.g. high school diploma) will be recognized.

28. Economist John Bishop found that New York State high school graduates achieved superior academic and labor market outcomes than graduates from other states, other factors held equal. See Bishop, J.H. (2000, Summer). Diplomas for learning: Not for seat time. *Economics of Education Review*, 19, 333–349.

29. For example, Germany offers the *abendgymnasium* and Fxrance the DAEU. See DAEU: le diplôme de la seconde chance. (1996, Octobre). *Le Monde de l'Education*, 241, 81–84.

30. U.S. Department of Education. (2010, April 9). Overview Information: Race to the Top Fund Assessment Program; Notice Inviting Applications for New Awards for Fiscal Year (FY) 2010, *Federal Register Notices*, 75(68), 18172. "To help improve outcomes in career and technical education, we are also establishing a second competitive preference priority for applications that include a high-quality plan to develop, within the grant period and with relevant business community participation and support, assessments for high school courses that comprise a rigorous course of study in career and technical education that is designed to prepare high school students for success on technical certification examinations or for postsecondary education or employment." (Note the ambiguity of the term "rigorous" here. Is it being used in the usual sense or in educationese?)

31. Richard P. Phelps & Mónica Silva. (2014). The effect of testing on student achievement, 1910–2010: Meta-regression analysis. Paper presented at the 9th Conference of the International Test Commission, San Sebastian, Spain, July 5, 2014.

32. See, for example, Eleanor Chelimsky, *Student Achievement Standards and Testing*, T-PEMD-93-1. Washington, DC: US GAO.

33. Harold W. Stevenson, Shin-ying Lee, and James W. Stigler (1986). "Mathematics Achievement of Chinese, Japanese, and American Children." *Science 231* (4739): 693–699; Harold W. Stevenson and James W. Stigler (1992). *The Learning Gap: Why Our Schools are Failing and What We Can Learn From Japanese and Chinese Education*. New York: Summit Books, pp. 13–27 in particular.

34. William Sanders pioneered the use of "value-added" measures in Tennessee and highlighted the importance of teacher quality in no-stakes for (anyone) tests. Thomas Kane (See http://www.brookings.edu/blogs/brown-center-chalkboard/posts/2014/05/29-incremental-education-reform-kane) and Erik Hanushek (http://dcps.dc.gov/DCPS/In+the+Classroom/Ensuring+Teacher+Success/IMPACT+%28Performance+Assessment%29/Value-Added) are among those who have promoted stakes-for-teachers/none-for-students policies.

35. Bishop, J. (1994). *The impact of curriculum-based examinations on learning in Canadian secondary schools* (CAHRS Working Paper #94-30). Ithaca, NY: Cornell University, School of Industrial and Labor Relations, Center for Advanced Human Resource Studies. http://digitalcommons.ilr.cornell.edu/cahrswp/255 ; and Bishop, J.H., Moriarty, J.Y. & Mane, F. (1997). *Diplomas for learning, not seat time: The impacts of New York Regents Examinations* (CAHRS Working Paper #97-31). Ithaca, NY: Cornell University, School of Industrial and Labor Relations, Center for Advanced Human Resource Studies. http://digitalcommons.ilr.cornell.edu/cahrswp/171 http://digitalcommons.ilr.cornell.edu/cgi/viewcontent.cgi?article=1170&context=cahrswp

36. See "The secondary school examination systems in countries in the SEAMEO Region." http://www.seameo.org/vl/library/dlwelcome/publications/ebook/exam/2ndintro.htm

37. See, for example, Linda Darling-Hammond and Laura McCloskey, "Assessment for Learning around the World: What Would it Mean

to Be 'Internationally Competitive?'" Unpublished manuscript, Stanford University.

38. *The Economist.* (2013, December 7). "School league tables: Finnished" Author. See also: Astela, et al. (2006, December). "The PISA survey tells only a partial truth of Finnish children's mathematical skills." Matilde, 29, 9; Kivelä. (2006, December). "Severe shortcomings in Finnish mathematics skills." *Matilde*, 29, 10; and G. Malaty. (2006, December). "What are the reasons behind the success of Finland in PISA?" *Matilde*, 29, 4–8.

39. In fact, Finland only de-emphasizes *external* testing, not accountability. A grade 9 test is high stakes and determines a student's fate—vocational or academic track in grade 10. Then there is a matriculation examination in grade 12 for the academic track, and only a small fraction—less than 50%—of those who pass the matriculation exam continue to state universities. In other words, it is not even sufficient to pass; one needs to pass it "well" to continue to university.

Further, slightly over 40% of Finnish students end up in the vocational track in grade 10, and about half in the academic one. About 9% drop out between grades 9 and 10.

Finally, there is a rigorous *internal* testing done by teachers every few weeks in Finland, with grades ending up in each student's file and counting towards the later high-stakes decisions.

40. Richard P. Phelps. (2005, February). Educational testing policy: Stuck between two political parties, *Yale Politic.* http://www.nonpartisaneducation.org/Foundation/YalePoliticArticle.htm;

Richard P. Phelps. (2007, Summer). The dissolution of education knowledge. *Educational Horizons.* 85(4), 232–247. http://www.nonpartisaneducation.org/Foundation/DissolutionOf-Knowledge.pdf; Richard P. Phelps. (2012, Summer). Dismissive reviews: Academe's Memory Hole. *Academic Questions.* http://www.nas.org/articles/dismissivereviewsacademesmemoryhole;

Richard P. Phelps. (2012). The rot festers: Another National Research Council report on testing. *New Educational Foundations*, 1. http://www.newfoundations.com/NEFpubs/NEFv1n1.pdf

41. Clifford Adelman. (1999). *Answers in the toolbox.* Washington, D.C.: U.S. Department of Education. http://www2.ed.gov/pubs/Toolbox/toolbox.html; Clifford Adelman. (2006). *The toolbox revisited: Paths to degree completion from high school through college.* Washington,

D.C.: U.S. Department of Education. http://www2.ed.gov/rschstat/research/pubs/toolboxrevisit/toolbox.pdf

42. Other scholars have corroborated Adelman's findings many times since. Perhaps most publicly, the testing company ACT published a series of research reports based on analyses of their own massive databases of the factors contributing to college success, under titles such as: *Crisis at the Core* (2004; http://www.act.org/research/policymakers/reports/crisis.html) (e.g., "Our research also confirms that taking and doing well in specific courses—such as Biology, Chemistry, Physics, and upper-level mathematics (beyond Algebra II)—has a startling effect on student performance and college readiness." (p. i); "Seventy-four percent of students who took Trigonometry and Calculus in addition to the three-course sequence Algebra I, Algebra II, and Geometry met the benchmark for college Algebra, as did 55 percent of students who took these three courses plus Trigonometry and one other upper-level mathematics course, and 37 percent of students who took the three courses plus Trigonometry (Figure 21). At 13 percent, students who took only Algebra I, Algebra II, and Geometry were no more successful at meeting the benchmark than were students who took less than these three years." (p.12)); *On Course for Success* (2005; http://www.act.org/research/policymakers/reports/success.html) (e.g., Figure 1.3 (p. 4)); *Courses Count* (2005; http://www.act.org/research/policymakers/pdf/CoursesCount.pdf) (e.g., Figure 2 (p. 5)), and *Rigor at Risk* (2007; http://www.act.org/research/policymakers/reports/rigor.html).

43. U.S. Department of Education, National Center for Education Statistics. (2013). *STEM in postsecondary education: Entrance, attrition, and course-taking among 2003–2004 beginning postsecondary students*, Report 2013-152, Washington, DC: Author, Table 7, p. 23.

44. PARCC.(2011,July29).Highereducationtohelpdevelopassessments. http://parcconline.org/print/higher-education-help-develop-and-implement-new-assessments

45. It is highly unclear what this actually means since, previous to Common Core, "beginning college algebra" was generally regarded as remedial, and we have no indications that "introductory statistics" is intended to be more than mathematics-free high school discussions. In today's better universities, a serious course in statistics commonly requires a solid knowledge of first year college calculus,

with strong recommendations that the student have had a course in linear algebra as well. But this level of background will take years to achieve for the vast majority of students entering universities under Common Core.

46. US Department of Education. (2010, April 9). Overview Information: Race to the Top Fund Assessment Program; Notice Inviting Applications for New Awards for Fiscal Year (FY) 2010, *Federal Register Notices*, 75(68), p. 18172.

47. See, for example, PARCC's "Frequently Asked Questions" (FAQ-forCCRDandPLD_Updated11-1-12.pdf), pp. 1-3.

48. See, for example, PARCC's "Frequently Asked Questions" (FAQ-forCCRDandPLD_Updated11-1-12.pdf), p. 4.

49. Many of the aptitude characteristics of the SAT have already disappeared (e.g., analogies). The complete transformation of the Mathematics SAT into a curriculum-aligned achievement test may have been inevitable (which does not make it any less regrettable). Indeed, some SAT critics deride aptitude testing in college admissions on the grounds that it failed to incentivize students to work harder in their high school courses. See, for example, Christopher Jencks, & J. Crouse. (1982, Spring). Aptitude vs. Achievement: Should we replace the SAT? *National Affairs*, 67. But, those particular incentives are not all that matter and, we believe, are easily outweighed by other incentives, a substantial lowering of standards in both high school and college, and a degradation of the quality of information provided to college admission counselors.

50. As might have been expected, new College Board PR staff is now busy responding to the concern of a decline in predictive validity due to the CCS alignment by assuring us all that there is nothing to worry about. See, for example, Emmeline Zhao. (2014, March 7). New SAT revision: 5 questions with Kathleen Porter-Magee. *Real Clear Education*.

51. Arthur G. Powell. (1997, Fall). "Student incentives and the College Board system." *American Educator*. Washington, D.C.: American Federation of Teachers.

7

The Road to a National Curriculum: The Legal Aspects of the Common Core Standards, Race to the Top, and Conditional Waivers

Robert S. Eitel and Kent D. Talbert,
with Williamson S. Evers

Introduction

Late in the afternoon on April 11, 1965, President Lyndon B. Johnson sat with his childhood school teacher, Mrs. Kate Deadrich Loney, on the lawn of the former Junction Elementary School in Johnson City, Texas. The bespectacled retired teacher and her famous former pupil had met for the signing of the Elementary and Secondary Education Act of 1965 (ESEA). With the President's signature, the federal government's role in elementary and secondary education began to increase rapidly. Congress formalized the federal government's power, establishing the U.S. Department of Education (U.S. ED) in 1979. Today, ESEA authorizes funding for key portions of school district budgets across the country. Despite this leverage, the Department has generally adhered to statutory limitations that disallow federal agency involvement in K–12 curriculum, courses, or instruction. Instead, U.S. ED has focused on issues such as aid for disadvantaged students, accountability, civil rights, and evaluation. Since 2009, this strict adherence has changed: Actions taken by the Obama Administration signal an important shift in the nation's education policy, with the Department placing the nation on the road to federal direction over elementary and secondary school curriculum and instruction.

With only minor exceptions, the General Education Provisions Act (GEPA), the Department of Education Organization Act (DEOA), and ESEA, as amended by the No Child Left Behind Act of 2001 (NCLB), ban federal departments and agencies from directing, supervising, or controlling elementary and secondary school curriculum, programs of instruction, and instructional materials.[1] ESEA also protects state prerogatives on Title I content and achievement standards.[2]

At the direction of the present Administration, however, U.S. ED has begun to slight these statutory constraints. Since 2009, through three major initiatives—the Race to the Top Fund,[3] the Race to the Top Assessment Program,[4] and the Conditional NCLB Waiver Plan[5]—the Department has created a system of discretionary grants and waivers that herds state education authorities into accepting elementary and secondary school standards and assessments favored by the Department.[6] Left unchallenged by Congress, these standards and assessments will ultimately direct the course of elementary and secondary study in most states across the nation, making states little more than administrative agents for a nationalized K–12 program of instruction and raising the question whether U.S. ED is exceeding its statutory boundaries.

This chapter has four parts. Part I analyzes the limitations that GEPA, DEOA, and ESEA place on the Department. Part II provides background on the rise of the Common Core State Standards Initiative (CCSSI), gives an overview of the Race to the Top Fund, and illustrates how the Race to the Top Fund has encouraged states to adopt Common Core standards. Part III reviews the components of the two awardees under the Department's Race to the Top Assessment Program that are working to develop assessments and align them with the Common Core standards. Part IV discusses how the Department is using ESEA waiver authority to consolidate the nationalizing effects of the CCSSI and the Partnership for Assessment of Readiness for College and Careers (PARCC) and SMARTER Balanced Assessment Consortium (SBAC) assessments. The final part provides conclusions and recommendations for policy-makers and interested observers.

Limitations Placed on the Department by Congress

Historically, legislative prohibitions on federal direction, control, or supervision of curricula, programs of instruction, and instructional materials have limited the influence of the federal government in the elementary and secondary school arena. Three laws currently in effect prohibit the kinds of actions entailed by Race to the Top's incentivizing the Common Core.

General Education Provisions Act

A long-standing law governing the administration of federal education programs, GEPA includes one of the first limitations upon federal involvement in curriculum.[7] Though the law has changed over the years from its earliest version, the substance remains the same. In its current form, the prohibition is a broadsweeping rule of construction:

> No provision of any applicable program shall be construed to authorize any department, agency, officer, or employee of the United States to exercise any direction, supervision, or control over the curriculum, program of instruction, administration, or personnel of any educational institution, school, or school system, or over the selection of library resources, textbooks,

or other printed or published instructional materials by any educational institution or school system, or to require the assignment or transportation of students or teachers in order to overcome racial imbalance.[8]

An "applicable program" is "any program for which the Secretary [of Education] or the Department has administrative responsibility as provided by law" but excludes Higher Education Act programs.[9] Under the prohibition, one must construe federal education programs not to grant authority to any "department, agency, officer, or employee of the United States" to exercise any "direction, supervision, or control over the curriculum, [or] program of instruction... of any educational institution, school, or school system."[10] The rule of construction against direction, supervision, or control also applies to the "selection of library resources, textbooks, or other printed or published instructional materials"[11] and reaches federal departments and agencies other than the Department.[12]

Department of Education Organization Act

Enacted in 1979, DEOA established the Department of Education as an executive branch department administered under the supervision and direction of the Secretary of Education.[13] Similar but not identical to the curriculum prohibition in GEPA, DEOA prohibits the Secretary and other officers of the Department from exercising direction, supervision, or control over curriculum, as well as over the selection and content of library resources, textbooks, and other instructional materials.[14] The one exception to the general prohibition is if such activities are "authorized by law."[15] Framed as a rule of construction, the prohibition states:

> No provision of a program administered by the Secretary or by any other officer of the Department shall be construed to authorize the Secretary or any such officer to exercise any direction, supervision, or control over the curriculum, program of instruction, administration, or personnel of any educational institution, school, or school system, over any accrediting agency or association, or over the selection or content of library resources, textbooks, or other instructional materials

by any educational institution or school system, except to the extent authorized by law.[16]

In addition to the direct language limiting the Secretary's and officers' authority in curriculum, Congress included clear statements in the law that the creation of a new Department of Education does not displace the role of state and local governments in education. Primary authority for education remains with state and local governments, as evidenced by Finding 4 of the DEOA: "[I]n our Federal system, the primary public responsibility for education is reserved respectively to the States and the local school systems and other instrumentalities of the States."[17] In addition, when it created the Department, Congress reaffirmed the limitations placed upon federal involvement in education:

> It is the intention of the Congress in the establishment of the Department to protect the rights of State and local governments and public and private educational institutions in the areas of educational policies and administration of programs and to strengthen and improve control of such governments and institutions over their own educational programs and policies. The establishment of the Department of Education shall not increase the authority of the Federal Government over education or diminish the responsibility for education which is reserved to the States and the local school systems and other instrumentalities of the States.[18]

The legislative history of the DEOA confirms the primary role of state and local governments in education. In testimony before the Senate Governmental Affairs Committee, Mary Berry, the Assistant Secretary for Education of the Department of Health, Education, and Welfare, warned that the federal presence in education "has and must continue to be a secondary role—one that assists, not one that directs local and State governments, which have historically shouldered the primary responsibility for...public education."[19] In like manner, Senator David Durenberger stressed the importance of Congressional oversight so as to preserve the diversity of state and local approaches to education:

The States have a rich mixture of programs to respond to their citizens' educational needs. A centralized approach to education would be fatal to this diversity...If Congress does not exercise proper oversight, State and local jurisdiction over education will be threatened by the federal government regardless of whether education is in a new department or remains a division of an existing department.[20]

Members of the U.S. House of Representatives also expressed reservations. Representative Leo J. Ryan described the enabling legislation as "the worst bill I have seen....It is a massive shift in the emphasis by the Federal Government from supporting the local efforts of school districts and State departments of education to establishing and implementing a national policy in the education of our children."[21] One can find a strong statement of concern in the Dissenting Views of Representatives John N. Erlenborn, John W. Wydler, Clarence J. Brown, Paul McCloskey, Jr., Dan Quayle, Robert S. Walker, Arlan Stangeland, and John E. (Jack) Cunningham: "[T]his reorganization...will result in the domination of education by the Federal Government.... [The legislation is] a major redirection of education policymaking in the guise of an administrative reorganization—a signal of the intention of the Federal government to exercise an ever-expanding and deepening role in educational decision-making."[22] These members concluded by raising the possibility of the Department becoming a national school board: "If we create this Department, more educational [decision-making] as to course content, textbook content, and curriculum will be made in Washington at the expense of local diversity. The tentacles will be stronger and reach further. The Department of Education will end up being the Nation's super [school board]."[23] With these criticisms in the record, the Department opened its doors on May 4, 1980.

Elementary and Secondary Education Act of 1965

Congress had set limits on federal involvement in elementary and secondary education well before the establishment of the Department. With language comparable to GEPA and DEOA, ESEA includes a rule of construction limiting the ability of federal officers and employees to mandate, direct, or control curriculum:

> Nothing in this Act shall be construed to authorize an officer or employee of the Federal Government to mandate, direct, or control a State, local educational agency, or school's curriculum, program of instruction, or allocation of State and local resources, or mandate a State or any subdivision thereof to spend any funds or incur any costs not paid for under this Act.[24]

Accordingly, ESEA denies authority to officers or employees of the federal government to mandate, direct or control curriculum or programs of instruction.[25] Additionally, ESEA goes further than GEPA and DEOA to limit directly the use of federal funds for a curriculum. Under 20 U.S.C. § 7907 (b), "no funds provided to the Department under this Act may be used...to endorse, approve or sanction any curriculum designed to be used in an elementary school or secondary school."[26]

The intent of Congress is clear: The federal government cannot mandate, direct, supervise, or control curriculum or programs of instruction.[27] Indeed, the legislative history of the DEOA underscores this, as does its statement of intent "to protect the rights of State and local governments...in the areas of educational policy" and to "not increase the authority of the Federal Government over education or diminish the responsibility for education which is reserved to the States and local school systems."[28] Yet, as explained below, the Department is evading these prohibitions and using proxies to cement national standards and assessments that will inevitably direct the content of K–12 curriculum, programs of instruction, and instructional materials across the nation.

The Common Core and the Race to the Top Fund

To appreciate the authors' concerns about the Department's incremental march down the road to a national curriculum, one must first understand the Common Core State Standards Initiative ("CCSSI"). The Common Core is a creature not of state legislatures but rather of two Washington D.C.-based organizations, the National Governors Association's Center for Best Practices ("NGA Center") and the Council of Chief State School Officers ("CCSSO"), which coordinated the CCSSI to establish voluntary, national elementary and secondary school education standards in mathematics and English language arts.[29] Other organizations provided advice and guidance concerning the direction and shape of the CCSSI; they include Achieve, Inc. ACT, Inc., the College Board, the National Association of State Boards of Education, and the State Higher Education Executive Officers.[30] In addition, the Bill & Melinda Gates Foundation and the Charles Stewart Mott Foundation provided financial backing, as did others.[31]

In developing the standards, the NGA Center and CCSSO consulted with representatives from participating states, a wide range of educators, content experts, researchers, national organizations, and community groups.[32] For purposes of development and receipt of public comments, the writers of the standards divided the standards into two categories: (1) college-and career-ready standards (which address what students are expected to have learned when they have graduated from high school); and (2) K–12 standards (which address expectations for elementary school through high school).[33] Common Core supporters released draft college-and career-ready graduation standards for public comment in September of 2009 and draft K–12 standards in March of 2010.[34] Announced on June 2, 2010, the final K–12 Common Core State Standards ("CCSS") incorporated the college-and career-ready standards.[35] This marked the final step in the development of the Common Core standards. After development, states began to adopt the standards. Currently, forty-five states, the District of Columbia, and two territories have adopted the CCSS in English language arts and mathematics.[36]

In early 2009, President Obama signed into law the American Recovery and Reinvestment Act (ARRA),[37] which provided funds for the Department's Race to the Top program, consisting largely of the Race to the Top Fund and the Race to the Top Assessment Program.[38] With $4 billion to disburse, the Race to the Top Fund attracted applications from forty-six states.[39] RttT attempts reform in four areas: (1) adopting internationally benchmarked standards and assessments that prepare students for success in college and the workplace; (2) building data systems that measure student success and inform teachers and principals about how they can improve their practices; (3) increasing teacher and principal effectiveness and achieving equity in their distribution; and (4) turning around the lowest achieving schools.[40] The RttT Fund also includes several "priorities."[41] Priority 1 is an "absolute priority" for a Comprehensive Approach to Education Reform.[42] Priority 2 is a "competitive preference priority" for Emphasis on Science, Technology, Engineering, and Mathematics (STEM).[43] Priorities 3–6 are "invitational priorities," respectively, relating to innovations in early learning, the expansion and use of longitudinal data systems, coordination of elementary and secondary education with postsecondary learning, and school level reform efforts.[44]

In order to participate in the Race to the Top Fund, U.S. ED required each state to adopt common K–12 standards.[45] The State Reform Conditions Criteria of the Race to the Top Fund required each state to demonstrate work toward jointly developing and adopting a common set of evidence-based, internationally benchmarked K–12 standards.[46] Indeed, the guidance to the peer reviewers of the Race to the Top applications points to an effort to compel a single set of standards: A state earns "high" points if it is part of a standards consortium consisting of a majority of states that jointly develop and adopt common standards.[47] Conversely, a state receives "medium" or "low" points "if the consortium includes one-half of the States in the country or less."[48]

The "internationally benchmarked standards" refer to a "common set of K–12 standards" that the Department defines as "a set of content standards that define what students must know and be able to do and that are substantially identical across all states in a [standards] consortium. A state may supplement the common standards with additional standards, provided that the additional standards do not exceed 15 percent of the state's total standards for that content area."[49] As their applications show, the twelve winners of the Race to the Top Fund competition adopted or indicated their intent to adopt the CCSS for purposes of meeting the requirement of "adopting internationally benchmarked standards."[50] U.S. ED did not need to mandate states to adopt the CCSS in order to participate in the RttT competition, as nearly every state had adopted, or was about to adopt, the CCSS— many induced to do so by the prospect of RttT grants. While remaining ostensibly neutral, the Department could rest easy in the knowledge that most states would come to the competition having already adopted or signaled intent to adopt the CCSS.[51]

Standards-Driven Curriculum, Programs of Instruction, and the Selection of Instructional Materials

A change to common K–12 standards will inevitably result in changes in curriculum, programs of instruction, and instructional materials to align with the standards. Secretary Duncan has noted the link between standards, curriculum, and assessments: "[C]urriculum can only be as good as the academic standards to which the assessments and curriculum are pegged."[52]

School districts, too, believe that new common standards require a change in curriculum. In September 2011, the Center on Education Policy published survey results finding that 64% of the school districts in states adopting the CCSS agreed or strongly agreed that those standards would require new or substantially revised curriculum materials in math; 56% similarly agreed for English language arts.[53] These survey results further show that 55% of districts in CCSS-adopting states have already begun to develop or purchase (or will shortly do so) new math curriculum materials aligned with the CCSS.[54] For English language arts, 53% have done so or will do so.[55]

The Department understands that the adoption of the Common Core standards requires changes in curriculum. It also knows that these standards will displace existing state standards—"replace the existing patchwork of State standards"[56]—and effectively nationalize not only state standards but also curricular content. U.S. ED published this exchange between the Department and members of the public responding to the Department's Notice of Final Priorities for the Race to the Top Fund:

> Comment: Several commenters recommended that we clarify the meaning of a "significant number of States" within a consortium [that develops and adopts a common set of K–12 standards]. One recommended that the number of States be set at a minimum of three if the quality of their common standards is comparable to the common standards developed by members of the National Governor's Association and the Council of Chief State School Officers. Others suggested that instead of a minimum number, the criterion should focus on the importance or potential impact of the proposed work.
>
> Discussion: The goal of common K–12 standards is to replace the existing patchwork of State standards that results in unequal expectations based on geography alone. Some of the major benefits of common standards will be the shared understanding of teaching and learning goals; consistency of data permitting research on effective practices in staffing and instruction; and the coordination of information that could inform the development and implementation of curriculum, instructional resources, and professional development. The Department believes that the cost savings and efficiency resulting from collaboration in a consortium should be rewarded through the Race to the Top program when the impact on educational practices is pronounced. And generally, we believe that the larger the number of States within a consortium, the greater the benefits and potential impact.[57]

The Department's concerns about "a patchwork of State standards" and unequal geographic expectations do not reflect a proper understanding of America's federal system, the role of the states in setting education policy, or the statutory prohibitions limiting the Department's involvement in curriculum matters. This view—that "the larger the number of States" in setting standards, the better[58]—underscores the Department's desire to herd the states into accepting the CCSS, which was arguably the only standards-based consortium with a number of states large enough to please the Department during the Race to the Top competition.

Several education leaders severely criticized U.S. ED for using the Race to the Top Fund to drive states toward the Common Core standards without regard to the thoughtful initiatives that may have been taken by individual states not participating in a consortium. Texas Education Commissioner Robert Scott expressed concerns about the CCSS leading to national standards and the eventual nationalization of schools.[59] In a November 25, 2009, letter to Senator John Cornyn of Texas, Commissioner Scott wrote,

> I believe that the true intention of this effort [Common Core State Standards Initiative] is to establish one set of national education standards and national tests across the country. Originally sold to states as voluntary, states have now been told that participation in national standards and national testing would be required as a condition of receiving federal discretionary grant funding under the American Recovery and Reinvestment Act (ARRA) administered by the [Department]. The effort has now become a cornerstone of the Administration's education policy through the [Department's] prioritization of adoption of national standards and aligned national tests in receiving funds.[60]

Commissioner Scott continued in that vein:

> With the release of the RTTT application, it is clear that the first step toward nationalization of our schools has been put into place. I do not believe that the requirements will end with the RTTT; I believe that USDE will utilize the reauthorization of the Elementary and Secondary Education Act (ESEA) to further the administration's takeover of public schools....[61]

Within four months of Commissioner Scott's letter to Senator Cornyn, the Department wrote that "[i]t is the expectation of the Department that States that adopt assessment systems developed with Comprehensive Assessment Systems grants [Race to the Top Assessment Program] will use assessments in these systems to meet the assessment requirements in Title I of the ESEA."[62] Like the requirement that a state participate in a Common Core standards consortium composed of a large number of states, the Race to the Top Assessment Program has also served to "grease" the nationalizing influence of these initiatives.

Race to the Top Assessment Program

Also authorized by ARRA, the Race to the Top Assessment Program provides $362 million in funding "to consortia of states to develop assessments…and measure student achievement against standards designed to ensure that all students gain the knowledge and skills needed to succeed in college and the workplace."[63] The new assessments seek to measure student knowledge and skills against a common set of college-and career-ready standards[64] in mathematics and English language arts.[65] The assessments also must measure student achievement and student growth over a full academic year, as well as include "summative assessment components" in mathematics and English language arts administered at least annually in grades 3 through 8 and at least once in high school.[66] The assessments must evaluate all students, including English learners and students with disabilities, and produce data (including student achievement and student growth data) for use in evaluating (1) school effectiveness; (2) individual principal and teacher effectiveness; (3) principal and teacher professional development and support needs; and (4) teaching, learning, and program improvement.[67] As with the RttT Fund, the RttT Assessment Program effectively promotes the Common Core standards. This program funds the consortia that are developing assessments that will, in turn, inform and animate K–12 curriculum and instructional materials based on Common Core standards.

The Race to the Top Assessment Program is not the federal government's first effort to establish nationwide testing. In his State of the Union Address on February 4, 1997, President Clinton proposed to "lead an effort over the next two years to develop national tests of student achievement in reading and math."[68] This provoked a strong congressional response. Congress prohibited the use of Fiscal Year 1998 funds to "field test, pilot test, implement, administer or distribute in any way, any national tests,"[69] required a detailed review of the Department's test development contract, directed a study and report by the National Academy of Sciences, and, most significantly, prohibited the federal government from "requir[ing] any State or local educational agency or school to administer or implement any pilot or field test in any subject or grade" or "requir[ing] any student to take any national test in any subject or grade."[70] Congress also included similar prohibitions on testing in ESEA and GEPA, with limited exceptions.[71] As carried out by the consortia, the RttT Assessment Program should raise similar concerns for Congress.

As a part of the RttT Assessment Program competition, each state within the applying consortium must provide assurances that it will adopt common college-and career-ready standards and remain in the consortium.[72] Thus, rather than permitting state and local authorities to use standards and assessments that uniquely fit a given state as required by ESEA, the RttT Assessment Program requires each state in the consortium to use common standards across the respective states of the consortium. The result is that the RttT Assessment Program moves states away from standards and assessments unique to a given state and into a new system of common standards and assessments across the consortia states. With this major shift (and so as to continue to curry favor with U.S. ED), participating (that is, most) states will now be compelled to change curriculum and instruction to align with the common standards and assessments.

On September 2, 2010, Secretary Duncan announced the winners of the Race to the Top Assessment Program: PARCC and SBAC.[73] With $330 million in federal funds, the consortia have begun to design and implement comprehensive assessment systems in mathematics and English language arts for use in the 2014–2015 school year.[74]

Through the RttT Assessment Program, the Department displaces state assessment autonomy with new common assessments for all states in the consortia, directed and influenced by $362 million in federal funds and program requirements.[75] As the Secretary stated, "[t]he Common Core standards developed by the states, coupled with the new generation of assessments, will help put an end to the insidious practice of establishing 50 different goalposts for educational success."[76] The Secretary has elsewhere underscored the far-reaching effects that the assessment consortia will have on curricula and instructional materials:

> And both consortia will help their member states provide the tools and professional development needed to assist teachers' transitions to the new assessments. PARCC, for example, will be developing curriculum frameworks and ways to share great lesson plans. The SMARTER Balanced Assessment coalition will develop instructional modules...to support teachers in understanding and using assessment results.[77]

Describing the work of PARCC and SBAC to include "developing curriculum frameworks" and "instructional modules,"[78] the senior leadership of the Department clearly understands that the assessment consortia will drive curriculum and instruction.

Significantly, in U.S. ED's formal award notices to PARCC and SBAC, it also announced supplemental awards of $15.9 million each "to help participating States successfully transition to common standards and assessments."[79] PARCC's top priority for this award is "to help its member states make a successful transition from current state standards and assessments to the implementation of Common Core State Standards (CCSS) and PARCC assessments by the 2014–2015 school year."[80] In supporting the priority, PARCC's strategy includes "[c]ollaborative efforts to develop the highest priority curricular and instructional tools."[81] Among other things, PARCC intends to use the funds awarded by the Department for instructional tools, model instructional units, model 12th grade bridge courses, and a digital library of tools[82]:

> The supplemental funds provide an important opportunity to...strengthen PARCC's plans by developing a robust set of high quality instructional tools that will support good teaching, help teachers develop a deeper understanding of the

CCSS and their instructional implications, and provide early signals about the types of student performance and instruction demanded by the PARCC assessments.[83]

[The supplemental funds will be used to] [d]evelop a framework that will define the priority tool set most important for improving teaching and learning and for supporting implementation of the CCSS and PARCC assessments. This priority tool set may include a mix of instructional, formative assessment, professional development and communication tools, for use by teachers, students and administrators.[84]

[The PARCC will] [f]ocus the development of tools on a set of robust, high-quality model instructional units that highlight the most significant advances in the CCSS and PARCC assessments.[85]

PARCC plans to use some of the supplemental resources to develop college readiness tools aligned to the CCSS and PARCC assessments, such as model 12th grade bridge courses for students who don't score college ready on the high school assessments, or online tools to help diagnose students' gaps in college-ready skills.[86]

PARCC's initial proposal calls for the development of a digital library of tools.... The broader set of tools in the library will provide choices and supplemental materials (beyond the instructional units) for teachers to use. The development of the library also will identify materials that can be used to inform the development of the instructional units or even become the instructional units, perhaps with minor modification.[87]

In its November 22, 2011 webinar entitled Model Content Frameworks for ELA/ Literacy, PARCC goes a step further, suggesting possible uses of model content frameworks to "[h]elp inform curriculum, instruction, and assessment" as member states transition to the CCSS.[88] Through its use of federal funding, PARCC also provides direct "Guidance for Curriculum Developers" to "us[e] the module chart with the standards to sketch out potential model instructional unit plans," and to "recogniz[e] the shifts in the standards from grade to grade and us[e] these shifts as grade-level curricula are developed and as materials are purchased to align with the curricula."[89]

SBAC notes that it will use its $15.9 million grant "to carry out activities that support its member states as they begin to implement the Common Core State Standards, including...curriculum materials[.]"[90] In its Supplemental Funding Scope Overview Table dated January 16, 2011, SBAC directly mentions the use of federal funds to support curriculum materials, as well as a digital library.[91] Under the supplemental award, SBAC intends to allocate federal funds—

> to develop curriculum materials, identify which efforts are aligned to the SBAC learning progressions, and define key approaches to teaching and learning[92]
>
> [to] contract with professional organizations, universities, and non-profit groups...to adapt their curriculum materials to SBAC specifications to upload to the digital library[93]
>
> [to upload] SBAC-approved curriculum materials...to the digital library.[94]

SBAC expects to create a "model curriculum" and instructional materials "aligned with the CCSS" paid for by federal funds.[95] SBAC will also require its member states to implement systematically the CCSS by fully integrating assessment with curriculum and instruction.[96]

Through these awards, which use assessments to link the Common Core standards of CCSSI with the development of curricula and instructional materials, PARCC and SBAC (as grantees of the Department) enable the Department to do indirectly what federal law forbids. The assessment systems that PARCC and SBAC develop and leverage with federal funds, together with their hands-on assistance in implementing the CCSS in substantially all the states, will direct large swaths of state K–12 curricula, programs of instruction, and instructional materials, as well as heavily influence the remainder.

These PARCC and SBAC supplemental funding materials, together with recent actions taken by the Department concerning ESEA waiver requirements, have placed the agency on a road that will certainly cause it to cross the line of statutory prohibitions against federal direction, supervision or control of curriculum and instructional materials– upsetting the historic structure of federalism.[97]

Conditional NCLB Waiver Plan

In 2011, state agitation about NCLB's accountability requirements and the slow pace of Congress in reauthorizing ESEA created a policy vacuum that the Obama Administration quickly filled through executive action. Building on its Race to the Top initiatives, this effort serves to cement the Common Core standards and PARCC-SBAC assessments in most states, setting the table for a national curriculum, programs of instruction, and instructional materials. With conditions that mimic important elements of RttT, the Conditional NCLB Waiver Plan will result in the Department leveraging the states into a de facto long-term national system of curriculum, programs of instruction, and instructional materials, notwithstanding the absence of legal authority in ESEA.[98]

On September 23, 2011, U.S. ED announced the Conditional NCLB Waiver Plan, allowing states to waive several major accountability requirements of ESEA "in exchange for rigorous and comprehensive State-developed plans designed to improve educational outcomes for all students, close achievement gaps, increase equity, and improve the quality of education."[99] ESEA lists specific items that a state must include in a waiver request to the Secretary of Education: (1) identification of the federal programs affected by the proposed waiver; (2) a description of which federal statutory or regulatory requirements are to be waived and how the waiver of those requirements will increase the quality of instruction for students and improve the academic achievement of students; (3) for each school year, identification of specific measurable educational goals for the state educational agency ("SEA") and each local educational agency ("LEA"), Indian tribe, or school affected by the potential waiver; (4) a description of the methods used to measure annually the progress for meeting these goals and outcomes; (5) an explanation of how the waiver will assist the SEA and each affected LEA, Indian tribe, or school in reaching those goals; and (6) a description of how a school will continue to provide assistance to the same population served by the ESEA program for which a waiver is requested.[100] The Conditional NCLB Waiver Plan does all this and much more.[101]

Critically, in exchange for receiving a waiver, the Department requires states to agree to four conditions: (1) adopt college-and career-ready standards[102] in at least reading/language arts and mathematics and develop and administer annual, statewide, aligned assessments that measure student growth in at least grades 3 through 8 and at least once in high school; (2) develop and implement differentiated accountability systems that recognize student growth and provide interventions for the lowest-performing schools and those with the largest achievement gaps; (3) develop and implement new systems for evaluating principal and teacher performance, based in part on student academic growth; and (4) remove burdensome reporting requirements that have little impact on student outcomes.[103] Each state must meet these conditions in order for the Secretary to grant the waiver application—a decision completely within the discretion of the Secretary under the Conditional NCLB Waiver Plan.[104]

The Department requires SEAs seeking waivers to make several decisions. Two of these decisions are especially questionable to those concerned about the Department's legislative limitations. First, the state must declare whether it has "adopted college-and career-ready standards" in reading/language arts and mathematics "that are common to a significant number of States" consistent with the Department's definition of such standards—in effect, the CCSS.[105] Alternatively, states may adopt such standards certified by its state network of institutions of higher education, as long as they are consistent with the Department's definition of such standards–the Common Core standards.[106] Second, in its application, the state must declare whether it is "participating in one of the two

State consortia [PARCC or SBAC] that received a grant under the Race to the Top Assessment competition."[107] If not, the state must represent that it is planning to adopt, or has already adopted and administered, "statewide aligned, high-quality assessments that measure student growth in reading/language arts and in mathematics in at least grades 3–8 and at least once in high school in all LEAs."[108]

The Conditional NCLB Waiver Plan provides two opportunities for states to apply for waivers– November 14, 2011, and February 21, 2012. On November 14, eleven states filed requests for waivers.[109] With few exceptions, each state declared that it has "adopted college- and career-ready standards in at least reading language arts and mathematics that are common to a significant number of states"—the CCSS.[110] (Minnesota adopted the CCSS for reading/language arts but not for mathematics, and Kentucky, the first state to adopt the CCSS in 2010, has adopted Common Core standards approved by its state network of higher education institutions.)[111] Ten of the initial eleven states filing requests for waivers participate in at least "one of two State consortia that received a grant under the Race to the Top Assessment competition"— PARCC or SBAC.[112] Another twenty-eight states and Puerto Rico informed the Department that they intend to apply for waivers by the second deadline of February 21, 2012.[113]

Given the states' near universal acceptance of CCSS and the common assessment consortia, U.S. ED's announcement of the Conditional NCLB Waiver Plan is not surprising. Indeed, to obtain a waiver, states must adopt and implement common standards and assessments. U.S. ED set the table in 2009 and 2010, using the Race to the Top Fund and the Race to the Top Assessment Program to entice competing states into accepting the Common Core standards and the assessment consortia. With an eye on the 2014–15 academic year, the consortia are using the Common Core standards to develop their assessments with the goal of writing content for curriculum, programs of instruction, and instructional materials. The Conditional NCLB Waiver Plan will ensure that nearly every state seeking a waiver remains forever committed to the

Common Core standards of CCSSI, PARCC-SBAC assessments, and the curriculum, program, and instructional changes that they inspire. Any state effort to untether from the conditions imposed by the Department in exchange for having received an ESEA waiver will certainly result in the Department revoking the waiver. Moreover, given the extensive compliance costs imposed by the waiver (California has refused to seek waivers on cost grounds), the likelihood of any state doing so after having spent significant funds required by the waiver conditions is minimal. Like the dazed traveler in the popular Eagles' song Hotel California, states can check out any time they want, but they can never leave.

Conclusions and Recommendations

Joseph A. Califano, Jr., former Secretary of Health, Education, and Welfare, once wrote, "In its most extreme form, national control of curriculum is a form of national control of ideas."[114] Unfortunately the Obama Administration placed the nation on the road to a national curriculum. By leveraging funds through its Race to the Top Fund and the Race to the Top Assessment Program, U.S. ED has accelerated the implementation of common standards in English language arts and mathematics and the development of common assessments based on those standards. By PARCC's and SBAC's admission, these standards and assessments will create content for state K–12 curriculum and instructional materials. The Department has simply paid others to do what it is forbidden to do. This tactic should not inoculate the Department against the curriculum prohibitions imposed by Congress.

The authors understand that the Common Core standards started as an initiative of the NGA Center and the CCSSO, but U.S. ED's decision to cement the use of the standards and assessment consortia through waiver conditions—a power that Congress has not granted in the waiver statute—changes matters considerably. Given most states' eagerness to escape the strict accountability requirements of ESEA, most states will agree to U.S. ED's conditions in order to obtain waivers. By accepting the Department's conditions, these states will be bound indefinitely to the Common

Core standards, PARCC-SBAC assessments, and the curriculum and instructional modules that arise from those assessments. As evidenced by the eleven states that have already applied for waivers, most states will accept the Common Core standards and the PARCC-SBAC assessment consortia conditions. Once this consummation occurs, U.S. ED will not permit a state to walk away from that commitment without the state losing its coveted waivers. Nor will many states turn away from the Common Core standards and assessments after making the heavy investment that these initiatives require. These efforts will result in a de facto national curriculum and instructional materials effectively supervised, directed, or controlled by U.S. ED through the NCLB waiver process.

In light of these conclusions, we makes seven recommendations:

1. Congress should immediately pass legislation clarifying that U.S. ED cannot impose conditions on waivers requested by states under ESEA.

2. The appropriate committees of Congress should conduct hearings on U.S. ED's implementation of the Race to the Top Fund, the Race to the Top Assessment Program, and the Conditional NCLB Waiver Plan to ascertain the Department's compliance with GEPA, DEOA, and ESEA.

3. Congress should review the curriculum and related prohibitions in GEPA, DEOA, and ESEA to determine whether legislation should be introduced to strengthen the ban on federal involvement in elementary and secondary curriculum, programs of instruction, and instructional materials.

4. Congress should request the U.S. Government Accountability Office (GAO) to conduct a comprehensive review of the elementary and secondary education programs of the Department, including programs implemented under the ARRA and ESEA, to identify those that fail to comply with GEPA, the DEOA, and the ESEA prohibitions, with the GAO submitting to the chairmen and ranking members of the appropriate committees a written report with specific findings.

5. Congress should require the Secretary to undertake a review of the Department's regulations appearing at Title 34 of the Code of Federal Regulations, as well as guidance relating to elementary and secondary programs, to identify those that fail to comply with GEPA, the DEOA, and the ESEA, with the Secretary submitting to the chairmen and ranking members of the appropriate committees a written report with specific findings.

6. Governors, State Superintendents of Education, State Boards of Education, and State Legislators should reconsider their respective states' decisions to participate in the CCSSI, the Race to the Top Fund, and the Race to the Top Assessment Program.

7. The eleven states that have applied for waivers under the Department's Conditional NCLB Waiver Plan should amend their waiver applications to delete U.S. ED's four non-statutory conditions and include only the statutory requirements of 20 U.S.C. § 7861.

Author Biographies

Robert S. Eitel served as deputy general counsel of the United States Department of Education from 2006 to 2009, working with General Counsel Kent Talbert. He is now vice president of regulatory operations at Career Education Corporation, a private occupational education company that owns and manages scores of colleges. Prior to joining the Department of Education, Eitel practiced law in New Orleans. He graduated with a J.D. from Tulane University.

Kent D. Talbert served in the United States Department of Education from 2001–2009, as Deputy General Counsel, General Counsel (chief legal adviser to the Education Secretary), and finally Acting Under-Secretary. He now practices law at his own firm, Kent D. Talbert PLLC. Before serving in the Department of Education, Talbert was the education policy counsel for the House Committee on Education and the Workforce, staff member of the Senate Committee on Health, Education, Labor and Pensions, and on the staff of United States Senator Strom Thurmond. Talbert graduated from Erskine College and the University of South Carolina School of Law.

Williamson S. Evers has been a fellow at the Hoover Institution since 1988 and a member there of the Koret Task Force on K–12 Education. He took a leave of absence from the Hoover Institute to serve as United States Assistant Secretary of Education for Policy from 2007 to 2009, and served as a Senior Adviser to United States Secretary of Education Margaret Spellings in 2007. Evers worked on content standards on two California commissions (in 1996 and 2010, when he served with Ze'ev Wurman) and has served on several boards of education. Evers received his bachelor's, master's, and doctoral degrees in political science from Stanford University.

Endnotes

1. 20 U.S.C. § 1232a (the General Education Provisions Act limitation on federal involvement in curriculum); 20 U.S.C. § 3403(b) (the Department of Education Organization Act limitation); 20U.S.C. § 7907(a) (the Elementary and Secondary Education Act limitation).

2. Though the American Recovery and Reinvestment Act, Pub. L. No. 111-5, 123 Stat. 115 (2009), and not ESEA authorized the Race to the Top Fund and the Race to the Top Assessment Program, Congress has repeatedly stated in ESEA that standards and assessments are the authority of states, not the federal government. See 20 U.S.C. § 6311(b)(1)(A) ("[A] State shall not be required to submit such standards [Title I content and achievement standards] to the Secretary."); 20 U.S.C. § 6311(e)(1)(F) ("The Secretary shall...not have the authority to require a State, as a condition of approval of the State [Title I] plan, to include in, or delete from, such plan one or more specific elements of the State's academic content standards or to use specific academic assessment instruments or items."); 20 U.S.C. § 6575 ("Nothing in this title [Title I of ESEA] shall be construed to authorize an officer or employee of the Federal Government to mandate, direct, or control a State, local educational agency, or school's specific instructional content, academic achievement standards and assessments, curriculum, or program of instruction."). ARRA did not change this language.

3. The authority for the Race to the Top Fund is §§ 14005 and 14006(a)(2) of the American Recovery and Reinvestment Act of 2009, Pub. L. No. 111-5, 123 Stat. 115, 282–283 (2009). See also Race to the Top Fund, Purpose, http://www2.ed.gov/programs/racetothetop/index.html.

4. The authority for the Race to the Top Assessment Program is §§ 14005 and 14006(a)(2) of the American Recovery and Reinvestment Act of 2009, Pub. L. No. 1115, 123 Stat. 115, 282–283 (2009). See also *Race to the Top Assessment Program, Purpose,* http://www2.ed.gov/programs/racetothetop-assessment/index.html.

5. The Department's ESEA Flexibility guidance is referred to throughout as a "Conditional NCLB Waiver Plan," given that the four "principles" that must be met to be eligible for a waiver are functionally "conditions." The four conditions, discussed in Part V are: (1) adopt college and career-ready standards in at least reading/language arts

and mathematics, and develop and administer annual, statewide, aligned high quality assessments that measure student growth in at least grades 3–8 and at least once in high school; (2) develop and implement differentiated accountability systems that recognize student growth, and provide interventions for the lowest-performing schools and those with the largest achievement gaps; (3) develop and implement new systems for evaluating principal and teacher performance, based on student academic growth; and (4) remove burdensome reporting requirements that have little impact on student outcomes. U.S. DEP'T OF EDUC., ESEA FLEXIBILITY 3–5 (2011), available at http://www.ed.gov/esea/flexibility.

6.   See supra notes 3–5.

7.   Elementary, Secondary, and Other Education Amendments of 1969 § 422, Pub. L. No. 91-230, 84 Stat. 121, 169 (1970), amending Title IV of Pub. L. No. 90-247. The corresponding current law provision is 20 U.S.C. § 1232a.

8.   20 U.S.C. § 1232a.

9.   20 U.S.C. §§ 1221(c)(1), 1234i(2).

10.   0 U.S.C. § 1232a.

11.   Id.

12.   Id.

13.   20 U.S.C. § 3411.

14.   20 U.S.C. § 3403(b).

15.   Id.

16.   Id.

17.   20 U.S.C. § 3401(4).

18.   20 U.S.C. § 3403(a).

19.   S. REP. NO. 96-49, at 10 (1979).

20.   S. REP. NO. 96-49, at 95 (1979).

21.   H.R. REP. NO. 95-1531, at 41 (1978).

22.   H.R. REP. NO. 95-1531, at 45-46 (1978).

23.   H.R. REP. NO. 95-1531, at 47 (1978).

24.   20 U.S.C. § 7907(a).

25. Though the last clause of this section of law was at issue in *School District of the City of Pontiac v. Secretary of the United States Department of Education*, 584 F.3d 253, 274 (6th Cir. 2009), in dicta, the United States Court of Appeals for the Sixth Circuit noted the first part of the text "prevents federal officers from controlling school curricula."

26. 20 U.S.C. § 7907(b).

27. 20 U.S.C. §§ 1232a, 3403(b), 7907(a). The authority for the Race to the Top Fund and Race to the Top Assessment Program is §§ 14005 and 14006(a)(2) of the American Recovery and Reinvestment Act of 2009, Pub. L. No. 111-5, 123 Stat. 115, 282283 (2009), and not ESEA. Accordingly, only GEPA and the DEOA are discussed in the analysis of the Race to the Top Fund and Race to the Top Assessment Program.

28. 20 U.S.C. § 3403(a).

29. See About the Standards, http://www.corestandards.org/about-the-standards (last visited Jan. 13, 2012); Frequently Asked Questions, http://www.corestandards.org/frequently-asked-questions.

30. See Process, http://www.corestandards.org/about-the-standards/process.

31. Nick Anderson, "Common Set of School Standards to be Proposed," Washington Post, Mar. 10, 2010, at A1.

32. While forty-eight states, the District of Columbia, and two territories (U.S. Virgin Islands and Northern Mariana Islands) participated in the process to develop the Common Core State Standards, the current number of states that have adopted English language arts and mathematics standards is forty-five, along with the District of Columbia and two territories (U.S. Virgin Islands and Northern Mariana Islands). See INTRODUCTION TO THE COMMON CORE STATE STANDARDS (2010), available at http://www.corestandards.org/assets/ccssi-introduction.pdf; In the States, http://www.corestandards.org/in-thestates

33. See Process, http://www.corestandards.org/aboutthe-standards/process.

34. Id.

35. See *Introduction to the Common Core State Standards* (2010), available at http://www.corestandards.org/assets/ccssi-introduction.pdf.

36. See In the States, http://www.corestandards.org/in-thestates (showing states that have adopted the Common Core Standards.

37. Pub. L. No. 111-5, 123 Stat. 115 (2009).

38. See supra notes 3-4; see also 74 Fed. Reg. 59,688 (Nov. 18, 2009); 75 Fed. Reg. 18,171 (April 9, 2010). This article discusses Phases 1 and 2 of the Race to the Top Fund, as well as the Race to the Top Assessment Program. The article does not discuss Phase 3 of the Race to the Top Fund, which distributed $200 million from Public 112-10, the Department of Defense and Full-Year Continuing Appropriations Act, 2011 ("FY2011 Appropriations Act"), to nine state finalists who did not prevail in Phase 1 or 2 of the competition. Nor does the article discuss the recently-awarded Race to the Top Fund grants for improving early childhood care and learning, authorized in the FY2011 Appropriations Act.

39. Alaska, North Dakota, Texas, and Vermont did not submit applications for either Phase 1 or 2 of the Race to the Top Fund competition.

40. 74 Fed. Reg. 59,688 (Nov. 18, 2009).

41. See 74 Fed. Reg. 59,836-59,837 (Nov. 18, 2009) for a discussion of the Race to the Top Fund priorities. Funding priorities are a "means of focusing a competition on the areas in which the Secretary is particularly interested in receiving applications. Generally priorities take the form of specific kinds of activities that applicants are asked to include in an application. There are absolute priorities, which the applicant must address in order to be considered for funding; competitive preferences, which the applicant has the option of choosing whether or not to address and for which they may receive additional points; and invitational priorities, which the applicant is encouraged but not required to address. Applications addressing invitational priorities receive no preference over applications that do not meet the priority." *U.S. Dep't of Educ., Handbook for the Discretionary Grant Process* 154 (2009)(emphasis added), available at http://www2.ed.gov/policy/gen/leg/foia/foia-hb01.pdf; 34 C.F.R. § 75.105(c)(1)-(3).

42. 74 Fed. Reg. 59,836 (Nov. 18, 2009).

43. 74 Fed. Reg. 59,836 (Nov. 18, 2009).

44. 74 Fed. Reg. 59,836-59,837 (Nov. 18, 2009). With respect to implementation of the ARRA, the Department first published its *Notice of Proposed Priorities, Requirements, Definitions, and Selection Criteria for the Race to the Top Fund* on July 29, 2009. Thereafter, it received comments from over 1,000 individuals and organizations, including teachers, principals, governors, chief state school officers, and others. The Department invited applications for Phase 1 of the competition on November 18, 2009, and for Phase 2 on April 14, 2010. Announced on March 29, 2010, Delaware and Tennessee won the Phase 1 competition. Phase 2 winners, announced on August 24, 2010, were the District of Columbia, Florida, Georgia, Hawaii, Maryland, Massachusetts, New York, North Carolina, Ohio, and Rhode Island.

45. 74 Fed. Reg. 59,843 (Nov. 18, 2009).

46. See the discussion of State Reform Conditions Criteria at 74 Fed. Reg. 59,843 (Nov. 18, 2009) and the definition of "common set of K–12 standards" at 74 Fed. Reg. 59,838 (Nov. 18, 2009) ("a set of content standards that define what students must know and be able to do and that are substantially identical across all States in a consortium. A State may supplement the common standards with additional standards, provided that the additional standards do not exceed 15 percent of the State's total standards for that content area.").

47. 74 Fed. Reg. 59,855-59,856 (Nov. 18, 2009); see also 75 Fed. Reg. 19,515-19,516 (Apr. 14, 2010) (emphasis added).

48. 74 Fed. Reg. 59,855 (Nov. 18, 2009); see also 75 Fed. Reg. 19,516 (Apr. 14, 2010).

49. See supra note 46.

50. Application of Delaware at B-3 (2010), available at http://www2.ed.gov/programs/racetothetop/phase1-applications/delaware.pdf; Application of Tennessee at 48 (2010), available at http://www2.ed.gov/programs/racetothetop/phase1-applications/tennessee.pdf; Application of District of Columbia, at 53 (2010), available at http://www2.ed.gov/programs/racetothetop/phase2-applications/district-ofcolumbia.pdf; Application of Florida at 73 (2010), available at http://www2.ed.gov/programs/racetothetop/phase2-applications/florida.pdf; Application of Georgia at 62 (2010), available at http://www2.ed.gov/programs/racetothetop/phase2-applications/

georgia.pdf; Application of Hawaii at 45 (2010), available at http://www2.ed.gov/programs/racetothetop/phase2-applications/hawaii.pdf; Application of Maryland at 75 (2010), available at http://www2.ed.gov/programs/racetothetop/phase2-applications/maryland.pdf; Application of Massachusetts at 52 (2010), available at http://www2.ed.gov/programs/racetothetop/phase2-applications/massachusetts.pdf; Application of New York at 24 (2010), available at http://www2.ed.gov/programs/racetothetop/phase2-applications/new-york.pdf; Application of North Carolina at 58 (2010), available at http://www2.ed.gov/programs/racetothetop/phase2-applications/north-carolina.pdf; Application of Ohio at B1-1 and B1-2 (2010), available at http://www2.ed.gov/programs/racetothetop/phase2-applications/ohio.pdf; Application of Rhode Island at A-8 (2010), available at http://www2.ed.gov/programs/racetothetop/phase2-applications/rhode-island.pdf; see also Letter from Dr. Kerri L. Briggs, State Superintendent of Education, District of Columbia, to Arne Duncan, Secretary, U.S. Department of Education, at 1 (July 29, 2010), available at http://www2.ed.gov/programs/racetothetop/phase2-applications/amendments/districtofcolumbia.pdf; Letter from Eric J. Smith, Commissioner, Florida Department of Education, to Arne Duncan, Secretary, U.S. Department of Education, at 1 (July 29, 2010), available at http://www2.ed.gov/programs/racetothetop/phase2-applications/amendments/florida.pdf; Letter from William Bradley Bryant, State Superintendent of Schools, Georgia, and Wanda Barrs, Chair, State Board of Education, Georgia, to Arne Duncan, Secretary, U.S. Department of Education, at 1 (July 26, 2010), available at http://www2.ed.gov/programs/racetothetop/phase2applications/amendments/georgia.pdf; Amendment of July 27, 2010, at 6, available at http://www2.ed.gov/programs/racetothetop/phase2-applications/amendments/hawaii.pdf; Letter from Nancy Grasmick, State Superintendent of Schools, Maryland, to Arne Duncan, Secretary, U.S. Department of Education, at 1 (July 30, 2010), available at http://www2.ed.gov/programs/racetothetop/phase2-applications/amendments/maryland.pdf; Letter from Mitchell Chester, Commissioner, Elementary and Secondary Education, Massachusetts, to Arne Duncan, Secretary, U.S. Department of Education, at 1 (July 26, 2010), available at http://www2.ed.gov/programs/racetothetop/phase2-applications/amendments/massachusetts.pdf; Letter from David Steiner, Commissioner of Education, New York, to Arne Duncan, Secretary, U.S. Department of Education, at 1 (July 27, 2010), available at http://www2.ed.gov/programs/racetothetop/phase2-applications/amendments/new-york.pdf; Letter from June St. Clair Atkinson, State Superintendent, Department of Public Instruction, North Carolina, to Arne Duncan, Secretary, U.S. Department of Education, at 1 (June 10, 2010), available at http://www2.ed.gov/programs/racetothetop/phase2-applications/amendments/north-carolina.pdf; Amendment of July 27, 2010, at 1, available at http://www2.ed.gov/programs/racetothetop/phase2-applications/amendments/ohio.pdf; Amendment of August 2, 2010, at 17 (at 10 in Minutes of Board of Regents for Elementary and Secondary Education), available at http://www2.ed.gov/programs/racetothetop/phase2-applications/amendments/rhodeisland.pdf

51. 74 Fed. Reg. 59,733 (Nov. 18, 2009) ("In [the Race to the Top Fund], the phrase "common standards" does not refer to any specific set of common standards, such as the common core standards currently under development by members of the National Governors Association and the Council of Chief State School Officers. The Department declines to make changes in order to endorse any particular standards-development consortium.").

52. See Remarks of Secretary of Education Arne Duncan delivered to State Leaders at Achieve's American Diploma Project Leadership Team: *Beyond the Bubble Tests: The Next Generation of Assessments* 4 (Sept. 2, 2010), available at http://www.ed.gov/news/speeches/beyond-bubble-tests-next-generation-assessmentssecretary-arne-duncans-remarks-state-l.

53. See Nancy Kober and Diane Stark Rentner, Ctr. On Educ. Pol'y, *Common Core State Standards: Progress and Challenges in School Districts' Implementation 4 (2011)*.

54. Id. at 6.

55. Id.

56. See 74 Fed. Reg. 59,733 (Nov. 18, 2009) for the Department's response to commenters' recommendations on the number of states within a consortium.

57. 74 Fed. Reg. 59,733 (Nov. 18, 2009) (emphasis added).

58. See supra note 65 for the award of high points to states that are a part of a standards consortium that includes a majority of the states.

59. Letter from Robert Scott, Commissioner, Texas Education Agency, to United States Senator John Cornyn (Nov. 25, 2009), available at http://www.edweek.org/media/common_core_standards_letter.pdf.

60. Id.

61. Id.

62. 75 Fed. Reg. 18,171-18,172 (Apr. 9, 2010) (emphasis added).

63. 75 Fed. Reg. 18,171 (Apr. 9, 2010); see also Cooperative Agreement Between The U.S. Department of Education and the Partnership for Assessment of Readiness of College and Careers 5 (2011), available at http://www2.ed.gov/programs/racetothetop-assessment/parcc-cooperative-agreement.pdf (award of $169,990,272 and supplemental award of $15,872,560); Cooperative Agreement Between the U.S. Department of Education and the SMARTER Balanced Assessment Consortium and the State of Washington (fiscal agent)5 (2011) available at http://www2.ed.gov/programs/racetothetop-assessment/sbac-cooperative-agreement.pdf (award of $159,976,843 and supplemental award of $15,872,696).

64. 75 Fed. Reg. 18,177 (Apr. 9, 2010) ("Common set of college-and career-ready standards" means "a set of academic content standards for grades K–12 that (a) define what a student must know and be able to do at each grade level; (b) if mastered, would ensure that the student is college-and career-ready...by the time of high school graduation; and (c) are substantially identical across all States in a consortium. A State may supplement the common set of college-and career-ready standards with additional content standards, provided that the additional standards do not comprise more than 15 percent of the State's total standards for that content area.").

65. 75 Fed. Reg. 18,171 (April 9, 2010).

66. Id.

67. Id.

68. Address Before a Joint Session of the Congress on the State of the Union, 33 WEEKLY COMP. PRES. DOC. 136 (Feb. 4, 1997).

69. Departments of Labor, Health and Human Services, and Education, and Related Agencies Appropriations Act, 1998 § 305(a), Pub. L. No. 105-78, 111 Stat. 1467, 1505 (1997).

70. Departments of Labor, Health and Human Services, and Education, and Related Agencies Appropriations Act, 1998 §§ 306-310, Pub. L. No. 105-78, 111 Stat. 1467, 1505-1507 (1997).

71. See 20 U.S.C. § 7909(a) ("[N]o funds provided under this Act [ESEA] to the Secretary or to the recipient of any award may be used to develop, pilot test, field test, implement, administer, or distribute any federally sponsored test in reading, mathematics, or any other subject, unless specifically and explicitly authorized by law."). Congress provided a limited exception for international comparative assessments administered to a representative sample of pupils under the Third International Mathematics and Science Study (TIMSS). 20 U.S.C. § 7909(b)); see also 20 U.S.C. § 1232j(a) ("[N]o funds provided to the Department of Education or to an applicable program, may be used to pilot test, field test, implement, administer or distribute in any way any federally sponsored national test in reading, mathematics, or any other subject that is not specifically and explicitly provided for in authorizing legislation enacted into law."). Here, Congress also provided a limited exception for TIMSS and other international comparative assessments administered to a representative sample of pupils. 20 U.S.C. § 1232j(b).

72. 75 Fed. Reg. 18,174 (Apr. 9, 2010).

73. See Remarks of Secretary Arne Duncan, supra note 52, at 1-11.

74. Id.

75. 75 Fed. Reg. 18,171-18,185 (Apr. 9, 2010).

76. See Remarks of Secretary Arne Duncan, supra note 52, at 4.

77. See id. at 7 (emphasis added).

78. See id.

79. Grant award notification letter from Joseph Conaty, Director, Academic Improvement and Teacher Quality Programs, Office of Elementary and Secondary Education, U.S. Department of Education, to the Honorable Charlie Crist, Governor, Florida (Sept. 28, 2010), available at http://www2.ed.gov/programs/racetothetop-assessment/parcc-award-letter.pdf. Grant award notification letter from Joseph Conaty, Director, Academic Improvement and Teacher Quality Programs, Office of Elementary and Secondary Education, U.S. Department of Education, to the Honorable Christine Gregoire, Governor, Washington (Sept. 28, 2010), available

at http://www2.ed.gov/programs/racetothetop-assessment/sbac-award-letter.pdf.

80. PARCC Proposal for Supplemental Race to the Top Assessment Award 1 (2010), available at http://www.edweek.org/media/parccsupplementalproposal12-23achievefinal.pdf.

81. Id. at 1.

82. Id. at 3-5.

83. Id. at 3.

84. Id. at 4.

85. Id.

86. Id. at 5.

87. Id.

88. See Partnership for Assessment of Readiness for College and Careers, Webinar: Model Content Frameworks for ELA/Literacy, at 14, (Nov. 22, 2011), available at http://www.parcconline.org/sites/parcc/files/PARCC%20MCF%20for%20ELA-Literacy%20Webinar_112211.pdf.

89. Id. at 17.

90. Press Release, SMARTER Balanced Assessment Consortium, SMARTER Balanced Receives Approval for $15.8 Million Supplemental Budget (Jan. 10, 2011), available at http://www. K12.wa.us/SMARTER/PressReleases/ApprovalSupplementalBudget.aspx.

91. SMARTER Balanced Assessment Consortium, Supplemental Funding, Scope Overview Table 14 (2011), available at http://www.k12.wa.us/SMARTER/pubdocs/SBAC_Supplemental_Funds.pdf.

92. Id. at 2.

93. Id.

94. Id.

95. Id. at 3.

96. Id. at 4.

97. See Part V for a discussion of ESEA waiver requirements; see also 20 U.S.C. §§ 1232a, 3403(b) for the prohibitions upon federal involvement in curriculum and instructional materials.

98. See 20 U.S.C. § 7861 (legal authority for ESEA waivers).

99. Dear Colleague Letter from Arne Duncan, Secretary, U.S. Department of Education, to the Chief State School Officers (Sept. 23, 2011), available at http://www2.ed.gov/print/policy/gen/guid/secletter/110923.html.

100. Id.

101. "College-and career-ready standards" are content standards for kindergarten through 12th grade that build towards college and career readiness by the time of high school graduation. A State's college-and career-ready standards must be either (1) standards that are common to a significant number of States; or (2) standards that are approved by a State network of institutions of higher education, which must certify that students who meet the standards will not need remedial course work at the postsecondary level. U.S. DEP'T OF EDUC., ESEA FLEXIBILITY 7 (2011), available at http://www.ed.gov/esea/flexibility.

102. Id. at 35.

103. 20 U.S.C. § 7861(a) ("The Secretary may waive any statutory or regulatory requirement of this Act...."). Noticeably absent from the Department's guidance is any in-depth explanation for its authority to require conditions-based waivers. In adding four conditions to the statutory requirements for a waiver, the Department has ignored Article I, Section 1 of the U.S. Constitution, which vests Congress, not the Executive Branch, with exclusive authority to make laws. The Administration recognized this several months earlier, when the Department took the position that college-and career-ready standards required a legislative change to the ESEA. See U.S. DEP'T OF EDUC., A BLUEPRINT FOR REFORM: THE REAUTHORIZATION OF THE ELEMENTARY AND SECONDARY EDUCATION ACT 7-8 (2010), available at http://www2.ed.gov/policy/elsec/leg/blueprint/blueprint.pdf. No authority exists in ESEA to permit the Secretary to grant waivers to SEAs in exchange for conditions. The Secretary unilaterally issued the Conditional NCLB Waiver Plan because Congress had not yet reauthorized ESEA. As President Obama stated on September 23, 2011, "Congress hasn't been able to do it, so I will." This statement is no legal justification for the Administration to add conditions to the law through executive action, particularly where, as here, the Department failed to

engage in the rulemaking required by the Administrative Procedures Act, 5 U.S.C. § 553.

104. U.S. DEP'T OF EDUC., ESEA FLEXIBILITY REQUEST 9 (2011), available at http://www.ed.gov/esea/flexibility.

105. Id.

106. Id. at 10.

107. Id.

108. Colorado, Florida, Kentucky, Georgia, Indiana, Massachusetts, Minnesota, New Jersey, New Mexico, Oklahoma, and Tennessee.

109. See ESEA Flexibility, http://www.ed.gov/esea/flexibility (last visited on Jan. 15, 2012) (listing ESEA flexibility requests received).

110. See Minn. Dep't of Educ., ESEA Flexibility Request of Minnesota (Nov. 14, 2011), available at http://www2.ed.gov/policy/eseaflex/mn.pdf; see also Kentucky ESEA Flexibility Request (Nov. 14, 2011), available at http://www2.ed.gov/policy/eseaflex/ky.pdf.

111. Colorado, Florida, Kentucky, Georgia, Indiana, Massachusetts, New Jersey, New Mexico, Oklahoma, and Tennessee are members of either PARCC or SBAC or both. See also U.S. DEP'T OF EDUC., ESEA FLEXIBILITY REQUEST 10 (2011), available at http://www.ed.gov/esea/flexibility.

112. See ESEA Flexibility, http://www.ed.gov/esea/flexibilty (last visited on Jan. 15, 2012) (noting a "Second Submission Window").

113. Significantly, California and Texas have indicated that they do not intend to apply for waivers.

114. Joseph A. Califano, Jr., *Governing America: An Insider's Report from the White House and the Cabinet 297* (1981).

8

National Cost of Aligning States and Localities to the Common Core Standards

By AccountabilityWorks

Sound public policy demands that any new proposal should be considered in light of its costs as well as its benefits. Historically, states have made considerable financial investments each time they have modified or adopted academic standards. Forty-five states and Washington DC, have agreed to adopt the Common Core Standards.[1] But few of the states that have adopted the Common Core Standards have analyzed and projected the costs of implementing the new standards. No state that has adopted the Common Core has released a cost analysis of the technology infrastructure and support to administer either of the testing consortia's online assessments.

This analysis aims for a mid-range projection of costs, neither overly optimistic nor unduly pessimistic. It relies on assumptions reflecting the years of experience states have now accumulated in implementing academic standards.

Method

This analysis is intended as a "middle of the road" estimate of the "incremental" (i.e., additional) cost of implementing the Common Core Standards based on actual state or local experience implementing similar initiatives. It does not include any expenses that might be criticized as lavish, but it also attempts to avoid unsupported optimism that new or untested approaches will lead to radically lower expenditures. Neither pessimism nor optimism provides a prudent basis for projecting overall, nationwide costs.

Our analysis focuses on vital components of standards-based system reform and on components for which substantial additional costs are likely. Assessment, professional development, and instructional materials are essential entailments of new academic standards. Each has substantial costs.[2] In these areas, our analysis draws on experience-based cost estimates by state or local school officials. In cases without a clear reason to prefer one cost assumption to another, we average the divergence between sources; in some instances, we weight proportionately in favor of sources based on a larger student population (e.g., a source based on a larger state is weighted more heavily than a source based on a smaller state). The other major element we address is technology infrastructure and support, which supporters and critics of Common Core both recognize as requiring significant new investments in light of the Common Core's reliance on online assessments. All student enrollment or teacher population data used in calculations have been drawn from nationally comparable tabulations by the National Center for Education Statistics (NCES).[3]

Our analysis does not address costs in areas where state and local practices and history vary too widely. For example, in recent decades, standards implementation in California has involved expenditure on a broad, public process that includes the development of state curriculum frameworks in each subject area as well as adoption of textbooks and other instructional materials. On the other hand, some states do not have a textbook adoption process and do not develop state curriculum frameworks to guide the implementation of state standards. Other states perform only some of these tasks or perform them only on a small scale. Such practices are not included as costs in this analysis because they do not reflect a consensus among states that they are essential to standards implementation.

States that have adopted the Common Core Standards reserve the right to add up to 15 percent academic content to reflect additional knowledge or skills. Because adding to the content will also require the expense of developing additional assessments, states will no doubt vary in taking advantage of this provision. In that light we do not include such costs in our analysis.

This analysis includes the major costs required for states to align their schools to the new standards, but it excludes the costs of any additional reforms that have been proposed to help students actually meet the Common Core Standards. States and local districts dispute whether such initiatives and school reforms should be supported through increased overall funding or through the reallocation of existing funds.[4] Such possible reforms may include more charter schools, lower class sizes, performance-based teacher compensation, and additional after-school programs. Attempting to select among these proposed reforms and identify these costs is beyond the scope of our study. Our analysis identifies only the "basic" costs of implementing the Common Core Standards. We do not attempt to track additional costs aimed at raising student achievement to higher levels.

Our study relies on two additional assumptions. First, states and districts that have adopted the Common Core will take their commitment seriously and will invest in the resources needed to implement it. Second, the two Common Core assessment consortia will develop their assessments within the cost parameters they have outlined, despite their ambitious goals, cursory planning, and major design shifts in test items.

All costs included in this analysis are divided into three categories:

- One-time costs
- Year one operational costs
- Ongoing annual operational costs for years 2 through 7

344

These costs are shown in Figures 1A and 1B.

Fig 1A. Total Projected Costs to Implement Common Core Standards (Billions)

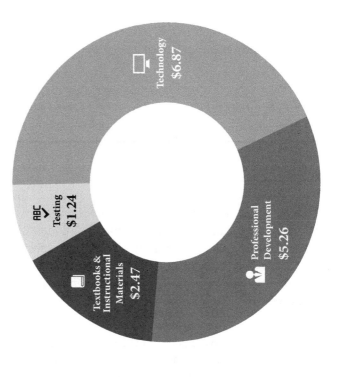

Fig 1B. Overview of Projected Costs to Implement Common Core

	One Time	Year 1 Operations	Years 2–7 Ongoing Operations (Annual)	Total of One Time & 7 Operational Years
ABC Testing Costs	$0	$177,234,471	$177,234,471	**$1,240,641,297**
Professional Development	$5,257,492,417	$0	$0	**$5,257,492,417**
Textbooks & Instructional Materials	$2,469,098,464	$0	$0	**$2,469,098,464**
Technology	$2,796,294,147	$326,042,312	$624,258,785	**$6,867,889,169**
TOTAL	**$10,522,885,028**	**$503,276,783**	**$801,493,256**	**$15,835,121,347**

One-time costs–including teacher professional development, aligned textbooks, and the technology infrastructure required for online assessment–are for activities that must be in place prior to meaningful implementation of Common Core instruction or assessment. Ideally, all such activities would have been implemented before school year 2014–2015, the first year in which students are to be assessed on their mastery of the new standards. Some "one-time" activities could be spread out over several years prior to 2014–2015. For example, the Washington Department of Public Instruction's analysis of local district costs assumes professional development for educators and administrators over multiple years; 25 percent of educators are expected to receive professional development in 2012–2013, 50 percent in 2013–14, and the remaining 25 percent in 2014–2015. Since states will vary considerably in their year-by-year rollout plans, we combine all such one-time costs into a single category and do not attempt to assign them to particular years.

We distinguish year one operational costs from ongoing annual operational costs for subsequent years. The first operating year includes administration of Common Core online assessments as well as technology training. An annual 20 percent replacement cycle for the added computer infrastructure is not projected until beginning in the second year of operations. A total of seven years of operating expenses are included in the cost analysis, a typical amount of time in between academic standards revision cycles in many states (i.e., a revision cycle triggers new one-time costs for realignment).

Information relevant or useful to this analysis was collected through November 15, 2011. Material that emerged after that date is unlikely to have been considered in developing this chapter.

Testing

Measuring student progress in meeting the Common Core Standards requires assessments. The U.S. Department of Education awarded grants to two parallel efforts to create such assessments. A total of $362 million was awarded to states: $186 million was awarded to states working with Achieve, Inc., in the Partnership for Assessment of Readiness for College and Careers consortium (PARCC), and $176 million was awarded to states working with the SMARTER Balanced Assessment Consortium (SBAC). Both efforts promise a new generation of breakthrough online assessments that will place a greater emphasis on innovative test questions and student higher order thinking skills.[5]

We project that the annual cost of assessment for states participating in the consortia will increase by a total of $177.2 million each year (see Figure 2). These are not one-time costs (which are covered by the federal grants to the consortia), but ongoing operational costs that will be faced each year. Over the seven-year horizon of this cost analysis, the total increase would be over $1.2 billion.

Fig 2. Additional Annual Testing Costs (Millions)

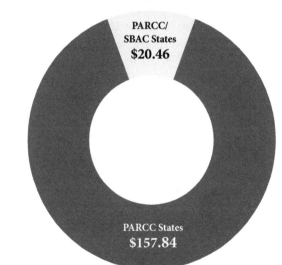

These figures are based on accepting at face value the cost targets for the two consortia. The goals and plans of the two consortia are ambitious, both with respect to innovative design as well as an assumption that all participating states will shift to online assessment. If either of these proves too challenging, the consortia could be faced with difficult choices that require significantly higher costs, greatly simplified assessments, or both.

Discussion and Assumptions

One area in which both consortia intend to change the face of assessment is computer-based scoring of open response test questions. Unlike multiple-choice test questions that are easily and reliably scored by computer-based systems, open response questions, such as short answer, essay, or even extended projects have historically been scored by trained individuals (known as "human raters") who have relevant expertise and qualifications. PARCC and SBAC share a goal of greater reliance on open response test questions and reduced reliance on multiple-choice test questions. Both PARCC and SBAC indicate that their projected costs assume that a majority of open response test questions will rely solely on computer-based "artificial intelligence" scoring algorithms without the involvement of a live person to review the answers. Only a sample of student answers to open response test questions is expected to be scored by "human raters." Statistical analyses would determine whether there is adequate agreement between expert human raters and the computer-generated scores.

Computer-based scoring of open response test questions is not a completely new idea. It evolved gradually from experimentation to live administration in schools over the last two decades. Nevertheless, current plans for the Common Core assessments contain two elements that would be quite new: the widespread use of exclusively computer-based scoring methods and the reliance on exclusively computer-scored test questions in high-stakes assessments.

Until recently, stakes for most state-mandated assessments were limited to public disclosure of annual results, aggregated at the school, district, and state levels. Some states also require students to pass a graduation test. A few states use assessment data in decisions on student grade promotion. Graduation or promotion assessments are truly "high stakes" testing environments. States that incorporate such elements in their assessment programs have stuck mostly to proven designs that can withstand legal challenges, which are not uncommon. Under the Obama Administration, the U.S. Department of Education has encouraged states and school districts to ratchet up the stakes for large-scale assessments by using results for the evaluation of teachers. For example, to receive Race to the Top funding, states had to promise to incorporate data on student performance to evaluate teachers and principals.[6] As of June 2011, twelve states had received RttT funds.[7] Other groups, states, and districts are experimenting with teacher evaluation systems that use student test scores as a measure of teacher effectiveness.[8] Given the substantial protections for public school teachers established in many state statutes as well as local collective bargaining agreements, significant legal challenges appear likely for tests that include exclusively computer-scored open response questions to evaluate teachers and determine either bonuses or negative consequences for nonperformance.

The per-student testing cost assumptions used in our study rely on PARCC and SBAC's own assumptions included in their approved grant applications and updated in some cases by our direct communications with each consortium. Reliable, current per-student testing costs for all U.S. states are unavailable. As an approximation, we rely on a "typical" per student state testing cost of $19.93, an amount recently calculated by a group of testing industry experts.[9] This amount is credible and broadly consistent with the testing industry experience of the contributors to this study. While this figure is very useful for generating nationwide projections, it cannot be used to analyze testing costs for any particular state, because individual state costs are highly variable. The most populous states (e.g., California) typically spend less per student. States with fewer students tend to spend more.

SBAC

In its grant application to the United States Department of Education, SBAC identifies per-student costs of $19.81for the summative assessments (required under federal law) and $7.50 for optional benchmark assessments. Since the benchmark assessments are not mandatory, we do not include their cost in this analysis, even though these assessments are probably an appealing component to many of the states in SBAC. The SBAC cost estimates were developed by the same group of testing experts that calculated a "typical" state per-student cost 12¢ higher ($19.93) than the SBAC estimate. We have no basis for calculating an alternative cost projection for SBAC and have adopted SBAC's official figures in our estimates. We are, however, skeptical that the $19.81 estimate is accurate given SBAC's ambitious goals for innovative assessment design.

PARCC

The PARCC assessment design described in its original grant application assumed four separate student assessments to be spread over the academic year. The results of the four assessments were to be combined to produce summative scores. In 2011, PARCC altered the plan to offer just two assessment components—both to be administered near the end of the school year—the results of which would be combined to provide summative scores. Under the new plan, one of the assessment components is expected to be entirely computer-based and the other will focus on extended performance tasks. PARCC now also intends to offer additional, optional diagnostic and formative assessments.

In its grant application, PARCC projected ongoing costs that ranged between $17 and $50 per student, depending on future decisions by the consortium regarding human versus computer-based scoring of open response test questions. The particular scoring approach described in detail in the application resulted in a cost of $32.68 per student, near the middle of its cost range.[10] As a result of a complete reworking of its assessment plans after its application was approved, PARCC now expects its per student costs to be somewhat lower, though it is not yet ready to commit to a particular figure.[11] For the purpose of this analysis, we accept that PARCC will find a way to reduce its costs below $32.68. We adopt as a reasonable estimate the midpoint between that previous figure and $17, the lowest end of the cost range included in the application, resulting in an estimate of $24.84 per student. In view of the considerable design changes so far, as well as the continuing lack of a commitment to a specific cost, we caution that either the final cost will probably be higher or that additional assessment design changes may be necessary in order to control costs.

States in both PARCC and SBAC

As of this writing, eight states are participating in both consortia and may end up choosing to implement either of the two assessment systems. For the purpose of estimating testing costs for these states, we assume that an equal proportion of the students in these states will end up in each of the two systems (i.e., effectively averaging the costs).

Other Operational Challenges

While online testing offers the promise of multiple benefits—such as faster scoring and no printing costs—state leaders with experience implementing online testing identify four significant operational hurdles:

1. **Technology infrastructure.** Infrastructure-related challenges include obtaining sufficient and secure bandwidth; acquiring the computers needed for testing; creating a suitable location and set-up for the testing computers; and dealing with the issues of the age and reliability of the equipment.[12]

2. **District expertise and support.** "'Few people understand how really challenging it is at the local level,' said one assessment director."[13]

3. **Open response test items.** One assessment leader who had difficulties scaling up online testing using constructed-response items said that he had observed similar problems in other states: 'Everyone I've met who says *Yes* [statewide online testing] *works like a charm*, answers *No* when I ask if their tests include constructed response.'"[14]

4. **Lengthened testing window.** The new assessments typically take more time for schools to administer because the limited number of computers creates bottlenecks. Having more stu-

dents take the same test on different days increases the risk of cheating.[15]

Implementation plans by PARCC and SBAC appear to be at odds with the "lessons learned" from previous experiences with online testing.

One lesson is "Start Simple: Begin with multiple choice test items before venturing on to more complex items or open-ended assessments like writing."[16] Yet both testing consortia tout groundbreaking, innovative open-ended items as a key feature of their online assessments. Current plans call for these items to be incorporated from the beginning, not phased in over time.

Another lesson is "Start Small: Stagger implementation of online assessments—gradually adding more subjects and grade levels—as districts and schools build their infrastructure and gain local expertise."[17] However, staggering implementation typically raises test development and scoring costs as well as technical hurdles because dual-testing systems must be created and operated. Psychometric equating to ensure comparability of paper and online assessment during the transition, for example, also adds significant work and expense. The current PARCC plan to implement online testing fully in all subjects and grades in the first testing year (2014–2015) promises to reduce costs and increase simplicity for the consortium. However, the lack of "phase-in" increases the challenge for local schools and districts, which must ramp up technology infrastructure and staff capacity quickly. As far as we could find, none of the states participating in either of the two Common Core testing consortia conducted a rigorous feasibility assessment on implementing online assessment.

SBAC plans to offer states the option of using a paper and pencil version of its tests during a three-year "transition period." While this allows school systems to delay the technology and support costs of implementing online testing, it presents the consortium with the costs and technical challenges of managing dual paper and online systems. There will be tension between ensuring comparability of the two assessments—an essential requirement—and the interest in "innovative" online test items that rely on technology for administration.

To help local systems struggling with the technology and support costs associated with implementing online assessment, SBAC also plans to allow schools a twelve-week testing window in which to administer its online assessment.[18] This raises concerns about the validity of the SBAC assessment. For test security reasons, most states currently do not permit schools more than one or two weeks to administer state accountability assessments, and some even require administration in a single day. It may be possible to address security concerns through the development of a large (and expensive) item bank and computer adaptive testing.

But other issues would remain. A twelve-week testing window would mean that some students would be tested nearly three months earlier than other students. This is nearly a third of a school year and represents a significant difference in the instruction students receive prior to testing. If students cycle through computer labs for testing with their classroom group (a typical scenario), teachers whose students were assessed near the beginning of the testing window would be substantially disadvantaged compared to teachers whose students were assessed near the end of the testing window. Under such circumstances, the use of student test results as a component of teacher evaluations, a policy encouraged by the Obama Administration, would be unfair to the teachers.

Even in schools and school districts, the fundamental units of accountability in most states, a twelve-week testing window and differences in technology would lead to advantages for some schools by giving them an average of nearly six weeks of extra instruction prior to testing. Differences in school technology often correlate with the relative affluence of the surrounding communities. The SBAC approach could favor wealthier schools by exaggerating differences between the skills of students in affluent and impoverished schools.

Professional Development

Professional development for teachers in the form of training on new academic standards is widely accepted as essential for implementation. Marshall Smith and Jennifer O'Day's seminal work on "Systemic School Reform" identified professional development as one of the key elements required to produce coherent, system-wide change in public school systems.[19] Since the experience of California and its curriculum frameworks in the 1980s, school reform leaders have advocated on behalf of systematic and in-depth professional development to address state academic standards.[20] Common Core advocates indicate that ongoing professional development is necessary to implement CCSS.[21] The urgent need for professional development programs was highlighted in a recent report by the Center on Education Policy, which surveyed 315 districts and found that fewer than half provided professional development for Common Core or planned to provide programs in the next school year.[22] Districts indicated that lack of funding and clarity from the State were the two biggest obstacles.[23]

We project a total cost for professional development of approximately $5.26 billion across the states that have adopted the Common Core Standards. This is a "one-time" cost for experienced educators that must occur before students are held accountable for meeting the standards. The professional development need not occur in a single year; states may choose to "phase in" the professional development over a defined period, reaching a certain proportion of the teachers each year. We also assume that teacher education programs will take responsibility, without needing additional funding, for reorienting their focus to prepare future teachers to implement the Common Core Standards. Figures 3A, 3B and 3C illustrate potential professional development costs for individual states participating in the Common Core assessment consortia. (Since the writing of this analysis, several states have begun to withdraw from either PARCC or SBAC or both.)

Fig 3A. Professional Development Costs for States in PARCC Only

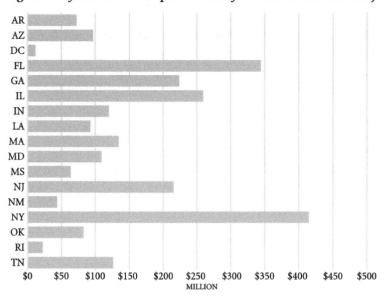

Fig 3B. Professional Development Costs for States in SBAC Only

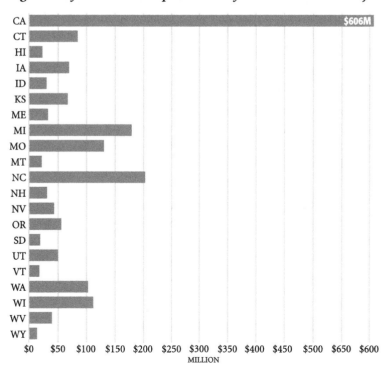

Fig 3C. Professional Development Costs for States in PARCC and SBAC

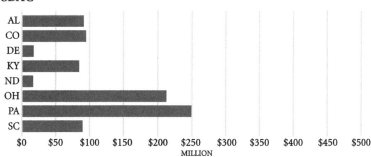

Discussion and Assumptions

We determined the cost of professional development for Common Core by first identifying a typical cost for professional development based on previous state experiences implementing academic standards, weighted by the relative size of the states. This cost was calculated to be approximately $1,931 per educator. This amount was then applied to the total number of educators in each Common Core state and aggregated across participating states. Cost information for professional development was secured for three representative states: California, Washington, and Texas.

We considered whether to assume professional development costs only for middle and upper grades teachers responsible for English and mathematics (e.g., not for science or history teachers). The state estimates we obtained did not limit training to only English and mathematics teachers.

Given the Common Core's increased emphasis on more challenging English Language Arts comprehension, it is reasonable that the responsibility for preparing students to meet the standards will be shared among all teachers. As a result, we assume that all teachers will require training on the Common Core Standards.

California

The California Department of Education has estimated the initial cost of professional development for the Common Core Standards at $2,000 per teacher.[24]

356

Washington

The Office of the Superintendent of Public Instruction (OSPI) of Washington conducted an in-depth analysis of the implementation of the Common Core Standards in that state. Local district and school costs associated with preparing teachers and other staff to implement the Common Core Standards were estimated at $165 million over several years.[25] This represents a cost of approximately $3,087 per teacher.

Texas

The Texas Education Agency (TEA) has estimated that implementing the Common Core Standards in the state would result in professional development costs of $60 million for the state and approximately $500 million for local school districts, resulting in a total professional development cost of $560 million.[26] This represents a per teacher cost of approximately $1,681.

Textbooks and Instructional Materials

Textbooks play a central role in defining the de facto curriculum in public school districts across the United States. What students are taught depends on the textbooks and other instructional materials used by their teachers. According to one study, "...80 to 90 percent of classroom and homework assignments are textbook-driven or textbook-centered."[27] Whether a state conducts a formal textbook adoption process or its schools make these decisions entirely on their own, the Common Core Standards are unlikely to be implemented in a coherent manner unless updated, aligned textbooks and other materials are obtained.

We project that states adopting Common Core will need to spend approximately $2.47 billion in one-time costs to obtain aligned English language arts and mathematics instructional materials. Such materials should be in place before teachers are expected to teach or students are expected to meet the Common Core Standards. Figures 4A, 4B and 4C illustrate potential textbook and instructional materials costs for individual states participating in the Common Core assessment consortia.

357

Fig 4A. Textbooks and Materials Costs for States in PARCC Only

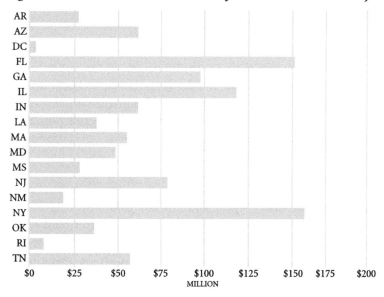

Fig 4B. Textbooks and Materials Costs for States in SBAC Only

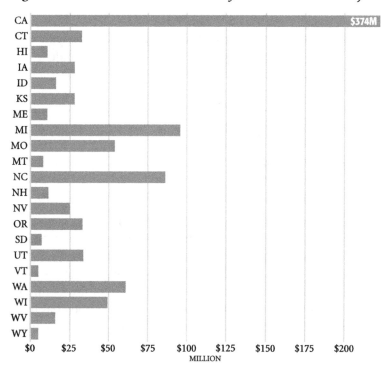

Fig 4C. Textbooks and Materials Costs for States in PARCC and SBAC

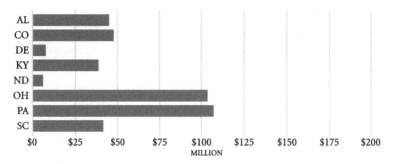

Discussion and Assumptions

Textbook lifespans are limited. All textbooks must eventually be replaced even if states do not modify their academic standards.[28] Estimates for the lifespan of K–12 textbooks vary, typically ranging from as few as 2 years to as many as 6 years.[29] School systems implementing Common Core, however, must ensure that all students have updated, aligned textbooks by the academic year in which students are to be tested on the new assessments. We assume that states participating in the two assessment consortia will roll out new assessments on time in the 2014–2015 academic year; therefore, updated instructional materials must be provided for all students no later than fall of 2014.

At a time of strained school budgets, when school systems might otherwise decide to delay normal textbook replacement purchases and tolerate increasingly worn but still usable materials, those in states implementing Common Core will not have that option. Instead, states working to ensure a serious implementation of the new standards will face a real, one-time cash expense for wholesale adoption of new Reading/Language Arts and Mathematics materials over the next two years (instead of a typical timeframe closer to four years). To account for the fact that some textbook purchases might have occurred anyway during this period, we conservatively adjust (reduce) this one-time cost by a factor of 50 percent. (N.B., given the nature of this estimate, some school systems will need to budget significantly more than assumed in this analysis in order to ensure that all of their students receive the materials they need.)

359

Once the up-front textbook costs are incurred, replacement of lost or worn out textbooks is a normal operational cost regardless of the standards; therefore, we do not include additional ongoing costs over the seven operational years of our analysis. In fact, districts implementing the wholesale adoption of new Reading/ELA and Mathematics instructional materials assumed here may expect to see some savings in their annual replacement costs for the following one to three years due to the recent purchase of new materials.

Individual state-by-state estimates in the nearby graphs illustrate potential costs, with the caveat that schools in states that negotiate bulk pricing for textbooks and other materials may incur lower costs than those in states that do not.

Estimates for the per-student cost of instructional materials vary significantly, in part depending on whether an estimate is limited to the textbook itself or also includes other materials. Our analysis averages two representative estimates for per-student cost of materials in each subject, English language arts and mathematics, and applies these averages to the number of students in states that have committed to the Common Core Standards.

One estimate, developed by the California Department of Education, is typical of the lower end of such cost estimates. The California DOE estimated an aggregate cost of $483 Million across all California local school systems.[30] When divided by the most recent available enrollment statistics for the state from the National Center for Education Statistics, the result is an estimated per-student materials cost of $77.19 across both Reading/Language Arts and mathematics.[31]

The second set of estimates, developed by the Florida Association of District Instructional Materials Administrators (FADIMA), is typical of higher cost estimates (though certainly not the highest). It is published with extensive documentation and detail and aims to be comprehensive, identifying a range of particular texts, consumables, manipulatives, and other potentially useful instructional materials from particular vendors, differentiated

360

by grade level. We excluded from this source the cost of remedial or "intervention" instructional materials because such materials already present in schools can more easily be adapted to a different set of standards. Based on this source, per-student costs ranged from $65.00 in elementary Mathematics to $144.17 for Kindergarten Reading/Language Arts (with other costs, including middle and high school, in between).[32]

Technology Infrastructure and Support

Costs for Common Core-related technology infrastructure and support include PARCC and SBAC's plans to implement online testing. State experimentation with online testing is widespread,[33] but broad implementation across all students participating in federally mandated testing is not common and will require additional substantial expenditure in improved technology infrastructure, training, and support.[34]

We project approximately $6.87 billion in increased local district technology costs for states planning to implement one of the Common Core assessments under development by PARCC or SBAC. This includes $2.8 billion in one-time, up-front costs, $326 million in additional costs in the first year of operation, and $624 million in additional costs for the remaining six years in the model. Figures 5A, 5B, and 5C illustrate potential technology costs for individual states participating in the Common Core assessment consortia. Since they are not based on a detailed investigation of available technology in every district in every state, they should be interpreted as illustrative.

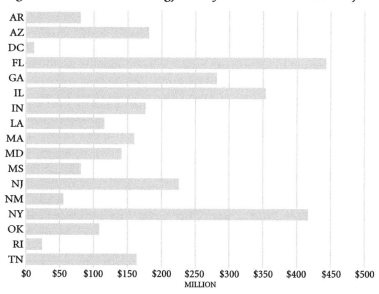

Fig 5A. Multi-Year Technology Costs for States in PARCC Only

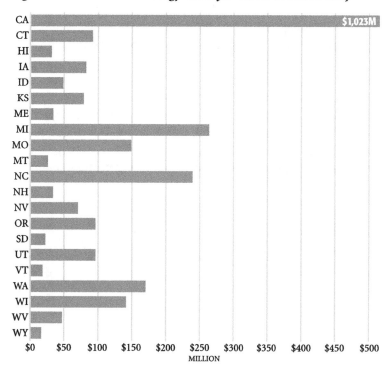

Fig 5B. Multi-Year Technology Costs for States in SBAC Only

Fig 5C. Multi-Year Technology Costs for States in PARCC and SBAC

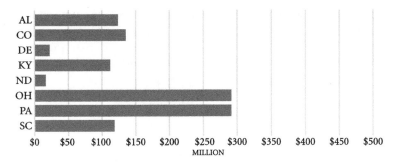

Discussion and Assumptions

South Carolina and Texas have published comprehensive feasibility studies of online testing.[35] These in-depth analyses, while developed independently, reached similar results. Based on surveys of available technology in local districts as well as expert analysis, both found that online testing would result in significantly higher costs. Reduced costs for printing, shipping and scoring tests were more than offset by increased costs in other areas, including, but not limited to, computers, hardware and bandwidth; staff training; staffing levels; innovative test items; and increased psychometric analyses.

There are four areas of significant technology-related costs, which we estimate based on the thorough analyses conducted for South Carolina and Texas. (In the most recent data available from the National Center for Education Statistics, South Carolina was comparable to the national average in the number of computers per student, while Texas was somewhat ahead.)[36]

Computers

While there are significant numbers of student computers in most schools, not all computers are in adequate working order and not all are available for online testing or located in environments suitable for such use (e.g., individual classroom computers). Statewide averages can also mask unequal distribution. Figure 5D summarizes a key finding of the South Carolina feasibility study that only a little more than half of all student computers in schools were available for online testing. To achieve an adequate (4:1) ratio of computers to students for online testing, 162,500 computers were necessary but only 100,372 were initially available (see Figure 5E).

Fig 5D. Computers Available to Students - South Carolina

Fig 5E. Total Computers Needed to Accomodate Electronic Testing - South Carolina

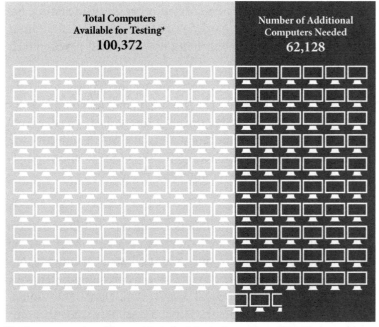

Total computers to achieve a 4:1 student-to-testing ratio = 162,500
⌨ = 1,000 Computers *Based on survey data.
Source: DRC SC Feasibility Report (2007) p. 6–12

We assume in this analysis that a 4:1 ratio of students to computers is necessary for efficient online testing (with testing windows of a couple of weeks), but that the initially available ratio is about 7.5:1. We also assume that approximately one-third of this difference can be made up by temporarily relocating or repurposing some of the other student computers during the testing period without excessive disruption or negative effects on other important uses (e.g., computer use in instruction). We also assume that the purchase cost of the additional computers is approximately $750, which includes not only the cost of the hardware but also installation and any necessary software; we use a lower amount than the $1,000 per computer figure used in the South Carolina and Texas feasibility studies because computer costs have a history of declining.[37] We further assume a 5-year depreciation schedule that is standard for computer equipment, which implies 20 percent annual cost for eventual replacement.

Wiring and Bandwidth

We expect that some additional electrical and network wiring will be necessary for the added computers. Similarly, additional proxy server machines will be required to support the bandwidth demands of the additional computers. We assume $2,000 in wiring costs and $750 for a student-level proxy server machine for each additional 25 computers.

Training and Technical Support

Teachers or other instructional staff who supervise students during testing will need to be trained to use the online testing system. We assume that one proctor will be necessary for every 30 students and that each proctor will receive three hours of training at a cost of $75 per hour. We only include training costs during the first year of operation, assuming that the training of replacement proctors in out years can be managed locally with existing resources.

Technical support will be required during online testing each year. We assume that 10 hours of support will be required for every 25 computers used for online testing at a cost of $30 per hour. Notably, we do not include the cost of supporting the added computers at other times during the school year.

Power

Computer usage during online testing will draw electrical power and incur utility costs. We assume that students at tested grades will participate in online assessment for approximately four hours each year at a cost of $0.11 per hour.[38]

Conclusion and Recommendations

Implementation of the Common Core Standards is likely to represent a substantial additional expense for most states. While a handful of states have begun to analyze these costs, most states have signed on to the initiative without a thorough, public vetting of the costs and benefits. In particular, there has been very little attention to the potential technology infrastructure costs that currently cash-strapped districts may face in order to implement the Common Core assessments within a reasonable testing window.

This nation-wide cost analysis is intended to illustrate the key expenditures necessary for implementing the Common Core. States and local communities can use it as a starting point in developing their own analyses of local needs and costs.

We recommend that states and local school systems considering Common Core:

- Analyze carefully the future annual costs of using the assessments being developed by the SBAC and PARCC consortia. Even though the development costs are covered by federal grants, some states will find—as California has—that annual operating costs may increase significantly.

- Develop a technology feasibility assessment to consider local readiness to implement online assessment for all students.

- Identify the resources necessary to provide fully aligned instructional resources and materials. The burden of stitching together conflicting instructional programs, textbooks and other materials with only "guidance" as support is unfair to teachers as well as students.

- Ensure that thorough professional development is provided to all teachers. Without sufficient teacher understanding of the standards and assessment expectations, students will not receive an adequate opportunity to learn the material on which they will be tested.

- Once the expenses have been identified and analyzed, states should encourage a public discussion of the potential benefits and costs of implementing the Common Core Standards. Each community must decide for itself, based on an appraisal of its own needs as well as a realistic assessment of the Common Core Standards initiative.

Appendix. The Cost of Common Core in California

We estimate that to implement the Common Core, California will have to spend more than $2 billion.

With the largest student population among the states, California will likely play a pivotal role in the implementation of the Common Core Standards. The decision by Texas, which has the second largest population, to reject the Common Core magnifies the importance of the rollout in California. A smooth implementation would help solidify the perception of Common Core as the dominant approach to standards-based reform, while a serious stumble in California might raise questions about its future.

Due to the prolonged economic downturn, California public schools are struggling with the effects of several years of flat or declining revenues from the state.

From the 2007–2008 school year to 2010–2011, the state budget for K–12 education has declined from $62.9 billion to $56.7 billion, a reduction of nearly 10 percent.

California's locally-developed academic standards have been judged at least as good as, if not significantly better than, the Common Core Standards by one of the strongest advocates for the Common Core: The Fordham Institute.[39] In English language arts, Fordham rated the California standards an "A", while the Common Core received only a grade of "B+". Similarly, in mathematics, Fordham graded California's standards an "A," while the Common Core received a score of "A–". Other national organizations have also judged California's standards to be among the very best. The American Federation of Teachers (AFT) judged California's mathematics standards, which were developed in a process led by top mathematicians, as "strong" (the organization's highest rating).[40] Since the development of its current standards, California has spent tens of millions of dollars each year to develop and administer assessments aligned to its standards at grades 2 through 11. The state further spent $1.6 billion to assist local districts with implementation. This included $800 million for state curriculum frameworks in each subject as well as adoption of aligned textbooks and instructional materials; due to its size, California commands the greatest attention of the publishers of textbooks and other materials. The state also spent $785 million for professional development to familiarize educators and administrators with its academic standards.[41]

Recently, the California Department of Education estimated a cost of $2,000 for each teacher for training on the new standards, with $237.5 million required to address only districts with "priority" schools in need of intensive assistance. The state department also believes that additional ongoing training would be necessary, as well as special training estimated to cost $118.8 million on applying the new standards to students who are English learners.[42] Based on the number of California teachers reported by the National Center for Education Statistics in the 2009–2010 school year, it is estimated that initial core training for teachers in all California schools would cost approximately $627.6 million.

The California Department of Education also estimated the cost to districts of implementing ELA and mathematics instructional materials that are "fully aligned" with the Common Core Standards at $483 million.[43] While the state department also estimates the cost of a second option with only partially aligned materials, a serious implementation of the Common Core Standards requires textbooks and other materials that are properly aligned to the new academic standards and accompanying assessments; teachers should not be expected to jump and skip through partially aligned materials while scrambling to fill gaps or rearrange out of sequence presentations of skills.

The state department further estimated that implementing the SBAC consortium assessments aligned to the Common Core Standards would increase California's state testing costs by approximately $10 per student annually, or $35 million each year. Over seven years, the increase would total $245 million. This would be added to the state's current testing contracting expenditure of approximately $54.3 million each year.

Because the SBAC assessment will be available exclusively as an online assessment, many California schools would need to make substantial expenditures in technology infrastructure and support to administer it. Based on typical school technology infrastructure and capacity, we project that California schools would need to make an initial, one-time investment of about $418.5 million in computers and other infrastructure as well as additional annual expense, assuming a testing window comparable to current state policy. Over a seven-year period, we estimate that the increased state expenditure for technology and support would total about $1 billion ($1,022.6 million).

For additional appendices that further detail the assumptions used in this study, please visit: http://www.accountabilityworks. org/news.php?viewStory=23

Author Biography

AccountabilityWorks - Theodor Rebarber is CEO of the nonprofit AccountabilityWorks. Rebarber previously was chief education officer of the charter schools management company Advantage Schools Inc., legislative director for United States Representative Steve Gunderson, and associate director for curriculum and assessment at The Edison Project. Rebarber was also Special Assistant to the Assistant Secretary for Educational Research Improvement at the United States Department of Education and a research associate at the Educational Excellence Network of the Vanderbilt Institute for Public Policy Studies. He earned a bachelor's degree from Wesleyan University.

Endnotes

1. The five states that have not adopted the Common Core are Alaska, Minnesota, Nebraska, Texas, and Virginia. The Common Core State Standards Initiative tellingly lists these five as "not yet adopted" states. See http://www.corestandards.org/in-the-states.

2. Francie Alexander, "Accountability and Assessment California Style." In *Education Reform in the '90s*, Chester Finn and Theodor Rebarber (Eds). (1992). New York, NY: Macmillan Company; Marshall Smith and Jennifer O'Day. "Putting the Pieces Together: Systemic School Reform," Consortium for Policy Research in Education Policy Briefs. (1991).

3. National Center for Education Statistics (NCES), "State Nonfiscal Survey of Public Elementary/ Secondary Education" 2009–10, v.1a, Common Core of Data (CCD)

4. For example, see Eric Hanushek. (October 2005)."The Alchemy of "Costing Out" an Adequate Education." "Adequacy Lawsuits: Their Growing Impact on American Education." Cambridge, MA: Kennedy School of Government, Harvard University; Susan Zelman, Projected Costs of Implementing the Federal "No Child Left Behind" Act in Ohio

5. Center for K–12 Assessment & Performance Management at ETS. "Coming Together to Raise Achievement. New Assessments for the Common Core State Standards." Updated July 2011. Princeton, NJ: ETS. (2011)

6. See part D(2) of the RTT criteria: "Improving teacher and principal effectiveness based on performance."

7. Michael Winerip. (June 2011). "Helping Teachers Help Themselves". *The New York Times*.

8. For example, a Gates Foundation project, Measures of Effective Teaching (MET), supports activities for the following groups: higher education (Dartmouth College, Harvard University, Stanford University, University of Chicago, University of Michigan, University of Virginia, and University of Washington), nonprofit organizations (Educational Testing Service, RAND Corporation, and the New Teacher Center), and several for-profit education consultants (Cambridge Education, Teachscape, and Westat).

371

In addition, the National Board for Professional Teaching Standards and Teach For America are supporting the project and have encouraged their members to participate. In addition, Gates also supports specific state activities via non-profit funding, for example Gates recently awarded $9.7 million to the Colorado Legacy Foundation to work with the state Department of Education on the implementation of new teacher evaluation systems; see "Gates Foundation Rolls $9.7 Million into Colorado Teacher Evaluation," *Denver Post* (June 13, 2011).

9. Barry Topol, John Olson, Ed Roeber of Assessment Solutions Group (ASG). "The Cost of New Higher Quality Assessments: A Comprehensive Analysis of the Potential Costs for Future State Assessments." Stanford, CA: Stanford University, Stanford Center for Opportunity Policy in Education. (2010) pp. 23–26.

10. PARCC: Application for the Race to the Top Comprehensive Assessment Systems Competition. (June 23, 2010). p. 248.

11. Laura McGiffert Slover, Senior Vice President, Achieve, Inc. Personal communication with Theodor Rebarber. September 19, 2011.

12. Grunwald Associates LLC. An Open Source Platform for Internet-based Assessment. (2010). 3.

13. Grunwald, 3.

14. Grunwald, 4.

15. Grunwald, 4.

16. Grunwald.

17. Grunwald.

18. Smarter Balanced Assessment Consortium. Computer Adaptive Testing.

19. Marshall Smith and Jennfier O'Day. "Systemic School Reform," Susan Furhman and Betty Malen (Eds.). "Politics of Curriculum and Testing." Philadelphia: Falmer. (1991); from the National Academy of Sciences a compilation of articles, reports, and testimony prepared by Alexandra Beatty, Rapporteur, Committee on State Standards in Education: A Workshop Series, Washington, D.C.: National Research Council. (2008).

20. See Francie Alexander, "Accountability and Assessment California Style." "In Education Reform in the '90s," Chester Finn and Theodor Rebarber (Eds). (1992). New York, NY: Macmillan Company.

21. From the AFT 2010 resolution: A Common Core: High Standards For All Schools. "...Whereas educational reforms important to the AFT, such as those detailed in "A New Path Forward" and "AFT's Pathway to Student Success"-including responsible, effective teacher development and evaluation processes; ongoing, job-embedded professional development aligned to staff needs for professional growth; and effective, appropriate assessments designed to further student learning- all depend first on having and implementing a clear set of standards that are specific, detailed and rigorous... RESOLVED, that the AFT continue to advocate for Common Core Standards and the development of aligned curriculum, professional development based on the curriculum, teaching materials, student intervention systems and assessments..."

22. Nancy Kober, Diane Stark Rentner, Jack Jennings, and Bruce Haslam. "Common Core State Standards: Progress and Challenges in School Districts' Implementation." Washington, D.C.: Center on Education Policy. (September 2011).

23. Kate Ash. "Common Core Accelerates Interest in Online PD," *Education Week.* (October 2011).

24. Tom Torlakson. California Department of Education Initial Estimate of Federal Waiver Fiscal Impact. Attachment 6. (November 3, 2011). p. 2 of 14

25. Jessica Vavrus. "The Common Core State Standards for English Language Arts and Mathematics: Analysis and Recommendations." Report to the Legislature. Sacramento, CA: OSPI. (January 2011; amended February 1, 2011). p. 29.

26. Richard Todd Webster, Texas Education Agency, chief of staff. (July 20, 2011).Personal communication with Theodor Rebarber.

27. Chester E. Finn, Jr. and Diane Ravitch. "Mad, Mad World of Textbook Adoption." Washington, D.C.: Thomas B. Fordham Institute. (September 2004). p.1.

28. A number of states and school systems are considering implementation of digital textbooks. The life cycle costs for such "virtual" instructional materials would be calculated quite differently from the assumptions described in this study. While some hope that

significant savings could be achieved as a result of such initiatives, the evidence so far is very limited. There is little doubt, however, that there would continue to be substantial ongoing materials costs, such as for periodic replacement of the technology hardware (e.g., e-reader or iPad) and for updates to the instructional content itself.

29. See, for example: Ahmed Tantawy, Brian Guernsey, Josh Lauman, Pranav Dharwadkar, Tapan Kamdar. PEARSON eTextBook Reader. Berkeley, California: Haas School of Business. p. 2

    Geoffrey H. Fletcher. "Making the Big Shift," *THE Journal.* (June 17, 2011) p. 1

30. Tom Torlakson. California Department of Education Initial Estimate of Federal Waiver Fiscal Impact. Attachment 6. (November 3, 2011). p. 2 of 14 http://www.cde.ca.gov/be/ag/ag/yr11/documents/bluenov11item05.doc

31. The state of California may use a figure of $75 per student for student materials cost, with the total state materials cost of $483 million based on a projected enrollment statistic from a later year than the 2009/10 federal enrollment statistics used throughout this analysis. Since the total cost figure for the state is the same, there is not a practical, material impact from this divergence. The 2009/10 California enrollment figure used here is drawn from the following source (and included as an appendix to this analysis):

    National Center for Education Statistics (NCES), "State Nonfiscal Survey of Public Elementary/ Secondary Education" 2009–10, v.1a, Common Core of Data (CCD)

32. Florida Association of District Instructional Materials Administrators (FADIMA).Instructional Materials Cost Analysis For Fiscal Year 2011–2012. (August 2010).

33. Grunwald.

34. The national organization of state directors of education technology have recognized the substantial technology infrastructure costs needed for the implementation of Common Core Standards and assessments. For a summary of the issues see: "High Stakes Online Testing Coming Soon!," *THE Journal,* (June 7, 2011).

35. Texas Education Agency. An Evaluation of Districts' Readiness for Online Testing (Document No. GE09 212 01). Austin, TX: Texas Education Agency, 2008; Data Recognition Corporation, South

Carolina Study on the Feasibility and Cost of Converting the State Assessment Program to a Computer-Based or Computer-Adaptive Format FINAL REPORT, (June 25, 2007).

36. US Department of Education. NCES Digest of Educational Statistics, 2010.

37. Ben Worthen. "Rising Computer Prices Buck the Trend." *The Wall Street Journal*, (December 13, 2010).

38. US Energy Information Administration. Average Retail Price of Electricity to Ultimate Customers: Total by End-Use Sector. (March 2011).

39. Thomas B. Fordham Foundation. "The State of State Standards-and the Common Core-in 2010." AFT.

40. Sizing up state standards. (2008).

41. Brian Edwards. "California and the "Common Core": Will There Be a New Debate About K–12 Standards?." Mountain View, CA: Ed Source. (June 2010).

42. Tom Torlakson. "California Department of Education Initial Estimate of Federal Waiver Fiscal Impact." Attachment 6. (November 3, 2011). pp. 8 and 9 of 14

43. Torlakson.